More Praise
Into the Sha[...]

D0482888

"*Into the Shadows* is a discerning testimony of the transforming power of God's gracious embrace. It offers proof that suffering-induced patience, produced in the presence of a loving family and a caring church, can lead to an enlargement of one's faith and a deeper wisdom about the world's cosmic and personal mysteries."

> —Steve J. Van Der Weele, Professor of English, Emeritus, Calvin College; Book Review Editor, *Christian Educators Journal*

"Walk with Bob and Roberta and the God who loves them into the deepening shadows of Alzheimer's. This eloquent story by a loving, creative caregiver will bless and inspire many."

> —Thea B. Van Halsema, Retired Dean of Students and Professor of Social Work, Reformed Bible College Author, *This Was John Calvin* and *Safari for Seven*

"Bob DeHaan writes with unusual clarity and fine Christian insight as he takes us on a journey into the mysterious world of Alzheimer's and how it affects both the patient and the caregiver. Remarkably the book brings a message of hope for caregivers because God's grace and love are greater than the disease."

> —Dr. Andrew J. Bandstra, Professor Emeritus of New Testament, Calvin Theological Seminary

"In Bob and Roberta DeHaan's deep and abiding love for each other and for God, the cruel onslaught of Alzheimer's disease has nearly met its match. This book details a painful—and in many ways victorious—personal journey into a relationship committed 'until death do us part.' It will bring tears to your eyes, laughter to your heart, and ultimately inspire the reader towards more grateful and gracious living."

—Rev. Joan Hemenway, D.Min., United Methodist Minister and Pastoral Educator, Yale-New Haven Hospital; Author, *Inside the Circle: An Inquiry Concerning Process Groups in Clinical Pastoral Education*

"This is a vivid and human portrait of a couple struggling with dementia. Robert DeHaan openly shares his deepest feelings as he provides his wife Roberta with a rich and loving existence despite her illness and decline. There are life lessons here for all of us."

—Madelon K. Krissoff, MD, Internal Medicine/Geriatrics, Senior Health Consulting, Grand Rapids, Michigan

into the shadows

robert f. dehaan

into the shadows
a journey of faith and love
into alzheimer's

 FaithWalk Publishing
Grand Haven, Michigan

Published by FaithWalk Publishing
333 Jackson Street, Grand Haven, Michigan 49417

Printed in the United States of America

08 07 06 05 04 03   7 6 5 4 3 2 1

This book describes problems common to many people who have Alzheimer's dis-ease. It is in no way intended as a substitute for competent medical counseling. The publication of this book does not constitute the practice of medicine nor is it an attempt to replace your physician. The author and publisher advise the reader to consult with a physician before administering any medication or undertaking any course of treatment. If you are on prescription drugs, do not change or modify your medication unless directed to do so by your physician. Changing dosages or sched-ules for medication on your own could lead to serious illness and even death.

Library of Congress Control Number: 2003100064
ISBN: 0-9724196-3-2 (pbk.: alk. paper)

To Roberta,
with whom I walked into adulthood
and shared more than fifty loving years.

To "Doc" John DeVries, who taught us
so much more than Chemistry;
and to the Rev. Ted Loder, who nurtured our faith for
more than three decades.

And to those who suffer from Alzheimer's
disease and their caregivers, I pray that this book
may provide comfort and encouragement
in their darkest hours.

Contents

Prologue

The professor was delighted with Roberta Timmer; the rest of us were frustrated but awestruck. He had spent the first period in our freshman mathematics class at Calvin College drawing a variety of curves and geometric figures on the chalkboard. After completing each construction he would ask if any of us could give its mathematical equation or formula, doing so, I suspected, to determine how mathematically challenged we were. Roberta was the only student who supplied one correct answer after another.

I was lovestruck as well as awestruck; and from that moment in our first math class, I had eyes only for Roberta. All other women faded into the background of my consciousness; none captured my whole being the way Roberta did. She was completely beautiful to me. I engaged in an old-fashioned campaign to woo her, having first, however, to weather some early storms as we both cleared our lives of prior romantic attachments.

Roberta's high level of academic performance continued throughout her college career. She made a point of seeking out the best minds on the faculty and, as often as possible, selected courses according to who the instructor was. I, on the other hand, selected courses to prepare myself for a career in science, regardless of the instructor.

Roberta's academic achievements did not interfere with her several extracurricular activities. After helping convert *The Chimes* from the monthly literary magazine that it had been for many years into a weekly newspaper, she became its first woman editor, a signal accomplishment. In the first issue of the 1946 school year, she wrote editorially, "Every Tuesday morning of the school year, *The Chimes* hopes to place in the hands of the Calvin students a peppy newspaper chock full of news, views and ideas which will interest all."[1]

Both of us were part of a coterie of students who made the organic chemistry laboratory our informal social and academic center. Besides conducting laboratory assignments, we gathered to compare notes, study for exams, analyze faculty members, and pass around campus news. Here we also heated soup in glass beakers over Bunsen burners as we ate our luncheon sandwiches.

Not only was Roberta a well liked and respected member of the student body, she also related well to faculty members. Spending hours playing chess with "Doc" John DeVries in his office in the chemistry lab, she unburdened herself of academic, social, and family problems.

Family problems formed a somber backdrop to Roberta's college life. During the summer of 1944, following her first year in college, she had moved with her parents from Grand Rapids, Michigan, to a small farm northeast of the city. The move was made, in part, to provide a favorable environment for her father, who was struggling at the time with severe depression. His illness had cast a pall over family life and was a major topic of discussion in Professor DeVries' office. While the move provided a measure of healing for her father and also afforded a pleasant home for Roberta, it laid on her the burden of finding a means of transportation to Calvin College in Grand Rapids, about ten miles away. Fortunately, being a favorite niece of several aunts and uncles, she could always rely on one of them for help in an emergency. An uncle who lived nearby and drove to work in the city offered her a lift to the starting point of the transit line, where she could board a bus that would carry her across town to the college.

In the early morning they would leave home through the fog that blanketed the river valley where the farm lay. Ascending to the rim of the valley, they would break out into a world gilded with the slanting rays of the rising sun. Although for most of the way they drove in the clear morning light, they would descend occasionally into the dark shadows of a fog-covered vale, only to emerge again into the bright world. Traveling in this manner they reached Roberta's destination, the bus stop.

Formal dating played only a minor role in our developing relationship. College life gave Roberta and me wonderful opportunities to grow together in natural ways on a daily basis. We took classes and studied together, worked late hours on the college publications, sang in the *a cappella* choir and the Messiah chorus, cut lab classes for bicycle rides around Reeds Lake on spring afternoons, and attended daily chapel and evening church services together.

One Sunday afternoon in the spring of our senior year, Roberta and I took a stroll in her uncle's apple orchard. In my pocket I fingered an engagement ring, and I was alert for the best moment to present it to her. Roberta may have sensed that this was no ordinary saunter. We found a place to sit to absorb the beauty of the April green grass and unfolding new leaves. To my delight, a robin with a bit of string in her beak lit on a branch near us. I knew this was the moment. Pointing casually to the bird, I cleared my throat and told Roberta that I was hoping we could do together what that robin was doing. I needed to say no more. From that moment we were engaged to be married. Our wedding took place on New Year's Day, 1948, and the photo on the next page captures our joy.

Through more than fifty years of our marriage Roberta was wonderfully occupied with her life, living with the élan of her college days. But when our marriage passed the half-century mark, she increasingly encountered minor moments of forgetfulness and dis-orientation, like the misty valleys on her early morning trips to college. These incidents became ever deepening shadows in our lives.

What follows is the story of the love we experienced during this terrible passage into Roberta's Alzheimer's disease, and of the love and grace of God that surrounded and upheld us along the way.

---

[1] David Timmer, "Censor, Censure and Sunday School: Changing Chimes," *Chimes*, February 19, 1971. Reprinted in *Chimes*, November, 2001, p. 16

I

Shadows in the Valleys

Although the shadows of Alzheimer's disease began closing in on Roberta in 1998, around the time of our fiftieth wedding anniversary when she was seventy-three years old, I ignored them as best I could. Her memory lapses were a bit of fog in the valleys, I thought. We often joined our older friends in lightheartedly calling them "senior moments." Who hasn't had them? Exercising her excellent verbal ability, she often danced around a forgotten word with a well chosen substitute. How interesting that in conversations the listener often realizes what the speaker wants to say while the latter is fumbling for a word that refuses to come out of hiding. When conversing together, Roberta often helped me by supplying the word I needed, and vice versa.

Ignoring my wife's problem was made easier by the message we gathered from the media and from the health letters of Harvard and Johns Hopkins medical schools to which we subscribed; namely that occasional forgetfulness is the normal concomitant of growing older and not something to worry about. A friend of ours told us of being teased by a friend about how forgetful she was becoming, to which she replied that she was simply *more precocious* than he! We, too, occasionally ribbed each other about who was aging faster.

1

Concentrating on the positive side of her life—her love of people, her willingness to be a friend to all, her joy in her gardens, her satisfaction in her therapeutic massage practice, and our life at church—we lived our days in the sunshine of God's love, disregarding the shadows.

I recalled a conversation I had with our pastor, the Reverend Theodore Loder, following a Sunday morning worship service. After talking of many things, he asked me how Roberta was doing. I wasn't sure whether he saw something in her behavior that caused him concern (he is an empathetic person) or whether he simply wanted to be updated on her life and times from my perspective. I mentioned Roberta's memory problems and that I thought she was losing her memory slightly faster than I was. "But," I said, "if you were to ask her how Bob is doing, she would probably tell you that she thinks he is losing his memory slightly faster than she is." Who was the more precocious?

I now realize that I lost an opportunity to make a connection with Ted that could have led to counseling with him later when I would need it. Although he was offering to discuss Roberta's condition, he was put off by my making a joke of it. I later found out from our friend, Sam Whyte, that he and Ted had discussed Roberta's painfully evident mental lapses, but that neither was able to raise the issue with me, fearing that he would be invading my privacy.

The problem of how to talk about the disease in its early stages with people who are facing its horrors is a difficult one and needs to be addressed by the medical profession, the church, and family members. I will discuss the problem in greater detail in the last chapter.

A Remarkable Life

Teaching was a lifelong calling for Roberta. Like many women in those days who were married to graduate or medical students, she had put me through a large part of my advanced training by teaching, in her case, high school mathematics. After we moved to Philadelphia, she continued her theological education, begun at Western Seminary in Holland, Michigan, by taking an internship in hospital chaplaincy. Later she taught for more than twenty years at the off-campus work/study program for college students that I had designed and directed in Philadelphia and which was called The Great Lakes Colleges Association's (GLCA) Philadelphia Urban Semester.

Linda Noonan, a former student who had been out of touch with Roberta for a long time, wrote her:

Dear Roberta,

It's been twenty years since I sat at your desk at the urban studies offices discussing phenomenology, Christianity, spiritual practice, and the meaning of life. I am now back in Philadelphia—just up the street from you.

I have been remembering and celebrating the deep and rich experiences and relationships which have formed me—and you are among them. You have been an important mentor to me— your presence and teaching touched me deeply two decades ago, and you have over the years remained an important part of my "cloud of witnesses"! I met you at a very fluid point in my spiritual development and you were, for me, an amazing model of commitment, integrity, and passion. I have vivid memories of conversations in your office, seminars, my first experience of yoga, and worship at your church and many other moments. I can't tell you how many times I have "consulted" my memory of you over the years!

So I have thought of you. And want to thank you. And give thanks for you!

Peace,

Linda

The congregation of the First United Methodist Church of Germantown in Philadelphia, in which we worshipped, loved Roberta. Having raised a family and maintained a marriage for fifty years, and being a well educated, professional woman, she was a role model to many younger women. Over the years she had invited scores of church folks to our home for a meal or late afternoon coffee, and offered massage sessions to many people during which

3

she relieved physical pain and spiritual distress. By being involved in many cutting-edge groups at church, as well as long established task forces, such as the Music Committee, the Evangelism Task Force, and the Education Curriculum Committee, Roberta also contributed to the church's institutional life. Serving as a member of the Coordinating Committee for the church's bicentennial celebration, she played a key role in the success of that event. Later she was one of the founders of the Bible discussion group that became a focus of our life at church.

No doubt some of our friends sensed that all was not well with her, but they did not talk to her or me about it, and may have ascribed her mental lapses to her loss of hearing, a deficiency that became serious enough to require her to use hearing aids years before she retired.

A Congenial Community

Never had we been surrounded by such interesting, caring and congenial neighbors as those in Cherokee Village apartments, where we moved in 1994 after we retired. Our closest ones were those who lived in the apartment units on opposite sides of the central driveway area, which we jokingly called *La Grande Allée*. Each unit offered a good view of the apartments across the way, so we could easily note each other's comings and goings, thus promoting continuous social interaction and neighborly gossip of a friendly sort. Spiritually, we were very close to our neighbors and had much religious life to talk about, being Presbyterian, Episcopalian, Roman Catholic, United Methodist, and Jewish. Their friendship and support sustained Roberta and kept her from withdrawing socially any faster than she did.

With parties, coffee klatches, and other informal gatherings, our apartment became one of the centers of neighborhood activity in the apartment complex. Roberta always preferred having friends visit us in our place rather than going to theirs, or holding a committee meeting in our rooms instead of in the church building. The book reading club to which we belonged also held some of their meetings in our apartment. She would gladly lay out a spread on

4

our dining room table to start a visit with friends or a group meeting with the fellowship of food.

About once a month in the late 1990s, we gathered with our neighbors in one of our apartments to have an "O-be-joyful" occasion, as our neighbor Grace Yocuma called it, with wine, cheese, cashews, fruit, and other goodies. Although Roberta always enjoyed having a group or committee meet in our apartment, it began to fall increasingly on me to prepare the place and lay out the spread that was an expected accompaniment of such meetings.

As time went on she gradually withdrew from active participation in church groups, such as in our reading group, and in the neighborhood, not only because of her increasingly serious hearing problem, but also because she was experiencing mounting difficulty following discussions that would be taking place in the group.

The front and side of our refrigerator were covered with notices, schedules of church meetings, entertainment events, and names of people (and their dogs) who we met in our apartment life. Unfortunately, this clutter of memory crutches was largely ignored and forgotten. (Memory aids tend to form an infinite regression, where notes to aid the memory are followed by reminders to read the notes, followed by ever more of the same.) Festooned with yellow tags, the refrigerator gave testimony to our failing memories, whether age-related or disease-induced. At this time we thought we were probably behaving in much the same way as many people of our vintage—adjusting to the problems of growing older.

A Devoted Gardener

Shortly after we had moved into our apartment, Roberta inquired among our neighbors whether it would be all right with the landlords if she were to dig up part of the lawn for a vegetable garden, in addition to the flower gardens already there. They responded, "You can do anything you want around here, as long as you don't ask them to do it." That was all she needed. Continuing her lifelong love affair with gardens, she put me to work digging out a small plot near the sidewalk, where she made preparations to grow her favorite vegetable, tomatoes. (When this groundbreaking chore was completed, however, I made it clear that in the future I would refuse to dig out any more sod, since my old back could no longer endure such heavy labor.)

Roberta called herself an avid gardener. Her several gardens in our apartment yard offered her a particularly appropriate expression of her selfhood. Helping things and people to grow was her lifelong vocation.

Growing irises, poppies, roses, lilies, and columbine also satisfied Roberta's artistic sense. Her appreciation of beauty and line found expression in the hues of the flowers and the curve of the white stone path through them. Moreover, her gardening extended the farming tradition of her family. When she wasn't engaged outdoors from April through October, she was actively engaged indoors (the rest of the year) perusing vegetable and flower catalogues, ordering seeds, and nursing tomato seedlings on the kitchen windowsill. Her gardens shaped her as much as she shaped them.

Even more, gardening was an expression of Roberta's spiritual life. Her garden was her trysting place with God. She wrote the following poems:

City Garden

1

A city garden
Here and now and I
Are quietly arranging
One another:
Small enough so we
Can meet a friend,
Large enough so God
Will join us here.
An ancient stone,
Place for being here alone,
An open path for creatures
Less and more who run
And fly and sinuate,
A flowering crabapple
To share surprise,
Vines and grasses move
The winds, live with bees.
Light and shadow touch
Each other into life.

2
Garden tomatoes
Spill into my Saturdays,
So, compost with you.

Later, upon reading the poems, my nephew Raymond Mulder, who had lived in Japan, pointed out to me that the second stanza was a haiku. Upon hearing that, my admiration for Roberta's gift of poetry rose to new heights. A gardener friend once told me that people who had grown tomatoes resonated with Roberta's haiku. (Tomatoes can be overwhelming at the height of the growing season, and by the end of the week, the gardener is ready to make fertilizer out of them.)

A New Profession

As she approached retirement age in the mid-1980s, Roberta realized that she would need a new activity to occupy her time. She found the answer in the profession of massage therapy. Enrolled in a training program she flew to Cambridge, Massachusetts, every third weekend for three years. After completing the program she launched a successful therapeutic massage practice that formed a bridge from her career as an adjunct college professor into retirement. It fit her temperament and values perfectly, bringing her into contact with people needing help, exercising her gift of healing, and gaining her professional standing in a status-conscious society.

For the next decade or more, Roberta practiced her art, laying her healing hands on scores of strained backs and sore shoulders. She became a significant presence in the lives of many people through her healing mission of massage and teaching. Her practice made a substantial addition to our family income even though she gave numerous treatments *pro bono*. To Barb Mortenson, a woman diagnosed with cancer, for example, she offered weekly sessions free of charge. Barb wrote the following note, which expressed the thanks of many other people whom Roberta helped:

Dear Roberta,

*Thank you so much for the months and months of mas-
sage. What a healing touch you have. You have made such
a difference in my recovery—your hands and your heart.
I'll miss seeing you while I'm working. You (and Bob of
course) remain in my prayers.*

Love, Barb M.

At a Crossing

For many years, attending the annual meetings of the American
Scientific Affiliation (ASA) had afforded us an intellectual oasis in
our summer season. The ASA is an association of Christian evan-
gelical scientists, engineers, academicians, theologians, and philoso-
phers who address issues of science and Christian faith. Not only
did the meetings offer three days of quality intellectual fare, they
also provided the occasion for renewing friendships with other
members, some of whom were former classmates from high school
and college.

Following the 1998 annual meeting at Cambridge University,
Roberta and I, with a group of other attendees, packed ourselves
into two tour buses and set off on a ten-day escorted journey to
places of scientific, Christian, and historic significance in England,
Scotland, Ireland, and Wales. These sites included Isaac Newton's
farm home, several historic churches, the famous Keswick conference grounds and church, cathedrals, castles, and museums. Seeing the *Book of Kells*, housed in Trinity College, Dublin, thrilled us
both. Throughout this rather demanding trip Roberta showed no
noticeable signs of forgetfulness or disorientation. In contrast, I was
the one who lost his wallet. The social interaction, the sites and
scenes, and the lectures stimulated her; and she gave no indication
of confusion.

At the ASA meeting a year later, however, the decline from the
previous year was perceptible. During one of the meetings that happened to be of great interest to me, Roberta whispered that she
needed to return to our dorm room, located on the far side of the
campus. Reluctantly, I gave her the key, wondering whether she

8

would be able to thread her way over and back through the maze of crosswalks. Although I sensed that I should accompany her, I did not want to miss the lecture and the discussion. Soon, however, my anxiety got the better of me, and I departed in the middle of the question-and-answer period to search for her. As expected, I found her on a crosswalk, looking around, confused. Although she was relieved to see me, she made no comment about her disorientation. This incident upset me, but I was relieved that, in social situations in the dining room and the residence, Roberta held her own and gave few if any noticeable signs of mental deterioration.

Yet, the disorientation and memory loss seemed gradually to be gaining ground.

A question of deep concern to me and probably to other seniors was this: When does a forgotten word, a disorientation, a slightly diminished ability to do daily tasks become a bona fide marker of Alzheimer's disease? It is not an easy question to answer. There is no clear transition point, and future brain research will probably show that the disease starts long before definite behavioral symptoms can be noticed. Because the onset of the disease is gradual and because the observation of one's loved one is often influenced by the wish not to believe what one sees happening, it is very difficult to determine when the disease may be present. Looking back on Roberta's behavior, however, I now recognize signs that I could not or would not interpret as symptoms of Alzheimer's disease at the time.

Memory lapses may not in themselves signify the onset of the disease, unless they occur frequently. But how often is frequent? It's a judgment call, requiring a comparison to be made with more-or-less normal friends and relatives and the person's prior behavior. Moreover, *what* is forgotten is as important as *how often*. A distant acquaintance of mine inexplicably forgot his children's names one day. That's a more significant symptom of the disease, I believe, than mislaying one's car keys. Disorientation in time and place may be more significant than memory lapses, and when they occur together with memory slips they begin to point to the disease. My experience, however, is that eventually there occurs a *defining moment* in a person's early-stage Alzheimer's disease, an event that puts all previous lapses of memory and disorientations into focus and, at least to the person's loved ones, marks the definite onset of the disease. Forgetting his children's names was such a defining moment in the disease of my acquaintance.

It was not possible for our immediate family to be deeply involved in the shadows that were gathering around my wife by our fiftieth wedding anniversary. Our children had long since left home, married, and established themselves elsewhere. We kept in contact by mail, telephone, e-mail, and occasional visits. Two daughters and their husbands who live in the vicinity of Philadelphia made visiting easy. The home of our oldest daughter, who lives in Ohio with her husband and three sons, offered a convenient overnight stop on our frequent trips to Grand Rapids to visit our parents, close relatives, and many lifelong friends. It was not until later that Roberta's increasing mental problems became evident to our daughters.

Roberta showed no signs of the disease when, on Memorial Day weekend in the year before I retired (1999), we made our annual trip to Lexington, Kentucky, to visit our son, his wife, and their four children to help them redecorate their house for selling. She was her old self. On previous visits we had always planned a little time alone with our grandchildren, by taking them to breakfast at a buffet restaurant. The trip to the restaurant on this visit was the last time that our grandchildren saw the grandmother they had enjoyed and the last time that she recognized them.

More Signs

One afternoon sometime after our fiftieth wedding anniversary, while working in my study, I heard a strange shuffling sound downstairs, like furniture being moved. Roberta called to me for help. I hurried down to find her staring at the carpet. There I saw four little pools of bubbling liquid by the dining room table. Horrified, I returned from the kitchen carrying towels with which I frantically scrubbed the froth. But the damage was done. Four bleached spots remained, never to be removed.

The damage that Roberta had done to the carpet troubled me

less than her reaction. She was impassive, expressing no surprise, remorse, or any other reaction to her mistake. Walking away from the mess, she gave no explanation nor did she want to discuss the matter. Was she in shock? Later she told me that she had failed to read the label on the bottle and had forgotten that the cleaner she had purchased through a catalogue was designed to clean tiles, not carpets.

This incident called to mind a previous accident in which she had inadvertently poured bleach over one of my favorite shirts. That time, however, she had been brokenhearted at her mistake, realizing how much I valued the shirt. In the light of this present mishap, however, I wondered whether a similar disorientation had been at work.

Although the spotted carpet represented another early indication of the encroaching disease, I discounted its significance. I did not want to believe that Alzheimer's was happening to Roberta.

Early in our married life Roberta had purchased a Singer sewing machine that became one of her prized possessions. I installed it on the cast iron Singer stand that she had inherited from her mother. On her machine my wife had sewed innumerable garments and had produced many other material projects throughout our children's growing years and later. It was to her what my table saw had been to me—an indispensable machine for raising a family and managing a household.

In the spring the Singer began telling her it needed a trip to the repair shop for routine maintenance and cleaning. Returning the machine in mint condition, the service man lauded the machine: "They don't make 'em like that anymore." Roberta agreed.

But Roberta never completed another sewing project with the machine. On her first attempt to sew with it, she tried to adjust the tension on the bobbin but soon had it so severely out of tune that it would not work properly. I was unable to correct her mistake, so it sat in the bedroom, abandoned.

Each morning in the late 1990s, Roberta managed to take a large assortment of vitamins, food supplements, and some prescription drugs along with her wake-up mug of coffee. She was especially concerned to provide herself with health products that were advertised to improve mental functions. Lecithin was one of these supplements. Every morning we sprinkled a generous helping of it on our breakfast cereal. I observed that she kept a checklist for her pill-taking routine, marking off the pills as she took them. Was this compensation for increasing memory loss? Again, a judgment call. We all make lists to keep us on track. By itself it did not signify much.

In sum, after our fiftieth wedding anniversary, numerous signs of Alzheimer's disease were appearing in Roberta's behavior, in what is usually described in the professional Alzheimer's literature as the first stage of the disease. She was becoming more absent-minded, had difficulty recalling names and words, was frequently forgetful, experienced difficulty in learning new information, was sometimes disoriented in unfamiliar settings. She had experienced minor but uncharacteristic lapses in judgment and behavior and had reduced her social activities both in and out of the home—all signs that the disease was well under way, disrupting and deleting the neural circuits of her brain.

Yet in other areas of her life, Roberta was reasonably competent. She was managing her social contacts at church and in the neighborhood rather well. Gardening was always more of an art than a science with her, so I couldn't tell if it was any less organized in 1999 and the spring of 2000 than before. She continued her massage practice into the spring of 2000. Cooking, shopping, and housework she did moderately well with some assistance from me. We enjoyed the spiritual experiences afforded by our church, we were conscious of God's goodness to us, and we lived in the sunlight of God's favor.

While signs of Alzheimer's disease were escalating in Roberta's behavior, I wanted desperately for them to be typical signs of aging, not symptoms of the dreaded disease. I convinced myself that Roberta was aging normally, even though, I admitted, perhaps a bit ahead of the curve. I looked the other way, toward areas wherein she was still proficient. Moreover, she showed no anxiety about her lapses and, as time went on, we no longer mentioned them.

Thus we were both in denial. It made life easier at the time and enabled us to carry on against the encroaching shadows.

II

The Defining Moment

I experienced two extremely bad days about the time of my retirement. The first occurred when I was diagnosed with prostate cancer. Coming face-to-face with the end of my days gave me one of the most fright-filled nights of my life. The second occurred when, lying in the recovery room of the hospital after mastoid surgery, I realized that the right side of my face was paralyzed. A nauseating dread spread through my body as I concluded that my facial nerve had been severed in the operation, leaving me with the prospect of a permanent disfigurement of my face. Fortunately, chemotherapy has kept the cancer at bay, reconstructive neural surgery has restored most of the mobility to the right side of my face, and my life goes on.

Neither of these two days, however, bad as they were, can compare with the despair that settled on me one Thursday morning in August, 1999. I was working at my computer around six o'clock when Roberta padded into my study looking sleepy and beautiful. We greeted each other with our customary smooching and compared notes on our night's adventures in our dream worlds. Soon, having had enough, she departed to the kitchen to brew a cup of wake-up coffee.

Later I heard her go into to her room to dress for the day's activities. To my surprise and dismay, she returned to me decked out in her Sunday attire—her lovely, muted yellow and blue summer suit. The sinking feeling I had experienced on my previous close encounters with death and disfigurement suddenly surged through me.

"You're all dressed up for church," I said, as casually as I could, my heart pounding.

"Why, yes," she replied, looking somewhat surprised at my comment.

"But it's not Sunday."

"Oh?" said she. "What day is it?"

"It's Thursday."

"Hmm." She paused. "Guess I made a mistake."

I searched her eyes for any sign of recognition of the significance of her time-disorientation. There was none. She left my study with no other comment.

It was different for me. Despair hit me like a physical blow to my midsection. Sitting with my head in my hands, I was suddenly overwhelmed with the hopelessness of Roberta's future. I could not fight back the specter of the bewildered, mindless person she was doomed to become. All I wanted to do was to gather her up in my arms, to run away and hide from what lay ahead. But I was numbed by despair in realizing that there was no escape for her.

This incident gathered past occurrences of momentary forgetfulness and fleeting disorientation and brought them together with stark clarity. Our former joking about who was aging faster, the reminder notes plastered over our refrigerator, my discovering her trying in vain to find her way back to me at the ASA meeting, four little pools of bubbling fluid on the carpet, the disabled sewing machine—each separate piece converged into a compelling picture. For several years I had been denying these signs and dismissing them from my consciousness. But they had not gone away.

That morning in August I was confronted with what I did not want to know. Confirmed by the upwelling of emotions associated with my earlier medical ordeals, my deepest intuitions told me without question that Roberta had entered into the shadows of Alzheimer's disease, and there was no turning back. It was the *defining moment* for me.

Yet, I had no reason to suppose that it was a defining moment for Roberta. I do not know when or if she ever had one. To her the disorientation may have looked like any other lapse she had occasionally experienced in the past, and which had not seemed to concern her.

But I would not be surprised if a defining moment comes in the early stages of the disease in almost every case, to the soon-to-be caregiver, the person being stricken, or both. Perhaps the moment comes long after symptoms of the disease had been visible but denied, when a person entering into the shadows of this disease and his or her loved one realize the awful future that lies ahead. So it was for me, but not for Roberta, as far as I knew.

Why was this incident so important to me? Why not one of the earlier incidents, say, when she stood bewildered on the university campus earlier in the summer? I can only guess at the answer. Perhaps the water had risen so high behind my dam of denial that the wall of my will could no longer restrain it. Maybe the quiet moment by ourselves in which it occurred gave it unusual force. Perhaps it was a wake-up call from God, exhorting me to deal with the realities of Roberta's life. Whatever the answer, I mark this as Dark Thursday, the day when I accepted the fact that she had already entered into the shadows of Alzheimer's disease and there would be no turning back.

Soon Roberta slipped out of the house dressed in her gardening attire. From the kitchen window, I watched her as she walked slowly in and out among her tomato plants, coffee mug in hand, tucking in an errant shoot here, plucking out a weed there, the classic picture of Roberta in her favorite surroundings. Was God joining her there at this time?

Through my tears I questioned, "Why, God? Why Roberta?" For a terrible moment, standing there in the kitchen, I harbored doubts about God's goodness to us.

The horror that lay ahead for Roberta continued to fill me with anguish as I contemplated her inexorable descent into the darkness, where past and future do not exist, only a bewildered present.

Endless questions, bouts of agitation, lost words, aborted thoughts, nameless fears, irrevocable shrinking of self—these were in store for her. The realization of her hopeless future would often shock me awake in the nights that followed. At times I had to look away from her to hide my tears. Never had I anticipated anything as dreadful as Alzheimer's disease happening to Roberta.

Alzheimer's struck two more blows in quick succession. On the following Monday, Roberta prepared a pasta dinner for our evening meal, a dinner menu that we have always enjoyed. When Roberta was still working on Monday mornings in her downtown massage treatment room, I had taken over the preparation of the evening meal in order to relieve her of the burden of this household chore. Pasta was the dish I loved to prepare. Since her retirement, however, she had reclaimed the preparation of the meal as a thing she wanted to do.

That evening she had cooked the pasta and covered it with the store-bought sauce we favored because it is so quick and easy to use. But Roberta had failed to heat the pasta sauce, serving a dish of steaming hot spaghetti covered with refrigerator-cold sauce. The mistake was obvious and couldn't be ignored. She offered to reheat the whole dish, which I concurred was a good idea. We ate in uncomfortable silence. Although we never discussed the meal, I surmised it was a frightening experience for her, coming as it did on the heels of the recent morning of her disorientation. In the past we might have joked about this incident. After Dark Thursday I wasn't able to do so. Nor could I bring it up for discussion with her.

The second incident, which followed shortly thereafter, could have come from a casebook on Alzheimer's disease. I opened the refrigerator door and reached for the yogurt I needed for the lunch I was preparing. When I opened the container I found myself looking at garbage. (Earlier Roberta had started the practice of collecting garbage and table leftovers in an emptied yogurt container, which she would dump at the end of a day or two into the trash can outside. The ancient garbage disposal in our apartment was unable to handle anything larger than tiny scraps.) Aware that Roberta had mistakenly placed the garbage-filled yogurt can in the refrigerator, I said nothing and later threw its contents into the trash.

16

Although Roberta's behavior leveled off after these episodes, I knew that she had set foot on a journey from which no one has ever returned, and I was to be her traveling companion and caregiver. I realized that she would need all the love and nurture I could bring to her. After my moment of doubt, I knew in my heart that only God's grace could sustain us, and I trusted that grace to carry us through to the end.

John Baillie[1] wrote a prayer that gave me the words with which to address God at this time.

O Lord my God, who dwellest in pure and blessed seren-ity beyond the reach of mortal pain, yet lookest down in unspeakable love and tenderness upon the sorrows of earth, give me grace, I beseech Thee, to understand the meaning of such afflictions and disappointments as I myself [and especially Roberta] am called upon to en-dure. Deliver me from fretfulness. Let me be wise to draw from every dispensation of Thy providence the lessons Thou art minded to teach me. Give me a stout heart to bear my own burdens. Give me a willing heart to bear the burdens of others. Give me a believing heart to cast all burdens upon Thee.

---

[1] John Baillie, *A Diary of Private Prayer* (New York: Charles Scribner's Sons, 1949), p. 113.

III

The Best Year of Our Lives

Following the events of Dark Thursday, I slogged through days of confusion and uncertainty. Despair sucked at my footsteps. Realizing that there was no hope for Roberta, medically speaking, I was hardly able to think about her future. Nothing could prevent the "one thousand subtractions" from occurring in her brain, as David Shenk characterized the disease in his book, *The Forgetting Alzheimer's*.[1] Nor could the demons of confusion, fear, and agony be prevented from taking up residence in her mind as her brain began to deteriorate. The hopelessness of her situation sometimes blotted out the sun, smothered my energy and will, and often woke me in anguish in the dark of the night.

Paradoxically, I remained stubbornly confident that the One to whom we belonged would uphold us on the coming journey. Although I was not confident that, as time went on, I would be able to respond effectively to the behavioral problems resulting from Roberta's disease, I did expect to receive help to meet those challenges. My confidence for the coming day grew as I voiced the following morning prayer:

*I thank Thee for the blessed assurance that I shall not be
called upon to face the tasks and interests of another day
alone or in my own strength, but shall at all times be
accompanied by Thy presence and fortified by Thy grace.[2]*

With it I was able to hold at bay the fiends of hopelessness and
sadness most of the day. Further relief came with my evening prayer.

*I bless Thee for Thy hand upon my life, and for the sure
knowledge that, however I may falter and fail, yet underneath are Thine everlasting arms.[3]*

The words "everlasting arms" are taken from Deuteronomy
33:26, "The eternal God is your dwelling place, and underneath are
the everlasting arms" (Revised Standard Version, 1952). The verse
was made into a hymn, "Leaning on the Everlasting Arms," by Elisha
Hoffman in 1887. This verse served as a sustaining hand reaching
out to me in the darkness of the stormy night that accompanied
Roberta's disease.

Exhausted, I would whisper thanks for those arms and for the
grace that had flowed into my day, hour by hour, minute by minute.

I tried to picture the changes that lay ahead of us. The mutuality of our relationship, knit together over the years, would gradually become unraveled. No longer would we share the workload as
we had since our college days. Our daily companionship—doing
chores around the house and yard, shopping, taking walks, working crossword puzzles—would become a thing of the past. Roberta's
dependence on me would increase until it became total. Control of
both of our lives would eventually fall completely into my hands.
The change in our relationship was already happening; even at that
moment it was I who was thinking about and planning for the future with little or no input from her. These considerations presaged
a radical restructuring of our lives.

Going Home

Despite the fact that we were surrounded by loving friends in Philadelphia, I began to hear the call of family and many an "auld ac-

quaintance" in Grand Rapids. Roberta and I both grew up and were educated there and had often said that we would like to spend our last days in that city. My two sisters lived there, as well as cousins, nephews, and nieces, to say nothing of friends from school and college days with whom we had stayed in touch over the years. Their voices became more urgent as I began to realize how much help and support I could count on from them as Roberta's condition would worsen in the future. I realized from the outset that without the help of family and friends I would not be able to give Roberta the care she would need.

There, too, were located the churches in which we had been nurtured as well as our *alma mater*, Calvin College, with its many community-oriented cultural and educational programs. The city is a foremost center of the Dutch-American community, with which we still strongly identified. I wanted us to be part of that mix.

Most important, the Holland Home retirement community was located in Grand Rapids. The fact that all four of our parents had spent their last days in its facilities increased its emotional appeal. Once we were accepted into the independent living section of the system, our health needs would be taken care of to the end of our days. Moreover, with its highly regarded Alzheimer's care program, it would be ideal for Roberta.

These circumstances exerted a tremendous pull to Grand Rapids, and tides of homesickness swept over me.

Another part of me, however, hung on to the forlorn hope that Roberta's decline would be slow enough to allow us to remain another year or two in Philadelphia before I would feel forced to move. Countless loving hands already supported us here. The thought of leaving this city, our church, and our neighborhood was almost unbearable, and I hoped to delay our departure as long as possible.

From the muddle of confusion and opposing thoughts gradually emerged the awareness that my first order of business was to deal with Roberta's immediate needs—especially to keep both her mind and body engaged with the real world as long as possible. She continued to be her customary self most of the time. To extend this condition as long as possible was my goal. Keeping our companionship alive, I continued doing the familiar things we had always done.

Moreover, I began to bring to our relationship a greater presence than I had ever done before, turning up the intensity dial on every activity. In many ways I adopted the frame of mind that had activated me in our courting days in college. I found more occasions to have fun with her, to laugh, sing, and play. The young lover returned in new form.

Although I knew that we could not prevail in the war against Roberta's disease, I was determined that we would win as many battles as possible. Helpless to prevent the disease as it advanced, I could, however, make her days as bright as possible, offering strength when she was weak, calmness when she was agitated, courage when she was fearful, consolation when she was forlorn—a light in the depth of her darkness. I decided that my new calling was to be an extension of the everlasting arms of the Almighty. This calling, I realized, would require my sustained efforts for a very long time.

Not that these realizations were clearly formulated at the time; I was only dimly conscious then. It was not until later that I understood more clearly what I had determined to do. Little did I understand, however, that my resolve would be tested to the utmost in the months and years that lay ahead.

Yet we did not always find it necessary to be actively *doing* something. Just *being* together was often enough to satisfy us. I knew her fulfillment lay not in activities per se, although they were important, but rather for both to be involved with each other, and to make every day count for something.

There were two situations, however, that imposed constraints on Roberta's life. Her lifelong struggle with *restless legs syndrome* (RLS) made travel difficult. Long automobile rides and extended airline flights were extremely uncomfortable and dampened her enthusiasm for travel. Although she was willing to undergo the discomfort of RLS if it was necessary (as, for instance, when in 1982 we had taken the long flight to Japan to visit our daughter Joanne and her family, who were spending a year there on her husband's academic exchange), she preferred to stay home or limit her traveling to short excursions that did not require sitting in a car or airplane all day. So I mapped out short trips rather than long excursions. Her RLS would add greatly to her discomfort in the years ahead.

In addition, Roberta had become afflicted with a progressive hearing disability shortly before she retired, eventually losing almost all of the hearing in her right ear and 40 percent or more in her left one. Hearing aids helped but made little difference in worship services, in other audience situations, and in informal groups where everyone seemed to be talking at once. She resisted going to Christmas parties and other social gatherings with our church friends and others. Committee work also became increasingly problematic for her. Her hearing disability added to the difficulty of sorting out signs of Alzheimer's disease from failure of hearing. (It never ceased to exasperate us how many people seemed unable to accommodate hearing disabled people, such as we were, by speaking louder or putting an edge to their voices so they could be more easily heard. Since I too have a severe hearing loss, almost comparable to Roberta's, I could fully empathize with her increasing reluctance to participate in group activities.)

For a while I reproached myself that it had taken Roberta's horrific illness to generate my conscious resolution to be more intensely engaged with her. Why had it not occurred to me in her uncle's apple orchard, when I asked her to marry me, that engagement meant that I should be engaged *with* her, not just *to* her?

Putting these thoughts aside, I turned my attention to Roberta herself and took inventory of her greatest passions as a guide to how I could enhance our relationship. Since Roberta was still doing things she loved to do and had been doing for years, one of my responses was to join more heartily in these pastimes than I had earlier. So I inventoried the situation:

- Gardening was one of Roberta's greatest passions. She liked to call herself an avid gardener.
- Our daily hikes over the trails of the Wissahickon Valley and on the sidewalks of the neighborhood provided the exercise she needed, as well as the beauty she craved.
- Day trips were preferred to long tours.

- Knowing the satisfaction Roberta derived from her massage practice and the friends that it brought into her life, I encouraged her to continue it as long as possible.
- Music and dance provided food for our spirits, and we scheduled as full a calendar of concerts and dance programs as we could manage.
- Visits from friends were constant sources of strength and love.
- Our spiritual life, as it was lived at church and in our home, was utterly essential to her well-being as it was to mine.
- I knew that Roberta wanted to show how much *she* cared for *me* as well as receiving love and affection from me. This became more important than ever as she became increasingly dependent on me.

These were more than mere activities that Roberta had enjoyed and commitments that she had made. They defined who she was at this time in her life—gardener, healer, friend, walker, artist, lover, daughter of God. I was determined, as her traveling companion and caregiver, to keep that core of herself alive as long as possible until the darkness would become complete and she would be called home.

At Home in Her Garden

The cool early morning was Roberta's preferred time to work in her four little gardens (two flower, one tomato, and one herb/vegetable). However, with her flowering plots growing adjacent to the sidewalk she was vulnerable to dawn strollers, out on an early constitutional with one or more dogs. Some wanted to tell her about the garden they or their mothers once had, others needed to ask for advice on various horticultural problems or wished just to "oooh" and "aaah" over her little jeweled "Edens." Wanting to be alone with her plants for awhile before the kibbitzers descended on her, she turned out ever earlier in the morning.

Later in the day, having washed the mud off her shoes, Roberta would enjoy conversing with neighborly people who continued to be drawn to her and her gardens. She was gratified by her friends' admiration for her tomatoes and vegetables and especially her flowers. The garden area developed into an informal communication center where one could find out what was going on around the neighborhood. When visitors asked for directions to our apartment, we simply told them to look for the apartment with the flower gardens.

I played a supporting role in her gardening in a more willing manner than ever, carrying bags of mulch more readily, cutting back invasive weeds without being asked, hauling the hose around the yard, and spending more time just walking through her garden and enjoying it with her. Working with her, I shared in the friendships she made with the neighbors, especially with two fellow gardeners from across the street.

Because it did not require verbal ability or abstract conceptualization—among the first victims of the disease—gardening was an ideal activity for Roberta. It is sometimes recommended as a first-rate activity for Alzheimer's patients. I later learned that the Holland Home dementia unit even has a greenhouse in which residents may tend plants of various kinds.

By October 1999, the time had come to put my wife's tomato garden to bed, so we took down the netting around the garden and pulled up the stakes that had supported the plants. After uprooting them, we set them in bundles at the curbside for the trash collectors to haul away. A pleasant pre-Thanksgiving Day celebration, this activity expressed our gratitude for a successful gardening year. After saving some green tomatoes to be fried for dinner, Roberta set the rest to ripen in the dark garage. There, some turned red as late as Thanksgiving Day, encouraged by the warmth from the steam pipes running along the ceiling. It was my hope that this would not be her last tomato garden, but that the following spring she might still be able to plant and care for another one. Gardening was so tightly woven into her life that, as long as it did not come undone, I believed that she would be healthy.

Roberta displayed her last two November roses in a vase for several days, after which they looked so sad she disposed of them With my heightened awareness of her problem I could not help seeing in the faded flowers the future that lay before us. She later brightened our apartment with marigolds and mums that still were blooming outside—divine grace driving back the shadows.

Happy Wanderers

Our walks over the rugged trails and through the magnificent forests around Wissahickon Creek complemented and extended Roberta's love of growing things. Jack-in-the-pulpits, trilliums, wild rhododendrons, the first green sprout in the spring, the last scarlet leaf in autumn—each gave her intense pleasure. Having always paid attention to small things, she was able occasionally to hear God's still, small voice in ordinary events, an ability that became surprisingly evident as her disease advanced. From her I learned to pay more attention to seemingly insignificant things and to find pleasure in the beauty of details. On the other hand, I was the one who stopped and admired the big panorama. The mighty sycamores struck me with awe; I was delighted by the frothy waterfall and wondered at the forces that shaped an unusual rock formation.

Climbing over and groaning our way under trees felled by the 1999 hurricanes, which devastated the Wissahickon woodlands, we would press on, reminded of how much flexibility our bodies had lost. We would complete our hikes with a burst of energy supplied by an orange or apple that we ate as we sat on a log or boulder at the halfway point. Our daily hikes in the woods provided a front seat in the natural amphitheater that no TV channel could match.

On a later day, just after sunset, she followed me, binoculars in hand, into an open field from which we observed the rare celestial event of the procession of planets in a line-up across the sky. To me the heavens do indeed declare the glory of God in a loud, clear voice. I needed this large perspective to maintain my orientation in the difficult days ahead.

An Autumn to Remember

While there were still some yellow and scarlet maples in late October, all the more resplendent against the backdrop of gray tree trunks, most of the trees had been fading fast and losing their leaves. After a cold wind storm, our walking trails were nearly obliterated under a carpet of leaves. As the cold snap continued, the colorful covering became a tawny brown and later a drab tan.

Yet, how green was the grass that sprang into view from underneath the leaves! That it could grow so green while all other plants had faded was one of the joys of late autumn. There is no more eye-popping emerald than the color of October grass. Again, being sensitized by Roberta's condition, I related the dying leaves and growing grass to our own situation—the fading leaves, her illness; the green grass, God's grace, still growing through the shadows.

On a cool morning that autumn, Roberta and I drove to the southern New Jersey shore for our annual walk along the ocean's edge near the old town of Cape May. Although one might hope to find the trees in colorful fall attire at this time of the year, the hue I expected to see on our drive was instead a lackluster brown, not unlike the color of military camouflage suits. Better known for its fields of tomatoes and sweet corn than for vivid autumn vistas, the Garden State, I held, could never match the autumn beauty of Vermont or Michigan.

But how wrong I was. We drove through one corridor after another of beautiful foliage along the Atlantic City Expressway and the Garden State Parkway. Colors presented themselves that we had not seen elsewhere—yellows, the hue of Spanish doubloons; reds, splashes of Burgundy wine; browns, fine tanned hides hung out to dry. The colors were more mature, as it were, than the flashy, adolescent shades of Vermont. I resonated deeply with them. Roberta, too, was enchanted.

The ocean had an even greater effect on us. We had often walked its shore and were always profoundly moved by its limitless expanse, its unending restlessness, its ceaseless waves lapping the sand. Perhaps some hidden part of us responded to this birthplace of life. The deep called to the deep within us, to paraphrase the Psalmist of old. Walking quietly along the shore with Roberta was a wholly soothing experience.

Lunch in the Lobster House brought us into an entirely different dimension of reality. There was no deep spiritual resonance here, only a succession of gustatory delights. Every kind of seafood on the menu found its way to our platters. Roberta was overwhelmed and, of course, boxed a good share of it, which we both enjoyed

27

later at home as a light evening meal. Such a day-long trip satisfied Roberta's travel desires in a way no extended tour could match.

A Career Ends, but a Full Life Continues

Roberta tapered off her therapeutic massage practice and finally retired from it completely in the spring of 2000, but not because of the onset of Alzheimer's disease. Her thumbs, crooked with arthritis from heavy demands made on them by her practice, finally gave out, and she was forced to discontinue the work she had loved so much.

Because she had been the assistant to Michael Korn when he launched the renowned "Philadelphia Singers," Roberta took special pleasure in attending the concert series of this choral group. A dance series, musical programs of various kinds, a string ensemble concert series, and operas of the Academy of the Vocal Arts comprised our entertainment menu. Providing peaks in what was already a high range of satisfying experiences, these performances and concerts also afforded contacts with friends we did not see on any other occasion.

Before each performance of the dance series, we had dinner with an extraordinary friend, Susan Ellis, and her mother, Anne, who also was a victim of Alzheimer's disease. After the meal Roberta would walk arm-in-arm to the theater with Anne, who would be chattering away in German, her mother tongue. Watching our two loved ones, Susan and I developed a quality of bonding that only caregivers of Alzheimer's patients can feel. Before the year was over, Susan stopped bringing her mother to the performances because she had become completely unable to grasp what was going on. At no time while Anne was with us, or when we talked about her, did Roberta indicate that she made a connection between what was happening to Anne and what was going on in her own life. I was never able to determine whether Roberta was aware that Anne had Alzheimer's.

One of the persons who increased our enjoyment of life was Sam Whyte, a most welcome guest in our home throughout the entire year. We loved him then and now as a brother. He and Roberta had earlier become fast spiritual friends when they served for two years as co-chairs of the Evangelism Committee of our church. Later, in the middle 1990s, we three, along with Marion Taylor, formed the Coordinating Committee for the church's bicentennial celebration, an intensely satisfying collaboration. Sam was also a co-founder of the Bible discussion group and a regular attendee. Hardly a Sunday went by that we didn't share our love of the Bible and other significant experiences with him.

Every several weeks on Thursday, we invited Sam for a visit after his day's toil as a faculty member at Montgomery County Community College. In front of the fireplace, with a glass of wine in hand and crackers and cheese close by, we shared conversation and fellowship. Our exchanges ranged widely and always included literary and theological subjects as well as news from church. Our minds and values were so closely tuned that seldom did disagreement arise on any issue. These get-togethers continued until we left Philadelphia. Sam's fellowship remains one of the most significant gifts God has given to Roberta and me.

We had the pleasure of entertaining several houseguests during that year. I valued these visits because they were the last time some of our friends would see Roberta as a reasonably whole person. Perhaps the most significant visit was that of our nephew and niece, Ray and Linda Mulder, who stayed with us for several days in October of 1999. Their visit would figure largely in one of the most important offers I received the following year when it became clear that we would need to relocate in Grand Rapids.

In the past Roberta had enjoyed the role of hostess during visits from friends or family. Her responsibilities, however, gradually became too great a burden for her and left her agitated and more tired than before. She said she was getting too old to handle them. While this was true, her confusion and agitation seemed to go beyond aging. Her response to these visits illustrated the difficulty of separating the effects of normal aging from the consequences of Alzheimer's disease. The challenge was not only how to separate signals of the disease from signs of normal aging, but also how to *accept* the signals of the malady. Roberta chose not to accept them and adopted aging as her explanation. I knew, however, that the shadows were closing in on her.

Our church was the linchpin of our spiritual life. It continued to provide a spectrum of opportunities for satisfying Roberta's and my most basic spiritual and social needs. Both were satisfied in the Bible discussion group that met on Sunday morning before the worship service, a gathering that Roberta helped start. Moreover, so important were the worship services to us that we seldom played hooky. As the spiritual dynamo in our church, the worship services generated much of our church's deservedly splendid record of promoting social, racial, and gender justice.

The most significant event in our church life, early in 2000, was the retirement of our pastor, Ted, after thirty-seven years of ministry. While the accolades he received at the retirement ceremonies were eloquent and wide-ranging, they hardly did justice to this man's spiritual influence on the lives of so many people, and in promoting social and racial justice in Germantown and the wider community. For Roberta and me he demonstrated what a pastor should be, and continued to be our minister *emeritus* after his retirement. His support was of inestimable value in the journey that lay ahead of us.

Corporate worship wove our lives into the tapestry of the Judeo-Christian faith, as no other activity could, and put us in touch with the saints below and those above every Sunday morning. Fellow church members who greeted us on Sunday went far beyond being friends; they were brothers and sisters in Christ. Through them a glint of heaven pervaded the building, and the air snapped with the presence of the Spirit on Sunday morning. We kept in touch with the Almighty directly through worship and, further, through the family of God who met with us and who inhabited the halls and rooms and sanctuary of our church. I did not realize until later what an important role our church family had played and would continue to play in our lives as Roberta's disease unfolded.

From the time Roberta and I retired from our full-time careers, a normal day for us went something like this: Roberta rose about six o'clock and brewed her wake-up coffee, took her daily medications, carried out her devotions, puttered in her gardens in season, and prepared breakfast. I had risen much earlier, spent my first hour drinking coffee, holding devotions, setting aside the rest of the time for e-mail correspondence, and working on my research on science and theology. We ate breakfast before eight, while checking out the weather channel. Ready to venture out into the world, we took our morning walk on the trails around Wissahickon Creek. After hiking a different trail every day we would spend an hour or so reading *USA Today*, or going shopping, which seemed to consume a larger fraction of our time as the days went by. Roberta enjoyed helping me make a shopping list, giving a suggestion here and there and following me around the market. This was recreation for us, and I did not hurry it.

As long as she could, Roberta took responsibility for breakfast and dinner; I undertook lunch preparation duties. Our favorite lunch menu consisted of sandwiches made with a thickly sliced, meaty Celebrity tomato from Roberta's garden and topped with a slightly thinner slice of onion, with a sprinkle of brown sugar over all, on a slice of nutty grain bread. A bowl of homemade soup and a glass of wine rounded out the menu.

We often watched the twelve o'clock news and afterward read to each other from books such as Thomas Cahill's *The Gifts of the Jews* and Amos and Gardiner's *Never Before in History*, a book on the contribution of the Protestant Reformation to the start of the American Revolution. Then we set aside time for our daily nap. Since we both rose early, we were more than ready for our siesta. Having taken a vigorous walk made the nap all the more delicious.

Waking refreshed in the afternoon, we followed Roberta's parents' custom of laying aside work for the rest of the day and relaxing to the background music of one of our favorite CDs, such as Wynton Marsalis on the trumpet. At this time we reviewed our mail, worked crossword puzzles, and occasionally played Scrabble™ or Rummikub™, the unspoken purpose of which was to retain our, and especially Roberta's, mental sharpness.

However, by the middle of summer 2000, we stopped playing those games. They were becoming too difficult for her, and she became upset by her inability to do well in them.

Completing a few chores and going outside, where we inevitably encountered a neighbor or two who came by to chat, we rounded out the afternoon's activity.

Coming down to the close of the day, Roberta would put together a dinner that we often ate while watching TV. Sometimes she would prepare a special dinner—a pot roast with potatoes and vegetables like her mother had made. Enjoying the greater formality of candlelight and all else that goes with such an occasion, we would eat in the dining room, sans TV. At such times we would engage in relaxed conversation that often turned to our earlier days of family life and former professional work experiences, as well as what was currently happening in the neighborhood and at church. Roberta never tired of recounting tales from her family life, her summers on her Uncle Kees's farm, and her walks with her father on the golf course across the street from her childhood home in Grand Rapids.

By that time, we were in a mood to spend an hour or two quietly reading, closing the house down, and getting ready for bed. We retired earlier than most of our friends and relatives. But then, we rose earlier than most of them did. Thus went a typical day in the middle 1990s. But by 1999 the routine began to deteriorate as Roberta's illness intruded more and more upon our lives.

As the year progressed I took over more of the decision-making and housekeeping in our home life together. Roberta's ideas gradually dried up, and she relied increasingly on my initiative in household affairs. I described some of these in an e-mail I wrote to my sister, Marguerite Mulder, in the spring of 2000:

Dear Marguerite,

I'm sure Roberta knows what is happening, but she is in denial, as they say in psychological parlance. I play along with this, not knowing what else to do. Over the past year, signs kept popping up. She sometimes forgets what we plan to do on a given day, and she keeps asking me repeatedly what they are, or I have to remind her about them again and again. She can't find the word she wants;

mostly she forgets nouns. She looks to me to supply them. She loses things and after finding them she again loses them.

The other day we were working on our finances, and I asked her to enter some figures into the calculator and then subtract others. However, she could not find the "subtract" button, although it is easy to see because all the function keys are in gray, and the numbers are in black. She just stared at the calculator, unable to make a move, until I told her to run her finger down the gray keys until she found the minus key. She had the same trouble with the "equal" key. After she went through the routine once, however, she was okay again.

That doesn't mean that she doesn't have her good days. Sometimes I feel that I must be mistaken, that she is indeed okay. When we are with others she generally holds herself together. You may not have noticed anything strange on your last visit, although when you look back on it you may recall that something was wrong. But inevitably she slips back into some unexpected disorientation, showing to me that the horrific disease has not gone away.

During the past year, I have tried as never before to make every day that has been given to us the very best day in our lives. I keep suggesting interesting places to go, things to do, nice things to see. Our daily walks are a Godsend. We do things to exercise our minds, especially crossword puzzles, Scrabble, Rummikub. On a piece of paper she keeps track of words that keep escaping her, that she must remember, like names of flowers and people. We have had some very good days, and we treasure them together. But there is no stemming the tide, I fear. We are in the days of our long farewell to each other.

Love,

Brother Bob

The End of the Beginning

Some months after the last ASA annual meeting we attended, in 2000, I asked one of Roberta's closest friends from college days, who had also been present at the meeting, if she had noticed anything strange about Roberta's behavior.

"I noticed that Roberta had been unusually quiet and withdrawn," she said, "but I felt this was due to her hearing problems."

Those who knew Roberta well made allowances for unusual behavior, not wanting to even consider the dreadful alternative. But Roberta's withdrawal was also part of her defense. Rather than betray her condition, she held her peace. By doing so, however, she revealed that she knew something was wrong, and very likely she recognized what it was.

By the middle of the summer of 2000, Roberta had clearly come to the end of the first stage of Alzheimer's disease, the stage she had already entered before Dark Thursday in August of 1999. Now she was showing more signs and characteristics of the disease: having increasing difficulty recalling names and words, being frequently forgetful and absentminded, having reduced ability to learn new information, and being disoriented in unfamiliar settings. Lapses in judgment were becoming more frequent, and social activities both in and out of the home were being reduced. She was gradually becoming less able to help me with making decisions in the ordinary affairs of life. I began handling household finances, making shopping lists, and deciding on the day's activities, chores she had always done herself or in which she had participated.

I realize now that I might have missed an opportunity, in the time given us after Dark Thursday, to connect with distant friends and relatives so they could see Roberta and enjoy time together while she was still in relatively good health. The death and funeral of my brother in September 1999 did give the extended family a chance to see Roberta before she began her precipitous decline. For the most part, I was intent on living life the way Roberta wanted it, close to home, doing the things she loved to do, and bringing to them the greatest vitality I could marshal. Yet in the back of my mind lurked the thought that I would soon have to arrange a trip to

Grand Rapids to check out the retirement communities that offered a continuum of care, including Alzheimer's care facilities. I knew that in the end we would have to make a move there for Roberta's sake as well as for my own.

Moreover, during the summer of 2000, many people we consulted about relocating told us that making a move as soon as possible was the right thing to do. In support of their advice, many recounted stories of how difficult it had been to move their parents when they had become too old or ill to do it themselves.

The year following Dark Thursday turned out to be one of the best in our lives. We had both done things we loved to do and had grown closer to each other than ever before. Yet I was also conscious that I would remember these wonderful days long after they were lost to Roberta, as the gift of memory was gradually plucked from her brain and mind, neuron by neuron, strand by strand, event by event, thought by thought, person by person. Thus the image of God would slowly be leached from her, one of its most beautiful bearers. Yet, I was confident that even to the very end a small glint of that image would continue to be reflected in Roberta's personhood.

---

[1] David Shenk, *The Forgetting Alzheimer's: Portrait of an Epidemic* (New York: Doubleday, 2001), p. 224.

[2] John Baillie, *A Diary of Private Prayer* (New York: Charles Scribner's Sons, 1949), p. 93.

[3] Baillie, *Ibid.* p. 21.

IV

Suffering Eased through Grace Revealed

People with Alzheimer's disease, like other older people, may suf
fer from additional age-related ailments, such as heart problems,
arthritis, diabetes, as well as the dementia itself. Roberta had a disease called restless legs syndrome (RLS) that during her lifetime
was not recognized as a bona fide illness. It was thought to be more
of a mental problem than a physical one. RLS and Alzheimer's working together compounded her miseries in the months that ensued.

Roberta recalled that as a child it was impossible for her to sit
quietly in church, as all children were expected to do in those days.
Despite her mother's best efforts to control her —"Why can't you
sit still?"—she continued to fidget throughout the worship service.
Nobody then had heard of restless leg syndrome (RLS) or what a
severe problem it was. Roberta suffered doubly: once, from the ailment itself; and second, from her mother's (and therefore some others') public disapproval. She continued to suffer from RLS the rest
her life.

As she matured into middle age, restless legs became somewhat less of a problem, perhaps because she was leading a physically active life. Upon retirement, however, it once again began to
afflict her.

An attack of RLS, which usually struck at night, would begin with a minor, involuntary twitch of a leg, followed by a period of relaxation lasting ten to fifteen seconds. Gradually the tremor would increase in magnitude, with shorter periods of relaxation in between. The movements were involuntary; try as she might, Roberta could not control them. Described as unbearable "creepy-crawly" sensations in the legs, these feelings cannot be adequately communicated by words, only experienced. They became worse at night, so agonizing that she found it impossible to lie quietly in bed. Since moving her legs was the only means of relieving the symptoms, she was forced to get up and pace the floor.

The newsletter of the national organization of restless-legs sufferers is aptly entitled, *Night Walker*, and the ailment is appropriately called the *sleep thief* because it is impossible for the victim or the sleep partner to slumber when an attack occurs.

After years of suffering, Roberta finally learned through her own research how to partially control her problem. She subscribed to *Night Walker* and contacted other sufferers for help. Upon discovering that caffeine exacerbated RLS, she stopped drinking coffee and tea. Iron and quinine tended to relieve it. Unfortunately, a side effect of the latter was an advancing hearing impairment. Since she already had a hereditary, age-related loss of hearing, she discontinued taking quinine. Until retirement, she had the problem under control aided by prescriptions of various sedative medications.

Roberta's primary care physician, like most doctors, knew little or nothing about the ailment when Roberta first presented her symptoms to her, and could offer her no help. Over the course of years, Roberta kept her doctor updated through information she gained from the national organization.

Sleep Thief[1] is a book about RLS that Roberta and I should have been reading in the fall of 2000, when she was again being troubled by this mysterious ailment. But we never even picked it up because we found the cover illustration—with its black background from which peered one large, unblinking eye—so disturbing. Roberta often remarked how much she disliked it. The wonder is that we allowed it to stay around so long. One afternoon in October, despite having a strong aversion to the cover of the book, Roberta picked it up and began randomly paging through it. She criticized this or that, or remarked, "Oh, we know that." At one point, however, she stopped and began to read aloud. The passage said that it was important to nip a restless leg attack in the bud. Rub the legs or take a warm bath, the book advised. The longer one lets an attack progress, the more difficult it is to remedy it. She let the passage go without comment, snapped the book shut, and laid it down.

That night, as I lay in bed with Roberta peacefully sleeping at my side, I felt a restful sleep lay ahead of us. Shortly after she dozed off, however, the first telltale twitch occurred. I groaned inwardly as she flexed her legs for relief, her restlessness following the usual pattern of increasing intensity. It was with a sinking feeling that I observed the sleep thief again robbing Roberta of her rest.

Recalling the events of the afternoon, I suddenly realized that I should have been following the suggestions that Roberta had read in the book. Already rather tardy, I reached over and began to massage her legs. Unhurriedly, I ran my hand up and down her thighs and calves, first one leg, and then the other. When one of them began to twitch, I pressed harder—but always slowly so as not to communicate anxiety or frustration. It is amazing how much love one can communicate by the laying on of hands, as Roberta herself had done many times while massaging someone's sore muscles. Could it have been what Jesus, and later his disciples, conveyed with their hands?

The harder I rubbed, the harder I prayed. In rhythm with my strokes I asked that my hands might bring peace to my wife's troubled body. It was a long session, and as this soothing massage continued, her restlessness subsided, her breathing became regular, and she fell asleep.

As I lay back on my pillow, the events precipitated by the book began to fall into place. With amazement I reviewed the entire sequence: first, our being repelled by the book and refusing to open it; second, Roberta's picking it up and paging through it for no apparent reason; third, her dismissing everything she looked at out of hand; fourth, her finding something that caught her eye for no apparent reason; fifth, her unexpected reading aloud to me the passage about leg rubbing, of all things; finally, my recalling the suggestion when it was needed. Later, when I tried to find the passage Roberta had read I could not locate it anywhere in the book. While I could find a sentence or two about leg rubbing or about bathing I never did see any that put these two together. Had she been ad libbing what I thought she had been reading?

Did all these events "just happen"? I do not believe so. Such a cascade of happenstance was not a mere coincidence, in my opinion. Since I hold a firm belief that intimations of God's presence are often unusually clear in a series of seemingly accidental occurrences, I could readily incorporate this day's events into my belief system. It was not just that my rubbing Roberta's legs eased her RLS, although that in itself was an answer to my praying. What was more noteworthy to me was the prior series of events that prompted me to do what I did. I interpreted it as the unfolding of grace, communicated through Roberta's sensitivity to little things that enabled her to pick up God's "still small voice" in the welter of stimuli that flooded her from the book with the desagreeable cover, and prompted her to "read aloud" what she did. Grace seldom comes in a thunderclap.

With a smile of thanks to the One behind all of this, I dropped off to sleep. Later I found one of John Baillie's prayers that expressed my feelings:

> *I thank Thee for every evidence of Thy Spirit's leading, and for all those little happenings which, though seeming at the time no more than chance, yet afterwards appear to me as part of Thy gracious plan for the education of my soul.[2]*

As time went on, leg massaging and later warm bathing, also suggested by the book, became standard treatments for RLS in our bag of home remedies.

---

[1] Virginia Wilson and Arthur S. Walters, M.D., Editor. *Sleep Thief, Restless Legs Syndrome* (Orange Park, Florida: Galaxy Books, 1996).

[2] Baillie, *Ibid.* p. 47.

V

The Breaking Storm

The year of grace following Dark Thursday came to an abrupt end after our return from a family visit to Grand Rapids late in the summer of 2000. The events of that trip seemed to trigger a rapid deterioration in Roberta's condition during that autumn. Since my main purpose for that trip had been to reconnoiter the retirement scene, Roberta and I had checked out several retirement communities that offered a continuum of care, from independent living arrangements through various levels of assisted living, and finally into special nursing and hospice. This continuum I considered to be a requirement of any retirement community to which we might apply. The Holland Home system looked especially good in that regard.

Upon our return, however, Roberta became increasingly vociferous about not wanting to leave Philadelphia. Even when I tried to avoid the subject, she kept niggling me about our plans, asking questions that I could not answer, such as when would we have to move, what would we take with us, what would we do with our beds and our reclining chairs? This was the first of a series of variations on a major theme that arose that autumn called *driven* or *obsessive behavior*. This behavior was triggered by a variety of situations and erupted many times during the fall of 2000.

41

Not surprisingly, my wife revealed an increasing need for stable surroundings. So it seemed the worst possible time for me to be thinking of changing everything that was familiar to her. Yet I felt an irresistible pull toward Grand Rapids, where my instincts told me our last days should be spent.

About that time my sister wrote me:

Dear Bob,

I am concerned about the pressures you must be living with in the light of what you wrote a few days ago about Roberta's attitude toward moving to Michigan—or anywhere.

I am all for you and agree with your original decision to come here. Maybe it is more important now than ever to do so.

At any rate—be assured that I am praying for you both and in particular that you can remain strong—and healthy—whatever the circumstances.

Love you much, dear brother,

Marguerite

Soon it became clear that an immediate move was out of the question, so I assured Roberta that we would not be moving for at least another year. That promise seemed to ease her mind. More importantly, we agreed to do what we had often done in the past, and should have been doing in the first place—to relax and wait for a clear answer to prayer as to what action to take. Like C. S. Lewis' characters in his *Narnia* stories, who were told by Aslan (the Lion representing Christ) that they would recognize the answer to what they needed to know when they came upon it, provided they stayed alert, so we waited and watched, trying to be confident that we would someday get a convincing answer as to when, where, and how to move. And we did, several months later.

Shoe Fetish!

As August wore on to September, Roberta's feet and legs became the new focus of her driven behavior, a more troublesome variation on the theme. Day after day she complained of having sore feet and legs over and beyond the usual symptoms of her RLS. While she never grumbled about restless legs—perhaps because she had lived with this problem all her life and had accepted it as an unchangeable condition of her existence like the color of her eyes—her constant complaining of sore legs and feet made me feel like screaming at times.

In response, I rubbed her legs and massaged her feet as she sat in her reclining chair. "That feels oh, so good," she murmured repeatedly. Nevertheless, her sore legs began to interfere with our daily walks, making them shorter and less vigorous. We opted for the smooth sidewalks of our Chestnut Hill neighborhood rather than the rugged trails of the Wissahickon woods.

Finally, we made an appointment with a podiatrist to have her feet and legs examined. The assessment revealed nothing more serious than a slight turning in of her left foot. The doctor suggested we try to find inserts for Roberta's shoes that might correct this condition.

That suggestion touched off a new round of obsessive behavior. Long before the doctor advised the use of inserts Roberta had been collecting and hoarding them by the basketful. She possessed all shapes and sizes, some for the arch, others for the toes or for the whole foot. At the doctor's suggestion we ordered one more special set from a catalogue and purchased yet another that could be obtained only from a sports store.

Roberta spent two whole evenings surrounding her chair with most of her shoes and the basket of inserts. She possessed many shoes, perhaps not in comparison with other women's wardrobes, but a lot according to my standards. She would stuff different combinations of inserts at random into one pair of shoes after another, and then would try them on. Not satisfied with finding certain inserts that fit some shoes to perfection, she would remove them and start over again. Soon everything lay in confusion on the floor, inserts scattered among disordered shoes.

I tried to slow her down, especially from removing inserts from shoes where they fit well. "There," I would say brightly. "Those fit perfectly. Let's set the shoes aside now." That did not work. She removed the inserts and started over again. There seemed to be no way to rein in this headlong obsession. It finally played itself out, and she retired out of sheer exhaustion.

I found, however, that there was usually an understandable, if not rational, foundation for what appeared to be Roberta's sometimes bizarre behavior. For a while she was constantly losing things—her comb, one sock of a pair, or a pair of shoes. When she found the lost item, she soon discovered that she had lost something else. It was as if she needed to be looking for and finding something all the time.

I once asked her why she wanted to find, in that case, her shoes. After a long silence she responded, "I'm so stupid." What did this mean? It meant, I think, that she was constantly reminded of how much her memory was failing, which she called "being stupid." That was more acceptable than being forgetful. So she had to keep on finding her possessions in order to show that she was not stupid, that is, not losing her memory. To find something she had to lose it first. Moreover, I believed that, underlying this driven behavior, lay a deeper current of *anxiety*—fear of Alzheimer's disease.

Misplacing things had become what I called her "obsession of the day." One evening she lost a shoehorn that she usually kept on the lamp table by her easy chair.

In an e-mail to our friend Sam, I described what was going on:

Sam,

Last night, sleeping in my own bed, I received an answer to prayer of the kind I am coming to expect. Roberta woke up about 3:00 A.M. with restless legs. With a sinking feeling I heard her pacing the floor in her bedroom, a sound that, although hardly audible, never fails to arouse me out of even the deepest sleep. It tells me that she is in profound discomfort from which I must help her escape if I can. After whispering a prayer for assistance, I got up and, taking her by the hand, guided her downstairs to the kitchen where I induced her to take a sedative with a glass of warm milk. I sat her down in her chair, massaged her legs for a while, and then just relaxed quietly next to her.

It was more than restless legs, however, that was driving her agitation. It was her lost shoehorn. Periodically, she broke out into a troubled search for it. This is her current favorite object to lose. She has two of them, identical in every way, one of which she keeps on the lamp table next to her easy chair so that it is available to her when she puts on her walking shoes, which she places next to her chair. The other one remains by her gardening shoes in the lower hallway. The one by her chair was lost this time. She adamantly rejected the one from the lower level that I offered her, hoping to trick her into accepting it as the lost item. Not to be fooled, she insisted on finding the exact one. So I laid the gardening shoehorn down on the lamp table, under her watchful eye, not knowing that a divine plan was being concocted to incorporate this move into a solution to her problem.

Soon the sedative began to take hold, and Roberta started to slow down. Returning to her bedroom upstairs, we prayed together. I also asked specifically to help my wife find her shoehorn. Although she seemed to relax somewhat as she lay in bed, she still hopped up now and again to rummage around for it. After a while I suggested, for luck of a better idea, that we try looking again downstairs. I switched on the light by her chair to help her sit down. There, to her delight she spotted the previously rejected gardening shoehorn lying where I had unthinkingly laid it and which she had forgotten about. The search was ended.

Clutching the lost shoehorn to her breast she returned with me to her bedroom where she contentedly laid it on her bedside table and went soundly to sleep.

Strangely, Sam, my love for her grows in proportion to her need for me. It's a different kind of love from what I had for her when she was whole and well; it is now more

protective and gentle. Her love for me, in turn, is grow-
ing every day, and she never tires of expressing it to me.

You are a friendly brother, and a brotherly friend.

Bob

Watching the TV weather report after breakfast the next morning, my eye happened to fall on the coffee table, where to my surprise I saw the original lost shoehorn. Being in the dark side of the
room, it had escaped our search. Since we couldn't find it, I believed that the divine back-up plan had been activated. This series
of coincidences attained the merciful goal of getting Roberta back
to sleep, which, heaven knew, is what she needed.

I offer this as a theological, not a scientific, interpretation of
the episode. The latter would involve a hopelessly complex calcu-
lus of causation, or would be written off as a series of chance occurrences. What happened was grace at work, I believe; and it is
grace that I continued to count on to get us through, not a rational
scientific understanding of the event.

How busy (in human terms) must the Master of the universe
be, making arrangements that look like coincidences all over the
world in response to prayers of millions upon millions of people,
not just now, but throughout all of history!

Losing Weight, and Her Way

At this time, Roberta was also voicing an ongoing complaint about
her aching stomach. Refusing to eat more than a token amount of
food, she lost sixteen pounds in three months. Food simply did not
interest her; and she resisted my efforts to increase her intake. Fearing a catastrophic response[1] such as screaming, striking out, crying, that Alzheimer's patients sometimes exhibit when pushed too
hard, I did not try to force her to eat as much as I knew she needed.
Since food was no longer a favorite topic of conversation, our meals
became such quiet affairs one might have thought we had taken the
vow of silence.

Her discomfort was so intense in September and October that
it spawned conversations tinctured with dark thoughts of death.

Although at one time in the past she had thought she would outlive me, and had purchased long-term care insurance to cover that contingency, she now told me she was convinced that she would die before I did. Although I agreed with her, I did not say that I believed it would be Alzheimer's disease that would deal the final blow rather than her stomach disorder.

So involved did we become with morbid thoughts that we both were swept into extended conversations about what life would be like beyond the shadows. At times we were sucked into a whirlpool of admittedly weird fantasies. I shared with her the idea that we would be walking down the corridors of the celestial palaces just as we had strode up the aisle on our wedding day, gazing at each other with unabashed adoration. (This idyllic moment in our wedding, caught by my father's camera, had become an icon for me of our married life.) These extremely emotional conversations drew us together in sometimes teary embraces in this eerie, psychedelic world.

On a Saturday afternoon late in September we met our daughter Eloise and her husband Pat Rogers for lunch at a neighborhood restaurant in Chestnut Hill. Being unable or unwilling to participate in our conversation, Roberta sat on the sidelines. Suddenly, out of nowhere, she announced in a sepulchral voice that she would be dying very soon. That was a conversation stopper. So obsessed with the end of her life was she that it was almost as if the Angel of Death were ever present by her side, ready to escort her out of this world at any moment. She needed to say what she did especially to Elo and Pat, whom she perhaps thought she was seeing for the last time. Before separating, Elo embraced her and said, "Goodbye, Mom. I love you."

We both decided it was time to make an appointment with her primary care physician, to discover, if possible, what was going on. I believed at the time that the stomach pains were psychological in origin but nonetheless real. I was aware of how often men, including male doctors, have wrongly assumed that women's ailments were imaginary. I was not about to make that mistake and ignore her problems.

Many months later I found a note that Roberta had evidently written to herself at this time, reproduced here.

> Thurs 8/24
> Woke at 6:15, rested
>
> Cancelled visit w Horstman
> Bob to Ali
> Appt Changes for RtDr to
> Wed Sept 6
> 9:15
> Sorted & wash a few things
> Made a new letter for Mike
> to gether
> o Will go to get letter of
> reference from Dr. Fabens.
> o Ask for Appt with Fabens
> Check over all. Ask ~
> ~~do ont Alzheimers~~, forgetting
> o losing ways... medications?

My heart clutched when I saw the words she had scratched out. Apparently, she recognized the probability that she had the disease and had decided to talk it over with her doctor, but later changed her mind. Nevertheless, she was prepared to talk about some of the specific tell-tale behaviors that may have seemed less threatening. The only problem we discussed with her physician, however, was her medications. After reviewing the box full of plastic pill vials, the doctor eliminated some of the redundant ones and others as well on the grounds that her stomach might be objecting to overmedication.

In addition, the doctor prescribed an ultrasound scan of Roberta's upper abdominal region. It was completed early in October, and the report indicated that no problem existed in that region of her body. Thereafter Roberta no longer complained about stomach pains, but she continued to lose weight because of her lack of interest in food.

I now possessed two plastic zip bags containing her medications to stabilize her behavior and moods, medications prescribed by three different doctors, none of whom gave me a schedule for administering them or, as far as I know, consulted with each other or coordinated their prescriptions. While this lack of coordination and loose oversight annoyed me, I nevertheless took over the management of her medications and organized them into morning and evening administrations.

Noises Off

Around this time, as well, Roberta began frequently to complain about her hearing aids and her loss of hearing in general. It was hard to tell, however, if she could not hear because of less-than-perfect hearing aids, because she had really lost much of her perception of sound, or because she didn't comprehend what was being said. Perhaps all three of the reasons were at work at one time or another. Her hearing loss, however, was real, having probably been inherited from her maternal grandfather who, she had told me, was almost totally deaf in his late years.

When I talked with her, she repeatedly said to me that she couldn't hear me. Strident at times, her complaints had a driven quality. Occasionally she also suggested that I was at fault for her hearing loss and that I should do something about it. One day she approached me as I was sitting in my easy chair reading a science journal. Leaning close, her face near mine, she said angrily, "I can't hear a thing that is going on around here."

"Oh?" said I loudly. "Like what?" (Stalling here, I was trying to get her to say more, not knowing what else to say.)

"Like everything. I just can't hear," she repeated.

"You can't hear anything?"

"No!"

A devilish question occurred to me. "Can you hear me now?" I asked in a quiet voice.

"No!" she snapped angrily.

49

This scenario, straight out of vaudeville, with such earnestness on her part, triggered an explosion of laughter in me. I pulled her down onto my lap and kissed her. "You're wonderful," I said, amidst my chuckles and her pleased confusion. I still smile thinking about it.

The Emptying

Roberta possessed a wonderful purse, an oversized fanny pack divided into numerous useful compartments. In it she carried her wallet containing folding money, her set of keys, a jack knife, a packet for plastic cards, driver's license, several combs, two ball point pens, the remote control for her hearing aids, and a pack of tissue. The utility of the bag delighted her and she valued it highly. It was her tool kit for her daily life, and in a real sense became part of her personal identity. "See how organized I am," it said.

In the period of a month the purse completely disappeared from her life. Its loss illustrates the emptying of the life of an Alzheimer's patient, the "thousands of subtractions" [2] that occur not only in the brain but also in daily life. The first resident of the purse to be evicted was her pet jack knife. She had lost it a few days earlier, after slicing open the wrapping of the take-out hoagie for our weekly picnic lunch that we enjoyed eating in our car parked by the bank of the Wissahickon Creek. After finding the knife later where it had fallen between the seats, she decided that she could no longer look after it and gave it to me for safekeeping. I was surprised at her voluntary surrender of her treasured object.

Later, after misplacing her keys, she also decided not to keep them in her purse any longer and gave them to me. Still later, we had been shopping when she reached into her purse for the plastic packet containing her credit card. It wasn't in its usual place. There ensued a frantic retracing of our steps to the stores where we had shopped, asking in vain at each one whether anyone had found her packet of cards. Disheartened, thinking fretfully of all the trouble we would have to go through to cancel and replace not only the credit card but all the others as well, we returned home. There, to our surprise and delight, we found the packet on the dining room table where she had been filling out a catalogue order that had required her credit card number. She did not object to my taking charge of her plastics.

At last her purse was emptied of everything but four combs, colored red, green, white, and black. These combs occupied her obsessive lost-and-found activities for an entire evening, nearly driving me to tears. She placed all four of them in her purse, then took out one and placed it on the windowsill in our downstairs bathroom where they were usually kept when she was not using them. She then retrieved it, and replaced it in her purse, all the while asking me if she was doing this the right way. I assured her she was. Again I was powerless to stop her. With four different colors to work with, it is not hard to imagine the large number of lost and found combinations she could conjure up. She simply wore herself out with this activity and finally retired to bed out of sheer fatigue. I, too, fell soundly asleep.

That wonderful purse, once bulging with the implements of daily life that helped define who she was, now hung limply on the back of a chair in my bedroom, hidden beneath a sweatshirt so that she would no longer worry about it. It was mute testimony of how her life was being emptied. She no longer needed or asked for it. By this loss was her life diminished.

I knew Roberta was rapidly unraveling, but I didn't know just how fast. Late in October I invited a nurse from our church to visit us to make an informal assessment of Roberta's condition over a cup of afternoon tea. She had been the head nurse of the Alzheimer's unit in a local retirement home before her retirement. Her professional experience and her long acquaintance with Roberta at church made her opinion extremely valuable.

After her visit, I asked her one question as I walked her to her car: "How long do you think it will be before I will need to commit Roberta to an Alzheimer's treatment center?"

"I would say probably within the next six months," was her reply. I was not surprised. But my alarm switch was reset by her answer. I would need to be in Grand Rapids in a half year if I wanted Roberta to be cared for in the Holland Home.

The Medication *Dans Macabre*

In the fall of 2000, Roberta was still aware that she worried passionately. One day after a long splurge of worrying she said in a matter-of-fact voice, "I think I'll go to the basement now to see what I can find to worry about down there." She grinned at her own joke.

Her refusal to take her medication, however, was no laughing matter. She gave me an extremely difficult time for a period of several weeks in October and November, after her doctor had revised the medication regimen. On a 3 x 5 inch card, I had written down the names of the four pills she was to take in the morning and labeled it the A.M. card. Doing the same for three evening medications, I labeled it the P.M. card. As I tapped each pill out of its plastic vial, I showed it to her, named it, told her why it was prescribed, and laid it carefully in a little glass dish. She then transferred all of the pills into her left hand, and in her right she held a glass of warm water that I had drawn for her.

The scene was now set for some of the most dramatic moments in our married life. First, she wanted to know why she was taking the pills; then she asked whether she had to; she insisted she didn't want to and she wasn't going to. Next she demanded to know why were there so many, why were they so large, on and on, round and round, until she came back again to asking why was she taking them. I pulled out every imaginable reason why she had to take them: because they would make her feel better, because they would relax her, she would sleep better. The strongest argument was that I was simply following the doctors' orders. This hassle sometimes went on for a half-hour or more.

The scene was worthy of a stage and an audience and would have drawn rounds of applause as the rebellious contrarian stood off the frustrated establishmentarian with her endless questions while he argued his case eloquently but futilely.

At one point, sensing that she may have been afraid of the pills and that they might look fearfully large to her, not just their normal size as they did to me, I asked her if they looked big. "Yes," she said, so fervently that I didn't doubt for a moment that this perception underlay in part, at least, her resistance to taking them. At times she may have feared that they might choke her.

Finally, with trembling hand, she would bring the pills up to her equally tremulous lips, flip them into her mouth, and wash them down in an instant. The hurried manner in which she swallowed the pills—reminiscent of the way we, as children, used to skitter past the entrance of the cemetery—reinforced my view that she was afraid of taking them. I thanked her with a hug for what was probably a genuinely courageous effort. We then proceeded either with the business of the day, or to the bathroom to remove our hearing aids, brush our teeth, and head for bed. After about a month, for no apparent reason, she stopped fighting the pill-taking routine and became very cooperative, for which I was profoundly grateful.

As time went on I began to perceive that the specter of fear was always at her elbow, whispering to her, for example, that "they" did not want her to do this, or "they" would be angry if she did that. Where did these phantoms come from? I wondered. Who were "they"? Her parents, aunts, and uncles with whom I was acquainted had never threatened her as far as I knew. I had no answer but hoped that perhaps eventually her behavior would give me a clue.

Her Last Garden on Earth

Early in October of 2000, I discussed with Roberta the task of putting her tomato garden to bed as we had done each autumn. Being in her city garden and closing it down for the year would be an engaging project for her, something she could genuinely help me with. It would be quite different from many of our activities where she was an onlooker, sometimes like a child, watching daddy at work.

Indicating no desire to ripen them, she picked the few remaining green tomatoes, and she dumped them in the trash can. Next I pulled out the plants, and she cut them into pieces to be bundled up and carried to the curbside for the morning trash collection. Finally, I pulled up the five heavy wire "pens" in which the tomato plants had grown, the most successful devices we had ever used for keeping the plants from sprawling all over—much better than tying them to bamboo stakes as we had done in the past. (The pens were collapsible, and I stacked them up, intending to hand them on

53

to our neighbor, Louise Weldon, for her tomato garden.) At last we were down to bare soil.

In former years, taking her garden apart had been a celebratory activity, a mini-Thanksgiving Day. This year, celebration seemed out of place. Memories associated with Roberta's tomato garden were coursing through my mind as we slowly disassembled it. How many tomatoes she had grown in her lifetime!

As I watched her cutting up the plants, I realized with a certainty that she would never plant another tomato garden, even while I chatted blithely about using these stakes and those frames again next April. This was the end of one of her signature roles in life. By springtime next year, when she would ordinarily be starting another garden (and probably trying to persuade me to enlarge one of them), we would be long gone from Cherokee Village apartments. Moreover, she would be past being able to engage in such activity. My heart wept with sadness as I said farewell to an essential part of Roberta while putting her last tomato garden to bed on that bright October afternoon.

We stopped doing other things, too. No longer did we take expeditions around the Wissahickon Creek gorge, where we had once walked an hour at a time. We quietly discontinued our traditional Monday picnic luncheon sitting in our car beside the Wissahickon Creek, munching hoagie sandwiches and listening to our favorite CDs. Once Roberta could no longer remember what to order on the hoagies, the custom dropped off our activity agenda. Soup making departed from her life without comment or farewell. Crossword puzzles became too difficult for her. Neither the news or the puzzles in the *USA Today* interested her any more. We didn't watch the "News Hour with Jim Lehrer"; it had become too unsettling and confusing.

I don't remember the final time we did any of these things, which is probably just as well. It was a wrenching experience to realize that an activity that had long been part of our life we would never do again. But I will always remember putting Roberta's last tomato garden to bed.

Although Roberta's world was contracting, our companionship was still strong. I found that Roberta responded well to calm talk and to my careful listening to her. We had a satisfying routine worked out where she helped me with some housekeeping chores, such as putting dishes away, or setting the table. She could dress herself if I selected her clothes, and undress herself if I cued her at each step. It was important for me to get enough rest, which I managed to do, so that I could be very much present with her throughout the day.

Roberta's driven behavior climaxed late in October in two related episodes. The first had to do with her SAS walking shoes. These are sturdy and comfortable shoes that she loved to wear. But for a while she could not remember what to call them—HAS, HAD, or SAH, she would say. Knowing that these were not the right names, she looked at me for help, and I would spell out, "S-A-S." Every time she wanted her SAS shoes, she went through the routine of wrongly naming them and then asking for my help.

Later I found yellow sticky tags on her bedroom chest of drawers and in other places with these words on them, "*SAS. Why can't I remember this?*" and "*Name of shoe SAS*" and this incomplete note, "*SAX—Sax shoes are dif—*". At one time she said more to herself than to me, "SAS shoes. You think that would be simple enough, wouldn't you? But it's not when your brain doesn't work right."

During this time she repeatedly asked me what was wrong with her. I told her that she had a sickness of the brain. I don't know if that meant anything to her.

The second episode had to do with *Aricept*, one of the medications prescribed for Roberta. A standard medication for Alzheimer's disease, it is prescribed to retard loss of short-term memory. It was listed on her P.M. medication card, and it was my practice to deliberately read off its name as I doled it out into her pill dish.

She latched on to the name of this drug one night, and it became absolutely essential for her to remember how to spell it. To do so she began a routine to commit its name and spelling to memory, a rhythmical recitation that sounded like a chant, or the recital of a grade school child memorizing the multiplication table. (She got the spelling wrong the first time and could not be persuaded to correct it.) Her mantra went as follows:

"*Air-cept*" (pause) "Aye-eye-are" (pause) "see-ee-pee-tee," (double pause);

"*Air-cept*" (pause) "Aye-eye-are" (pause) "see-ee-pee-tee," (double pause);

I could hear her pacing the floor, "*Air-cept*" (pause) "Aye-eye-are" (pause) "see-ee-pee-tee," (double pause); intoning this rhythmical cadence, seemingly unable to stop, almost hypnotized.

It drove me frantic to hear this unending recitation from a woman whose verbal skills had been so admirable. I queried, "Don't you think you know that word now?" It took several more attempts before I broke through and stopped the compulsive recital. After that evening, however, she never did it again.

Brief, Shining Moments

An occasional island appeared in this sea of turmoil. Early in November, I wrote the following e-mail to my sister.

> *Dear Marguerite,*
>
> *Last week I had three wonderful evenings with Roberta. On Tuesday, we spent an hour after dinner just chatting about what was happening to us. We talked about the wonderful times we have had in this apartment and about our great neighbors, Roberta's gardens, our walks around the Wissahickon Valley. She doesn't remember the exact physical environment of these walks, but enjoyed hearing about them.*
>
> *This kind of talk always leads back to the long life we led in our Haines Street house. We have so many wonderful memories of that place, too. Roberta was very alert during this chat, and could recall much of what we were talking about.*
>
> *On Wednesday evening I sat in my rocking chair, very close to her, and started to ply her with questions about her early life, especially about her summers on Uncle Kees' farm with her brother, Jack. She opened up and poured forth a flood of events. Her love for her Uncle Kees and Aunt Dorothy and her brother was very clear. I've*

heard many of these stories before, but it was good to revisit them. Again, she remembered quite well many of the events, and even added some things I had not known about.

On Friday night we just sat on the couch and necked, as we used to call it in our college days. We didn't talk a lot; we simply sat there feeling close to each other physically and spiritually. During such times she does not talk about her immediate problems, which is a relief to both of us. I, of course, will treasure these times forever.

Love to you,

Bob

Roberta's behavior and moods began to level off, thanks to the medication the doctors prescribed for her. (I have nothing but admiration for scientists when it comes to the medications available to Roberta.) Her sleeping pill worked wonders. A couple of her morning pills put her in a more positive, optimistic mood than she had been previously. One day I made a pot of white bean soup, from a mix that comes with the beans, herbs, and spices all in the package. While making it, I kept up a running patter with her, much as a mother does to a little child who looks on in amazement at what the mother can do. I enjoyed these oases, as did she.

I usually knew what she was talking about, provided I could correctly guess what was bugging her at the moment. Since she could not remember nouns very well, she substituted the word "thing" or "things" or "stuff" for the specific object or situation. For people whose names she had forgotten, she said, "them." So I needed to know who and what "them" and "things" were. If I know what she was anxious about or afraid of at the time, I could usually name the object or person. "Them" often referred to her doctors or someone at church. "Things" depended more on the context. The startup of a sentence she could not complete sometimes gave me a clue to what she wanted to say, and I then could help her finish the sentence.

I was sure that Roberta's decline was particularly noticeable to those who hadn't seen her for several weeks at a time. But to me there was a continuous line from the person she had been to the one she was becoming; and I must say that, frustrated as I sometimes became, I continued to find her company enjoyable, even at a much different level from before. As our daughter once said to me, "You have to take her as she is, not as she was." That was so true. My worst bouts of depression occurred when I allowed myself to think back on the Roberta who was.

Early in November, I wrote the following e-mail to my network of family and friends describing an incident that happened about that time.

Dear Support Group,

The other night I woke up after the clock had passed the midnight hour with the sense that Roberta was not in her bed. I checked it out, and sure enough, the blankets were thrown back, and her bed was empty. This could mean trouble. I recalled the number of accounts of Alzheimer patients wandering around indoors and getting lost out-of-doors during the night. I also remembered a previous night of Roberta's wandering when I had come downstairs to find the kitchen being alarmingly hot, the oven broiler turned on. I have since pulled the oven control knob off the stove and placed it in a dish on the back ledge of the stove.

So I tiptoed down the stairs expecting the worst. Instead I found Roberta sitting on the couch with a small spread of food on the coffee table in front of her. She had sliced up an apple, peeled a banana, and placed a few donut holes on a plate. With soft lamp light shining over the scene, it was a romantic tableau. She welcomed me with a smile, and held out a coffee mug to me.

"Come here," she said. "I thought you might like some coffee."

I sat down next to her, and sipped the hot water in the mug. She drew a coverlet over our shoulders and cuddled up to me. While I munched donut holes and apple slices

we chatted amiably about nothing much in particular.
She was relaxed and companionable. After some time I
suggested that we might like to return to bed since it was
still dark outside. She readily agreed and we trundled
up to her bedroom. She seemed thoroughly content and
was soon sleeping soundly.

A little glimmer of her generous personhood momentarily
shone through the dark night of her sickness. She loves
me and wants so much to show in this romantic way
that she can still take care of me, as I do of her.

Bob

To Sleep, Perchance to Dream

Sleep deprivation was one of the most severe problems I faced before Roberta was provided with good medications. There were two nights in a row, late in September, when I got only four hours of sleep, being kept awake during the night by her RLS, and being thwarted from taking an early afternoon nap by her constantly waking me to ask if I was sleeping all right. By the third day, I thought that if this went on one more night I might do something horrendous to her. There may be no worse torture than sleep deprivation.

All those who have been responsible for the daily care of a loved one with Alzheimer's disease know that enormous and unrelenting stress is engendered in the process of caregiving. When sleep deprivation drains emotional, physical, and spiritual resources, one reaches the point of thinking of committing mayhem. The pressure is increased even more when one's beloved slips into the disease as rapidly as Roberta did.

Desperate for a nap, I called Phyllis Strock, our neighbor and friend from church. Fortunately, she readily agreed to sit with Roberta while I sacked out. I cannot tell how grateful I was to her for giving me this break, the most profound ninety minutes of sleep I had in weeks.

Her task was not easy. Roberta kept wanting to come upstairs to see how I was doing, Phyllis told me. Later, commenting on her experience, she said in Roberta's presence, "I had to keep dancing with you, Roberta, to keep you from waking Bob." What a resource-ful woman! She also reported Roberta's saying, "You're nice and all that, but you're not Bob DeHaan."

Life with Roberta was not without its lighter side. She often showed flashes of her old sense of humor and fun. Some of her one-liners were wonderful.

One morning in October, we were sitting in the living room. I was slowly drinking my coffee, chatting with her about nothing at all. Suddenly she got out of her chair, walked past me on her way to the kitchen, calling over her shoulder as she might have done to an audience, "Hold your applause, everyone. I just got out of bed!"—as if, having made a significant pronouncement, she were striding off stage, and would return with something even better. Where that came from, I did not know. Was she hallucinating?

Another time, after we had engaged in an affectionate embrace, she said, "I love you so much, in spite of the fact that you still have a long way to go." Take that!

She once made a poignant comment on her confusion, saying, "Trouble is, I don't know what I don't know."

One afternoon, a car started to pull out in front of us as we were driving down Germantown Avenue. As we swerved and drove by, she growled with exaggerated belligerence at the offending driver, "Watch out! People are tough where we come from." (Her people were among the gentlest in the world.) "You tell 'em, Roberta," I encouraged. She grinned in a pleased, I-guess-I-told-him sort of way.

Another time, quite happy with herself after a bowel movement, she looked down into the toilet and commented, "Some people know how to do it, don't they?" After finishing going to the toilet another time, she muttered, "Nothing to it."

One day I felt like reading before indulging in our longstanding tradition of taking an after-lunch nap. It was a dark, rainy day, and so I had to turn on the floor lamp at the end of the couch. I usually tell Roberta when I am going to do something like this so as not to surprise her and to give her a chance to object if she feels so in-clined.

I said, "I'm going to turn my light on. For just a little while."

Her retort: "For just a little Wawa?" (Wawa is the name of a chain of convenience stores that populate corners of neighborhoods in the Northeast. They say that you know you're from Philadelphia if you can say, "Wawa" and not think it funny.)

I groaned at her pun. Roberta smirked.

One night we were saying our evening prayers after a rather exasperating day. I prayed, "Forgive me for being gruff with Roberta today. Tomorrow help me to be a better caregiver, a better husband, a better lover . . . " At this point she broke in, "Wow! You're going to be pretty tired by the end of the day."

The Nightmare Returns

Each morning upon waking, however, a sickening awareness would sweep over me not unlike what I felt years before in the recovery room after my botched mastoid surgery, when I realized my facial nerve had been severed and my face would be forever paralyzed. Now the awareness would engulf me, like the fog rolling in from the sea, smothering me under the realization that this nightmare was not going to go away with the redeeming light of morning.

How could I stay afloat in the midst of the waves of depression that sometimes threatened to sweep over me? How does one gird himself for the tasks of such days? Where can strength be found to carry on? I needed a way to prepare each day for the task of caring for the woman I loved who was in such desperate straits.

Friends and relatives advised me to find respite, take regular breaks, go for a walk, head for the library, join an Alzheimer's support group, take care of myself as well as Roberta. However, I felt physically strong and on top of my task as her caregiver. In one sense, as I told friends, taking care of my wife was not unlike my professional work as an educational administrator. There were problems to be solved, and goals to be attained, and I went about solving them as expeditiously as possible. Administration involved stress, and I was used to it.

Moreover, my love for Roberta made it relatively easy to shrug off the stress so that I would be able to continue caring for her at home. I did not want to give her up. In the morning my goal was to be able to look back on the day at bedtime, and to say that it had been a good day, a time of grace in the midst of another day's journey into the shadows.

At a deeper level, however, what I found myself needing was not so much respite, although that was important, but rather spiritual *comfort*, in its original sense of the word, meaning *strengthening*. I continued to find strength in reading John Baillie's *A Diary of Private Prayer*. In the morning I prayed,

> *"I thank Thee for the blessed assurance that I shall not be called upon to face the tasks and interests of this day alone or in my own strength, but shall at all times be accompanied by Thy presence and fortified by Thy grace."[3]*

Surprisingly, hymns arising from my childhood and youth appeared unbidden on my lips. I found myself singing "Does Jesus Care?," a rather sentimental hymn that I sang at the time as much as a challenge to show me as a rhetorical question. The answer came in the chorus, "Oh, yes He cares, I know He cares." Under less trying circumstances this would have seemed like "wearisomely explicit pietism," as C. S. Lewis might have called the song.[4] In my condition, however, it became important that Jesus cared.

Ted consistently counseled and preached, "You don't need to be afraid," during our life at our church in Philadelphia. "God will take care of you." Delivered again and again, this message shone like a lighthouse on a dark night at sea. One of the first sermons I and my young family heard from him when we first arrived in Philadelphia thirty some years before was on the topic, "Fear not." We needed that. Roberta and the kids were scared by the big bad city. What he preached gave us something to hang on to and encouraged us to move ahead.

I had come to experience a little more of what it meant to constantly live in the presence of God. I brought myself into frequent contact with Him/Her, (God was as often more feminine than masculine during those days), and on a much more familiar basis than ever before. When an answer-to-prayer-like coincidence occurred that reset my start button, I would murmur, "Thanks, pal." When I was stretched too far, as when RLS hit Roberta hard, I would suggest, "I could use a little relief right now." While the relief did not necessarily come in a surcease of RLS, what did often happen was that an extra gush of energy would surge through me and carry me through the crisis. These were amazing experiences.

Strength also came from our various families—my children, sisters, nephews and nieces, neighbors, other relatives, and church family—with many of whom I communicated regularly through the Internet. I began to gather a list of names of friends and relations in my computer address book to whom I would issue periodic e-mail updates on Roberta's condition and how I was faring. The very process of writing the experiences helped relieve the stress. The feedback I would receive from these people was uplifting. Their support, encouragement, suggestions, and prayers conveyed through return e-mails helped me stay afloat in the midst of the upsurge of depression that occasionally endangered my stability. I found that stress and fear need not merely be endured; with the help of others, faith can actually grow at such a time.

Black Monday: The Diagnosis

Toward the close of autumn, the message of Dark Thursday played itself out. Things had not been going well with Roberta, and I asked for an early appointment with her primary physician. Upon taking one glance at Roberta and asking some general questions, the doctor began to ask the standard questions[5] that form the in-office, preliminary, informal diagnosis of Alzheimer's disease—What day is it? What year? Who is our president? Who was president before him? Roberta looked helplessly at me, unable to answer any of them. Then the doctor gave her a sheet of paper with the instructions to fold it and place it on the table at her side. Roberta folded it neatly, and held it in her hand until the doctor retrieved it. I wept inwardly to see this erstwhile bright woman unable to complete these simple two-step instructions, so diagnostic of Alzheimer's disease.

The doctor wrote out a prescription for a sedative, but more important, an order for an MRI (brain scan) and an appointment for a consultation with a neurologist to evaluate the MRI report afterward. These were threatening appointments because of the verdict I expected them to deliver, and I approached them with qualms. There could be no more denial after them, I was sure. They were, however, steps that needed to be taken medically to confirm Roberta's disease. I knew that the brain scan was necessary to rule out other possible causes of her dementia, and also for future use in filing for benefits from her long-term care insurance policy.

I was also worried that the MRI would be terribly trying for Roberta, being stuffed into a dark tunnel with waves of noise crashing on her head. In order to help her deal with the anticipated trauma, I sought the advice from nurses at church. They suggested that I give her a sedative and take a relaxing walk with her before the procedure was to take place and not to explain what was about to happen until just before entering the clinic. I followed their advice and sat through the MRI procedure with my hand on Roberta's leg to let her know I was present. It was completed without any adverse response from her.

After the visit to the neurologist's office, where Roberta once again failed the office diagnostic test, the doctor wrote out the dreaded, but not unexpected words—*"Diagnosis: Alzheimer's disease."* If my defining moment marked the Dark Thursday of our lives, the medical diagnosis on November 13, 2000, denoted the Black Monday. The road on which we were journeying was now clearly marked, and as we left the doctor's office, I took a deep breath knowing we would both need a fuller measure of grace and more support from those everlasting arms than ever before.

---

[1] Mace, Nancy L. and Rabins, Peter V., *The 36-Hour Day* (New York: Warner Books, 1991), pp. 37-43.

[2] David Shenk, *The Forgetting Alzheimer's: Portrait of an Epidemic* (New York: Doubleday, 2001), p. 224.

[3] John Baillie, *A Diary of Private Prayer* (New York: Charles Scribner's Sons, 1955), p. 93.

[4] C. S. Lewis, *Letters to Malcolm: Chiefly on Prayer* (New York: Harcourt Brace & World, Inc., 1964), p. 31.

[5] There is a short series of standard questions, called a Folstein Mini Mental State Examination, which doctors ask in their offices of patients suspected of having Alzheimer's disease. The questions comprise a brief diagnostic test. See Folstein, M. F., Folstein, S. E., & McHugh, P.R. 1975, "Mini-Mental State: A practical method for grading the cognitive state of patients for the clinician." *Psychiatry Research*, 12, 189–98.

VI

A Light through the Shadows

Following the dreadful diagnosis, Roberta continued trying to grasp what was happening to her, leading us to some wrenching conversations. She would often ask me if I knew what was wrong with her. Never having the heart to tell her point blank that she had Alzheimer's disease, I said that something was going very wrong with her brain. She once said, "Three times a day I think, there, I've got hold of it." She paused. "Then I don't." At another time she remarked, "Sometimes I feel like it's going to get better again." After a pause she said softly, looking into my eyes, "But it won't, will it, Bob?" The fear and despair in those words was unfathomable.

"No, it won't, Roberta," I said.

(Weeks later, as I typed this, I found myself both applauding her courage and weeping over the hopelessness of the struggle she was waging against the clouds of confusion that were engulfing her.)

Roberta sensed that our time together was short. Earlier she may have thought it was because of her physical ailments. At this time she knew, I believed, that it was the mindless disease that was encompassing her. We were led into seasons of profound oneness of spirit, in which we often simply clung to each other as we sat on the couch. Knowing nothing else to do, I would hold her close to

65

me in an attempt to shield her from the malevolence of the disease. Doing so, I realized that my arms needed somehow to serve both of us as the everlasting arms.

At times like these I hated Alzheimer's disease with every fiber of my being. Why did this evil happen to my beloved? The mystery of suffering may be an engaging theological and philosophical problem to some academics, but to Roberta and me the suffering of Alzheimer's was an unending descent into the valley of the shadow of death. The Psalmist may have feared no evil there. But I did. There was nothing, *nothing* I could do to help her, except to hold her tightly and whisper that I loved her and that God did, too.

But there were seasons of refreshing. One day in November, our daughter Christy visited us and, after a time of pleasurable conversation, she offered to play some hymns on the piano and invited us to sing along. At first Roberta demurred, but she soon joined in, and we all sang heartily to Christy's accompaniment. Later she showed us a model that her husband, Burt, had assembled of their new second home they had built in the Pocono Mountains. They have always loved the mountains. I was happy that they now had a home there. We talked some more, hugged each other, and then she went on her way. This was Christy's farewell to her mother.

I loved to waken Roberta in the morning after she had had a good night of sleep. She was beautiful, with an innocent look of happiness at seeing me, not unlike the expressions our children had once worn upon waking. As she greeted me, her voice had its former vibrance.

Later in the day her world of confusion would again blanket her, and her voice would take on a breathy, raspy quality, as if she had to force herself to talk. Her face, too, had a different look, described by John Bayley as follows.

> *The face of an Alzheimer's patient has been clinically described as a "lion face." An apparently odd comparison, but in fact a very apt one. The features settle into a leonine impassivity which does remind one of the king of the beasts, and the way his broad expressionless mask is represented in painting and sculpture.[1]*

The lion in the paintings of *The Peaceable Kingdom*, by Edward Hicks, where the king of the beasts is pictured lying down with the lamb, clearly portrays that look. Such was the way Roberta's features were changing.

Helping Hands

As we approached Thanksgiving Day, I received a most remarkable offer, one I compare in magnitude to an offer I received in 1947, when our friend and my mentor, Dr. Douglas Blocksma, offered to get me into the doctoral program at the University of Chicago where he was an administrator. That offer launched me into my doctoral studies and into my career in higher education.

The offer in the fall of 2000 came from my nephew and niece, Ray and Linda Mulder. Ray, then retired, had been an extremely successful businessman. He knew how to think big, having served for five years in Japan as the vice-president of operations for Amway Corporation, and having held other high-level positions for the company in other countries.

His offer was this: He and Linda would drive to Philadelphia in his SUV, pick up Roberta and me, and transport us back to Grand Rapids. There they would make the lower level apartment of their large house available to us to live in until we could find a more permanent residence. Whatever clothes and things we needed for this interim stay they would load in their vehicle (their SUV was a monster). Later we could move the rest of our household goods into storage in Grand Rapids.

Not only that, but he also strongly suggested that we make the move immediately after Thanksgiving Day, basing his recommendation on the precipitous deterioration in Roberta's condition, about which I had kept him and other relatives apprised by e-mail.

Ray's offer was extremely appealing, even more so after I received the following e-mail from Linda immediately after Thanksgiving Day. It is one of the most important factors in solidifying my decision to relocate in Grand Rapids, a decision that Roberta, of course, was quite incapable of helping me make.

Dear Uncle Bob,

Thanks for your continued messages regarding your situation! I am, of course, reading the non-private ones, but so far Ray has been doing all the responding. You will hear from him today, too, but I wanted to share a few thoughts with you.

I have been imagining the two of you being here and want to assure you that we will embrace you and at the same time leave you alone to live your lives. This is uncharted territory for all of us, but we CAN and we WANT to do this—have you live in our home during your transition. [She then gave a detailed description of the lower level of their house that they proposed to turn over to us.]

This is my report for now—please keep your questions, thoughts, concerns coming our way.

We love you!

Linda

With such an invitation I became more fully committed than ever to make the move. I wrote Ray and Linda my thankful acceptance of their offer. From then on the only question became, When? To pull up stakes immediately after Thanksgiving Day did not seem possible. There just wasn't enough time. So we settled, over the course of several e-mails, on soon after Christmas, most desirably early in January, 2001.

Ray's offer, Linda's invitation, and our subsequent correspondence were the unambiguous answer to our prayer for guidance. "We would know." The door, for which we had been praying, watching, and waiting, stood wide open. Roberta and I walked through it arm in arm. Occasionally I stopped what I was doing just to smile over the divine intervention. The answer was the first fruits of a cornucopia of divine kindness that was to be poured into our lives in the months to come, through family and friends, who lit up the journey into the dark shadows with their love and support.

But could Roberta make the move without having it precipitate a crisis or a calamitous decline in her condition? We would be on the road two days and a night. Would her RLS make it impossible for her to sit quietly in the vehicle for miles on end? Would she be able to sleep in a strange bed in an unfamiliar motel?

To forestall a crisis, I kept her informed of the e-mail correspondence I had with Ray and Linda, reading their notes and explaining them to her. She raised no questions about them and had none of the negative response to the move that she displayed at the end of the summer. She loved Ray and Linda and remembered their visit of the previous October. When I explained that I would be sitting by her side in the back seat of their vehicle and would continue to help her in the new apartment in their house, she seemed content with the idea.

While the move would undoubtedly be difficult for Roberta, I believed that the main consideration that got through to her was my assurance that I would not leave her. While doing what I was doing was discouraged in the literature on Alzheimer's disease that I had been reading, I came to believe that as long as I was present all the time as an anchor in her life, she would not be hurt by the disruption. As with young children, the stability and constancy of the main person in her life was more important than an unchanging physical environment.

The reactions of our friends at church to our announcement that we were definitely planning to move soon after Christmas ranged from frank approval to consternation. Those who approved did so because, they said, we were still young enough to enjoy the new surroundings. One couple told of the trauma of moving their ninety-year-old mother to a retirement home, whereas she could have been moved much more easily when she was ten or fifteen years younger. The consternation, of course, grew out of the realization that our regularly occupied pew would be vacant every Sunday and that our voices would no longer be heard in the song service, in committee meetings, and in the fellowship hall.

Upon hearing of our intentions to relocate, our Cherokee apartment neighbors mourned the imminent loss of Roberta and me and the splendid camaraderie we had enjoyed for so long. They had observed Roberta's decline, however, and understood her need for special care. They respected my decision that the best care for her could be obtained in Grand Rapids. To make the most of the remaining time, all of us intensified our relationships, chatting more often and increasing the number of late afternoon "O, be joyful" occasions.

Family Farewells

Soon after Roberta was diagnosed with Alzheimer's disease, I informed our children of the result via e-mail. They immediately made plans to visit us. Although they had suspected that their mother had the disease for some time, they realized that this would be the last time they would see her as a relatively well person. They wanted to come, in effect, to bid her farewell. Visits around the Thanksgiving holiday were best for them.

Thanksgiving Day itself was a day of mixed blessings for Roberta and me. On the plus side, we enjoyed a wonderful dinner, just by ourselves. I happened to have two small lobster tails in the freezer, purchased for a party that had never taken place. It was a grand meal. She enjoyed the lobster to a point, and then declared she had had enough. I was delighted to finish off what she couldn't.

On the downside, however, our visit that afternoon to our daughter Christy's suburban home—where our other daughter and son-in-law, Joanne and Omer Prewetta, and two of their sons were staying during the holidays—was a disaster. I had enticed Roberta to drive out to join the Thanksgiving festivities there. She had flatly rejected the idea, and as I towed her along, she never stopped telling me that she didn't want to do this. Unfortunately, by again failing to realize how deeply ingrained and easily triggered were her fears and confusion, I had precipitated this explosion of negativity. I should have anticipated that she would see this gathering as a maelstrom of loud talking and laughter that she would be unable to understand. How would she know that they were not laughing at her? My telling her that it would not be a long visit did not address her fear. Had I started earlier to talk about it, helping her to recall

70

and visualize our daughters and their families, and working slowly up to the visit, emphasizing that I would help her, I believe she would have agreed to it, or at least would have been less negative.

Upon being greeted by our two daughters and the rest of their families, Roberta immediately announced to one and all that I had tricked her into coming, and that I had said we would stay only ten minutes. She refused to take off her jacket, and sat glowering in a chair with her cap tugged down over her eyebrows, waiting to be taken home. The one bright spot was her recognition of our grandson. "And you're David," she said with a smile. Both he and Christy smiled in return.

I chatted with each beloved family member there, catching up with our three grandsons, of college, high school, and middle school age. Our daughters had retired to the kitchen and soon emerged with pumpkin pie, topped with whipped cream, and a mug of Postum on the side. Roberta would have none of it. She kept staring at me the whole time, muttering occasionally, "Ten minutes are up." I held my own until I had talked to each grandson. Then, with my wishing them all a Happy Thanksgiving over my shoulder, we made our exit.

Consumed by my frustration, I could not stop myself from berating her for what I called her unseemly behavior on our drive home. She took it quietly.

As soon as we drove into our driveway, she asked, "When are we going home?" I answered by walking her through our entire apartment, pointing out the dining room table, directing her attention to her bed and massage table, checking out the kitchen. Even though she finally settled down, she continued to pop up occasionally with the same question. Our unhappy visit may have raised confusion about what and where home was. Perhaps because she felt satisfied that she had exerted her selfhood by resisting me, she slept soundly all night and was still snoozing into daylight hours on Friday morning.

The day after Thanksgiving, having left their sons to roam the Chestnut Hill shopping district, Joanne and Omer arrived, Joanne toting her flute with which to serenade her mother. After performing a short concert she played some hymns for us to sing along with. Flute music expressed well the sweet sadness of that moment.

71

Afterwards we purchased a take-out lunch from the Chestnut Hill Farmer's market and, joined by the boys, ate a delightful lunch in our apartment. Joanne embraced her mother in a long goodbye. I could feel her body throb with sadness in our own farewell embrace. Although her taking leave of me was only until our next visit, that of her mother's, I feared, was for the rest of this life.

Early in December, our son Philip and his wife Mary came for their farewell visit. A violinist, Philip played a mini-concert for his mother, accompanied on the piano by Mary. Afterward we sang some favorite hymns with Roberta joining in readily. Mary showed us photos of the plot of rural land they had purchased and were clearing, along with Mary's plans for the house they intended to build on it. Roberta didn't show much interest in them; the conversation was flying past her. They embraced their mother as they bade her farewell. Standing outside by their car, we three prayed and continued our farewells, anguished over Roberta's condition.

Soon after Thanksgiving Day I wrote the following e-mail to my network of relatives and friends:

Dear Friends and Relatives,

The past week was a wonderful one for me. (I went on to describe visits from Christy, Joanne, Philip and their families). *While these visits were refreshing for me, they were problematic for Roberta. She had to work hard at remembering their names. The activity swirling around her left her confused and terribly anxious.*

So on Saturday we reached an oasis of quietness. Roberta slept long, we breakfasted slowly, and dressed without haste. I puttered around the house, emptying waste baskets and cleaning the kitchen cupboards. She follows me around and gives me what help she can. Her attention span is very short, so she doesn't stick with a task for long. For example, when I was making fresh tomato sauce for pasta the other evening she asked if she could slice up the tomatoes. Delighted with this initiative, I put her to work. After cutting two slices she walked away from the job without a word.

Late in the afternoon, I played a CD of Perry Como. On his first song, "Round and Round," we were standing near each other. She reached out her hands to me and we started dancing. She was relaxed and embraceable—like old times.

I often sing while doing chores; and more often than not, Roberta joins in harmonizing as we sing. The other day I was singing an old favorite hymn, "God Will Take Care of You." Although a little sentimental, it contains a fundamental promise for a Christian. She sang her alto part while I took the melody. When we got to the chorus I sang at the top of my voice, partly to control the quaver in it, and partly to challenge God to come through.

Roberta is no longer interested in why she cannot do things that she used to be able to do, nor understands what is happening to her. She no longer seems to care or has given up the struggle. She is much less agitated now, and easily falls asleep. The medication is responsible for much of her calmness. I have mixed feelings about it. On the one hand, her agitation is hard to deal with, but her unresponsiveness is also difficult to bear. But this is the direction the ailment takes, I presume.

She is eating somewhat better. I received advice from an experienced nurse to include ice cream for dessert as often as possible. "Lots of calories in it," she said. Now, however, it is difficult to find old fashioned ice cream that isn't "light." Still, I feel that she is no longer losing weight.

Roberta asked an interesting question one day recently. "How come we aren't having any fun when we are having so much fun?" That's really quite profound. Not having fun is our somber journey through the shadows. Having fun is grace.

Best regards to you all.

Bob

I e-mailed my sister the following note:

Dear Marguerite,

One of the ministers in our congregation, Dick Cox, preached a very encouraging sermon for us on Sunday. He examined each of the four angelic appearances at about the time of Jesus' birth—to Zechariah, father of John the Baptist, Mary, Joseph, and the shepherds—and pointed out that the message of each angelic appearance was: "Fear not." This assurance sank in deeply.

After the service, as Roberta and I were walking up the avenue to our parked car, she commented on Dick's sermon, saying, "Well, we heard all that before." She sometimes fired an intuitive shot into the air like that when she didn't understand what was going on.

"Well, maybe," I said. "But Dick was saying something very special to you and me. He told us, 'Roberta and Bob, do not be afraid.' He was looking right at us when he said that. He was telling us that what the angels said when Jesus was born is also meant for all of us, especially you and me."

"Oh," she said. "That was nice. I didn't realize that was going on."

Now, as I prepare to move ahead into the next, and probably last stage of our lives, I again hear the message, "Fear not." My time in Germantown and our church began and ended in that motto. After that sermon on Sunday, I am again encouraged to move on.

I know it's a tricky business to discover signs of God's approval, especially when they confirm what you already want to do. Yet Ted has often said that God is sneaky, or ingenious, as I like to say, and gives us subtle signals, sometimes in out-of-the-way places, that He watches for us to decipher and act on. I took that to be the case with the message, "Fear not."

I love you so much, dear sister. Hope to see more of you in the future. But we must continue to e-mail each other even then, like I do with friends at our church here, even though I see them every Sunday.

Brother Bob

Early in December, Roberta and I were returning from a late afternoon shopping trip at the supermarket. Toting a shopping bag, I trudged up the walkway from our car to the apartment as she followed, also lugging a sack. Since she is sometimes confused as to whether I remembered to lock the car, I stopped to show her how I did it with my remote key.

"Watch how the parking lights flash on when I lock it," I said. After this exhibition of modern technology, I pointed out the little red light on the dashboard.

"That blinking light tells you that the car is locked and the burglar alarm is on," I said. She made no comment. If she was mystified by this electronic magic, she didn't show it.

Gazing out the kitchen window later in the evening, I looked at the miniature airplane beacon on the dashboard of the parked car. "Come over here and see something on the car," I called to Roberta. After looking carefully she finally located what I was pointing at.

"What does that blinking light tell you?" I asked, expecting her to repeat what I had taught her about locking the car. Without a moment's hesitation she responded dryly, "That it's alive." She turned on her heel and walked away, unimpressed by my wonder working and leaving me amazed at her interpretation of the car's life.

At the close of each Sunday worship service in December, after we had made it known that we were leaving for Grand Rapids early in January, we would be surrounded with fellow parishioners who wanted to wish us well, give us a pat on the shoulder, or enclose us in a long embrace. Roberta took this all in, but she could stand just so much of it and then needed to escape.

One time, after leaving one of these sessions, we walked down the aisle toward a group of prominent church women engaged in animated conversation. They broke it up in order to greet Roberta.

Again there was hugging and expressions of appreciation for all that Roberta had done in church over the years. One of them was especially effusive. "Whenever you walk into church, it's like a beam of sunshine, gleaming through the window."

Roberta took a long look at her, turned on her heel, saying loudly enough for all to hear, "Nice try," and stalked away. I didn't look back, but I had the feeling that the women were smiling at her audacious put down.

Roberta and I were in the eye of the hurricane in early December. After the leading edge of the storm had battered us all fall, the winds had died down, the storm surge had passed, and we enjoyed a season of respite. Although I realized that more tempestuous times lay ahead when the trailing edge would catch up with us, I enjoyed the peaceful breather with Roberta while it lasted. She slept almost around the clock at night. During the day she dozed occasionally. Her appetite was slowly returning, and I thought we had halted her weight loss. She usually enjoyed a short walk with me after she got over her first protests about going outdoors.

As far as she was able to, Roberta helped me and did exactly what I asked of her. Rarely, if ever, did she show signs of anger or frustration at not being able to remember how to do something she had set out to do. After washing dishes, she sometimes forgot what cupboard a certain plate went in. When I pointed out to her where it belonged, she simply said, "Oh, yes. I forgot." Or, "Oh. That's right."

Often, being unable to finish a sentence that she had started, Roberta and I would try to guess at the word she could not recall. If neither of us succeeded, she simply abandoned the effort with, "Oh, I just can't think of that now."

I felt at times like the lead dog as I went around the house doing chores, with her tagging after me. Once she said, "Why am I following you this way?" I responded, "I don't know. Sometimes you act like a little puppy." She laughed and agreed, "Yep. I'm like a little puppy."

She got back at me on one occasion for reminding her for several mornings in a row to wash her face and under her arms before getting dressed. Later in the afternoon I was in the bathroom, splashing some water on my face after having performed a heavy task.

76

From behind me came this cheery voice, "Don't forget to wash under your arms." Turning around, I saw her standing in the doorway, grinning.

What C. S. Lewis wrote fits the scenario. "Any patch of sunlight in a wood will show you something about the sun which you could never get from reading books on astronomy. These pure spontaneous pleasures are 'patches of sunlight' in the woods of our experience."[2] This patch of sunlight showed what a sweetheart Roberta was to take care of most of the time.

One event early in December, however, jarred me out of my tranquillity. I had been completing the application form for Roberta's future admission into the Holland Home dementia care center in Grand Rapids. It was the most heart-rending task I had undertaken since Black Monday. Doing it surreptitiously, because I didn't want her to ask what I was doing, only increased the pain. I felt treacherous, as if I were signing her life away while she was sleeping. Moreover, she had no say in this momentous decision I was making for her. I had to push hard on the pen to finish the task, sign the questionnaire and the application form, and seal it in the envelope. I kept telling myself that this can't be the way our marriage, our life together, was going to end.

On the landing of our stairway hung the photograph that is the icon of our marriage. The road ahead had been paved with promises. That was then. Where are those promises now?

However, I would allow myself only a certain amount of grieving. I realized that, carried too far, mourning would become self-indulgence. So I put my mind to the thought of *tough love*. Making a reservation for her at this time was necessary for what would inevitably transpire in the future, when I could no longer take care of her.

With that determination I posted the application.

---

[1] John Bayley, *Elegy for Iris* (New York: Picador, USA, 1999), p. 53.

[2] C. S. Lewis, *Letters to Malcolm: Chiefly on Prayer* (New York: Harcourt Brace & World, Inc., 1964), p. 91.

VII

Before the Move

I was now confronted with the huge task of packing our household goods for the move to Grand Rapids. Organizing for the move became my top priority once the decision was made, the mode of travel assured, and the deadline for moving set (only seven weeks down the line). Yet the euphoria I felt about having decided the how, where, and when of the move soon gave way to mounting anxiety about how to go about making it happen.

Books were the easiest items with which to start. I could begin anywhere since a stack of them could be found on almost every flat surface in our apartment. They disappeared into boxes, and the pile of cartons grew like a Tower of Babel.

Occasionally, as I was trying to stuff one more book into a box, or hoisting a hefty carton to the top of the tower, Roberta would comment, "That won't work, will it?" I wanted to think that she was not being negative, but rather that she thought she was being cute, making one of her clever statements that often had such humorous effects. Yet before she became ill she would never have needled me that way. I don't recall ever hearing her say anything to anyone that would have been the least bit discouraging, and I ascribed her doing so now to the impaired judgment that resulted from the disease. Still, her comments annoyed me and I covered my rising ire by saying stubbornly, "Oh, yes it will. You just watch me."

Not surprisingly, the place looked neater. But I did not see myself making any progress whatsoever on the larger task of preparing the bulk of our goods for the move and disposing of the rest.

A helpless onlooker most of the time, Roberta gave me little assistance. While I worked at packing, she took to sitting in her chair, watching and dozing. How I missed her strong body and go-for-it attitude that had seen us through many other difficult moves in our life.

Having most of the books packed, I began to grow discouraged and to doubt that I would be able to complete this endless packing and downsizing job that lay ahead of me. Maybe Roberta was right. Perhaps the whole idea wouldn't work.

I began having a recurring dream of being lost on the outskirts of a decayed urban area, walking down streets that ended in brick walls, not knowing how to advance to some hazy destination that always lay just beyond where I thought it was. This dream always told me I was on the verge of a crisis.

Packing was not the only problem that fueled my bad dreams. I was confronted with the task, among others, of mailing batches of change-of-address notices to two scientific journals, several popular science magazines, two health letters, a long mailing list of friends, several charities, a bank, and a number of insurance companies. This did not include my landlord, cable TV, and utility companies that also required notification of my date of departure. I foresaw hours of time being swallowed by these tasks.

Dismay began to fill my heart as I looked down the road ahead.

More Helping Hands

A voice sounded on the phone one morning, It was that of Sue Rardin, friend and member of our church. "Good morning Bob. This is Sue. I'm calling to make you an offer you can't refuse."

"You don't mean that, Sue," I said smiling.

"I do. Tell me what you need to have done and I'll do it."

Knowing what a well organized and energetic woman she was,

I immediately said, "If you will fill out and send off this pile of change-of-address cards, I will be very grateful." She promptly agreed, and thereby put an end to my recurring dream.

Further dispelling my discouragement, Susan Jensen, who Roberta had sponsored when she joined our church several years before, arrived one afternoon to help me organize my packing efforts. How did she know that organization was my greatest need? Seeing how disheartened I was, she told me that no one thinks at the outset that it is possible to make the move they have set out to make. It always appears to be overwhelming. "But somehow," she said with a smile and a pat on my shoulder, "they all make it."

As a professional organizer, helping elderly people downsize and move into smaller quarters when their large homes became too much for them, Susan not only helped me win the packing game, but she also saw to it that we survived the trauma of downsizing and getting rid of the rubbish and second-hand stuff. I could not have managed these operations without her help from the first of December into late in January, 2001, when the movers were scheduled to load most of our possessions on the van for the move to Grand Rapids. Moreover, in her newly launched vocation, she was able to obtain a hefty discount on our moving bill from the company she located for us.

Packing items from the linen closet, I came upon container after container of assorted pills—calcium, phosphorus, iron, vitamins, "Memory Well" pills, and many forms of ginkgo. I emptied them into a shopping bag in order to recycle their plastic containers. The bag was nearly half full when I finished.

Earlier I had received in the mail a package of knee-high hosiery and a bill for $17.50. After paying the bill I added the packet to the dresser drawer, which I had discovered was already overflowing with panty hose, thigh highs, and knee highs. When I received a similar package and bill about a month later, I surmised that Roberta had been drawn into a club arrangement. So I returned the package with a threatening note that I was about to report them to the Better Business Bureau. No more packages arrived.

The mess in our basement was almost beyond description. Part of the clutter consisted of a box containing more than a half-dozen

81

packages of waxed paper and still more of plastic wrapping material. I gave all of this stuff to Susan, who will not need to replenish her supply for years to come.

How long Roberta's hoarding behavior had been going on I didn't know. The variety and quantity of memory pills suggested that she was concerned about the decline of her ability to remember longer than I originally thought, perhaps for several years.

While all this activity was swirling around her, Roberta was keeping track of what I was doing by writing down what she knew was happening. Although confused, she was following the events more than I realized. Below is a note written by her that conveys how she was trying to keep up with the world that was leaving her behind.

Early in December, as Roberta still strolled along with me on short walks around the neighborhood, down several blocks to a *cul de sac* and back again, I continually pointed out things around us for her to look at. My aim was to keep her engaged with the world, rather than staring fixedly at the ground ahead of her, as she increasingly did those days.

Soon, however, even short walks became too much for my wife, and she willingly let me go solo, provided I did not stay away too long. Thus, she lost a once-loved lifelong activity, victimized by the "thousands of subtractions" occurring in her brain.

They Came Bearing Soup

Roberta and I were great "soupsters," as we sometimes called ourselves. Her specialties were vegetable, pea soup with Indian spices, and carrot soup. Mine were gazpacho, onion, and mushroom soups. Perhaps there was nothing quite as satisfying as making a pot of soup you enjoyed creating and had prepared well, and having your loved one express endless enjoyment eating it, savoring each spoonful, commenting on the subtle flavors, remarking on the difference from the last batch. For years, Roberta and I performed this ritual of appreciation for each other.

During the season of packing, however, there was no need for either of us to practice our soup-making talents, even had Roberta been able to do so. Friends knew we were in the midst of packing and brought in their specialties for our benefit—chicken soup with an Indian curry, Kosher turkey soup, vegetable soup, and several containers of turkey soup from Thanksgiving Day feasts. Our refrigerator was filled with these welcomed containers, and we ate well.

Roberta's rapid decline was painfully evident in church, to neighbors, and to friends. By December, she no longer made coherent comments in the pre-service Bible discussion group that we attended every Sunday. She slept through most of the meetings, and continued dozing through the worship services. Afterward we would be surrounded by friends who wanted to embrace Roberta and tell her how much they loved her and would miss her. Because she knew the difference between *being friendly* and *being a friend*, she had bonded with many people not only at church but elsewhere. Many of them were returning her love with their own expressions of caring at this time. The tributes they gave to her were deeply gratifying to me. Roberta had cast her bread of love upon many waters, as the wise preacher had counseled, and it was returning to her in kind.

Caring for an Alzheimer's patient is a very earthy experience at times, not unlike minding young children. Raising four children with Roberta had prepared me somewhat for this aspect of care. (What parent hasn't been squirted in the eye while diapering an infant son?)

When Roberta woke up one morning and was still lying in bed, her first comment was, "I'm so confused." She went on, "I don't know what happened. I got up last night and went in there," pointing to the bathroom.

Getting out of bed, she walked into it with me. Reaching down to the towel bar on the wash stand, she pulled one of her underpants off it. It was soaking wet.

"Uh, oh," I said. "Did you wet it?"

Worried that she had also soaked her bed too, I hustled back to the bedroom and felt along the sheet. It was dry.

Checking her nightgown, I found that it too was dry. As she took it off, in preparation for getting dressed, I was surprised that she was wearing dry underpants. Here was a mystery.

"Where did you get those?" I asked.

"Oh, in my . . . " Not being able to complete her sentence, she made some rolling-over motions with her hands in the direction of her dresser. The action suggested something that was full to overflowing—the drawer in which she kept her underclothes.

Then it dawned on me what had happened. She had used the toilet in the night without taking off her underpants. Yet some part of her brain still functioned well enough to instruct her to hang up her wet ones and go to her dresser drawer for a fresh pair. What a weird disease is Alzheimer's!

Christmas was approaching apace. The candlelight service at church on the Sunday before Christmas had prepared us in the past for this holy day. On the day after the candlelight service, Phyllis, our neighbor who had saved my sanity by dancing with Roberta while I napped, e-mailed me the following message:

Dear Bob,

I think about you and Roberta a lot. I saw you out in the audience for the Christmas concert. Wasn't it fun?

I keep thinking about you having to say goodbye to so many familiar things and people. It must really be hard. I will miss having you here in the 'hood.

That's it for now. Lots of love,

Phyllis

I responded with a return e-mail:

Phyllis,

You're wonderful. Believe me, I will miss the 'hood, too. You and our other neighbors are, bar none, the best we have ever had.

Yes, the candlelight service was beautiful. Roberta enjoyed it, too. But she had to be persuaded to go to it. As she sat in her easy chair before the service, we had this amazing conversation, which I report to you, more or less verbatim.

Bob: "It's time to get ready for the Candlelight Service."

Roberta: "Do we have to go?"

B: "No, we don't have to. But I think you will like it."

R: "I don't want to."

B: "I know you don't. What would you rather do?"

R: "I just want to sit here in my chair."

B: "I can see that."

Then I drew close to her.

B: "But it's not good for you to sit all day in your chair. You need to get out once in a while. You need to do different things to stir yourself up. That's why it's a good idea to go to candlelight. Besides you will love the music. It will be all music. No preaching."

At this point she must have thought I was praying. She started to pray herself.

85

R: "Dear God, I am sorry that I get in Bob's way. I know he has a lot of things he wants to do and can't because he has to take care of me. I know he's right. I know I have to get out. I want to do the things to help him. But I can't. So help me to do better, God."

She paused. I brushed the tears from my eyes, and murmured, "Amen."

Yes, Phyllis, candlelight was beautiful. And Roberta enjoyed it.

Bob

That day, one week before Christmas, was our daughter Joanne's birthday. We forgot completely about it, as we did Eloise's in September. We will probably not remember Phil's in February, or Christy's in July. These are not the only important dates we missed. The Philadelphia Singers concerts, the string quartet programs, the Academy of the Arts opera series, the dance series, and the Drama Group's play at church—they all slipped by us like ships in the fog. We saw none of them.

I e-mailed the following to Sam after a most interesting episode with Roberta:

Sam,

I need confirmation on a bit of doggerel from Mark Twain. Here's why. The other day Roberta and I were returning from a shopping trip at Super Fresh market. We were walking up the stone pathway from the driveway to the apartment each lugging a bag of groceries, she right behind me. Since she dislikes being gone from home I was chanting for her benefit, "Coming home. Coming home" (to the melody of "Going Home" from Dvorak's famous New World Symphony).

From behind me came an unexpected response, an intervention, but in perfect cadence, without missing a beat, "... Indian meal shorts." (Where in her befuddled brain did this fragment come from? Probably from her early family life when her father read many classics to her.)

Catching on to her switch in lyrics, I followed by chanting, maintaining the rhythm, "Skunk water, skunk water . . . "

" . . . swaller these warts," she concluded, precisely on the beat.

I turned around and together we guffawed at our serendipitous recollection and recitation of a scene from Tom Sawyer, *I believe it is.*

Here's where I need your help. 1) Is the incantation from that book, and 2) what is the scene? (These questions sound a little like the opera quiz that Milton Cross used to conduct on the Saturday afternoon broadcast of the "Texaco Opera," don't they?) As I recall, it is from Tom Sawyer *and is a scene in the cemetery in the dark of the moon where Tom and Huck Finn were trying to get rid of some warts by this incantation.*

Can you corroborate this?

Thanks,

Bob

Roberta remarked, again and again through her tears, that she was so confused and that she didn't know what the matter was and what to do. Each time she did so, I would cradle her, and sway her slowly in my arms, telling her that I would take care of her no matter what happened. This helped for a while; she was freed from confusion. I was prepared to hold her as long and often as necessary to relieve her of the horror of being confused and unable to clarify it.

As the holiday approached, our Cherokee neighbor, Ronnie Snowden, from across *La Grande Allée*, invited us along with neighbor Louise for Christmas dinner. I brought a baked ham and baked potatoes, new ventures in cooking for me. For dessert I added Sam's magnificent applesauce cake, his annual Christmas gift to Roberta and me. I also brought real whipping cream to slather on the cake, a delicacy not often served in these days of fluffy foam squirted from a canister. All morning I worked to prepare these goodies.

Louise brought a humongous spinach salad and a vegetable stir-fry. Our hostess provided appetizers, wine, cider, and delicious dinner rolls.

Roberta, however, was agitated throughout the meal and repeatedly told me she wanted to go home. She was overstimulated by the laden table, the passing of dishes, and the lively chatter. Efforts to include her in our conversation failed. She and I finally left, but not before we both had eaten our desserts. Sam's cake still tasted good to her.

The next evening, after watching "The News Hour," I suggested that we serve up the ham from yesterday's meal, along with some broiled, small, red-skinned potatoes sprinkled with rosemary, and steamed zucchini. She agreed, but added the comment, "I wish I could be your wife and make dinner for you." The statement became the theme for the night.

"It's okay," I said, trying to reassure her as we walked to the kitchen. "Come out and help me."

While I was cutting up the potatoes before broiling them, she came close to me and said, "I wish I could be your wife and do the things wives do to help you. But I can't. I'm just in your way."

Then she added, "You don't want me to get close to you."

"Why do you say that?" I asked.

"I'm just in your way," she repeated. "People don't want others to get too close to them."

"Any time you want to get close to me, come ahead. I want it that way. But sometimes I have things to do that take me away."

I really meant that. I was so conscious of her being on a journey of no return that I wanted to spend every moment that remained being close to her.

She drew near to me. I wrapped her in my arms and held her tightly.

Then she did something she had never done in my presence since the ravages of this disease struck her with such force in August; she wept. Her body shook with the force of her sobs. The realization of her inability to act in the role of my wife as she had done in the past seemed to overwhelm her. She turned on herself. Her only thought was that she got in my way.

I held her teary face up to mine.

"I wish I could help you," I said, kissing her tears.

"I know you can't," she replied through the mist. Then she said something she had never uttered before or since, "It's not fair." Knowing immediately that she was not complaining about the injustice of the situation for herself, I realized that her complaint was made on my behalf. She wanted me to know that she appreciated the care I was giving her, that she accepted her dependence on me, and that she was sorry that her illness was unfair to me. I could only hold her close and weep with her.

Yet she continued to do the few small things she could do in a wifely manner. She loved to spread the coverlet over me when I was preparing to take a nap. She would carefully tuck in my feet to be sure they stayed warm. She would hover over me until she was sure I was comfortable. On occasions as I was working on the computer, she would bring me slices of apples. They have always been her special delight, and because of this I have learned to enjoy them, too. Yet her overall life was in my hands, not hers, and she knew that mutuality of our relationship was long gone.

Later that evening, after she had just taken her pills and we were standing by the sink, she said, "I can smell the . . . " But she was unable to finish the sentence. She pointed at the little cup from which she drank the water to wash down her medication.

"Do you mean something in the cup?"

"Yes."

Then we started the guessing game.

"Is it water?" I asked.

"No."

I brought up every food word I could think of: orange juice, milk.

"No, it's not food."

This went on for some time: I suggesting words, and she rejecting them. Shortly, I ran out of words, and let her think on her own. At one point, she said, "Come on, Roberta, don't be so stupid." She continued standing, eyebrows drawn together in concentration. I held my breath. Was she going to be able to come up with the word she was searching for, or would she have to give up in another little defeat?

At long last she said with satisfaction, "Smoke! That's it. Smoke. The cup smelled like smoke."

I couldn't imagine where that smell came from. For her it was real. More important—she called up the word by herself.

I clapped her on the back. "Nice going. You remembered it."

Alzheimer's lost that battle.

Two days after Christmas our daughter Christy, her husband Burt Todd, and their son David came for an early dinner. Christy brought the food—remains from her holiday feast: ham, scalloped potatoes, broccoli, and salad. I furnished the ice cream bars for dessert, a favorite with them. It was a pleasant visit.

That evening we removed our hearing aids, brushed our teeth, undressed and we were ready for bed. I asked Roberta to please shut off the table lamp by my easy chair. Heading toward it confidently, she soon faltered as she came within arm's length of it.

"You'll have to come here and do it," she said. "I don't know how." The switch is out of sight underneath the shade.

"Here, let me show you how to do it, and then you'll have learned something today," I replied.

I pointed out the button switch on the lamp. "Push that button, and the light will go out."

She did so, and it went out.

"There, now you've learned something."

"Yes, I've learned something," she repeated. "But by tomorrow it may be gone."

"That's true. You have a good forgetter."

"That's right. I have a *very* good forgetter."

Sequel: The next evening I asked Roberta to switch off the same lamp. She went directly to it, fingered the switch, and turned it off.

A Season of Giving, and Receiving

I was amazed that so many friends, mostly from our church and our neighborhood, came to our aid with help and encouragement while we were preparing to leave Philadelphia. The feeling was not unlike that produced in the days when group dynamics and growth groups were all the rage, when as a trust exercise, I was physically elevated on the hands of fellow group members and gently rocked back and forth above their heads. Placing myself in the hands of others was both relaxing and energizing as well as gratifying for the strong hands and arms underneath. In a similar way the arms of our friends lifted us and supported us. I could think of no clearer manifestation of God's grace, the "everlasting arms" working to uphold us.

Besides those who donated soup by the quart, other friends came with sandwiches and sat down to eat lunch with us. A stream of others brought frozen dinners, delivered a large fruit basket from the United Methodist Women, gave both Roberta and me a massage, offered the book, *The 36-Hour Day*, for me to read, went shopping for us, hauled our waste paper to the recycling center, gave informal medical advice when asked, purchased underclothing for Roberta, gave neighborhood parties for us, sat with Roberta when I needed to leave the apartment, and dropped by late in the day to chat awhile and give us their support and encouragement. A half-dozen people offered help that I, unfortunately, could not get sufficiently organized to accept and use. I was overwhelmed by this outpouring of love and support.

The pastoral staff at church was unstinting in its efforts to assist and support us, bringing the sacrament of communion into our home when we were unable attend worship, and planning the reception following the worship service on the last Sunday before we left.

Other friends took items off our hands that we would never use again—no small favor, indeed. It is harder than one thinks to get rid of things in this material-rich society. Many things we sold or donated: Roberta's word processor, her hot paraffin bath, massage table, sewing machine, double bed mattress, quilted comforter, spinet piano, some of my power tools, a bin full of scrap wood, and gardening equipment and supplies. Clothing and miscellaneous stuff went to the Salvation Army. To our church I donated the garden hose and some power yard tools. Most of my shop tools and equipment went to my son-in-law.

The mixed feelings I had on parting with these possessions were probably the common lot among all people at this stage of life who are downsizing. It was like bidding old, faithful friends farewell, sorrowing that I would never meet them again, yet feeling a certain exhilaration at having lightened my load of unneeded impediments.

Roberta was only partly aware of what was going on, although I consulted her before disposing of anything that belonged to her. I thought that material possessions did not mean much to her anymore, even though occasionally she objected to my giving away so many things.

My wife continued to cycle through seasons of worrying. Seemingly she was quite aware that she was on a worrying kick. We had been invited to a gathering at the apartment of Henry and Grace Yocuma. Three days before the date Roberta was already declaring that she did not want to go to the party. "We don't have to go to the party, do we?" She kept badgering me with this. Finally I said with asperity, "Don't worry about it now. It's still three days off." "That's the trouble," she joked, "I now have three days of worrying to do."

One of the most painful experiences was to have Roberta starting to tell me something, speaking confidently and forcefully at first, and then hitting the chasm of lost memory, unable to complete what she started to say. Her struggle would be determined, accompanied by deep breathing, intense staring, and scraping noises in her throat as she endeavored with might and main to articulate what she wanted to say. Her voice was forced, almost croaking. I longed for her to succeed. During the pauses, I would try to suggest the word she was looking for. Sometimes I succeeded. At other times I didn't, and then she would stop me and I would realize I was only confusing her and disturbing her efforts to remember what she wanted to say.

Here is an approximate account of one such conversation, which took place in bed following a day of packing our goods and giving things away.

R: "I want you to know . . . " (pause)

B: "Yes?"

R: After several more repetitions of "I want you to know . . . " followed by, "It's all right with me if you . . . (pause)

B: "Yes?"

R: "It's all right with me . . . "(pause)

B: "If I . . . ?"

I was lying with my face close to her head. I smelled the scent of her hair. But my mind was dwelling on the awful things that were happening inside her brain, just below my cheek, and my anger rose again that this should be her fate.

R: "It's all right with me if you use those . . . " (pause)

B: (Guessing) "Quarters?"

R: "No. Just a minute, let me think." (pause, hard breathing) "It's all right with me if . . . " (pause)

B: "I buy those things?"

R: "Yes." (pause) "No. Not that." Starting over yet once more, "It's all right with me . . . " (pause)

I was weeping inwardly to feel her straining and struggling.

B: "I'm not sure what you mean. I'll try to guess."

R: Once more: "It's all right with me . . . "(pause)

B: A sudden inspiration: "Do you mean if I give those things away?"

R: "Yes. It's all right with me if you give those things away."

Her body relaxed as she settled down in my arms, having succeeded in saying what she wanted to say. But even more important, she had restored the mutuality of our relationship for this situation, at least. She was at one with me, agreeing to have me give all these things away, and anything else I might donate in the future. She had made this statement on her own initiative.

She did not always succeed. Sometimes she would just give up and say, "Oh, I can't think of that now." But on this occasion, our mutuality was too important for her to surrender. For a moment it was like old times.

VIII

An Anniversary to Remember

It was the middle of the afternoon on the last day of the year 2000. Roberta was sitting in her chair with the electric space heater pouring warmth over her, unaware that this day was, traditionally, a day of celebration for us. She had recently told me she was always cold, not in a complaining voice, just as a matter of fact. Holding her hand as I sat next to her I had the following conversation with her:

Bob: "Do you know that tomorrow is our wedding anniversary?"

Roberta: "Is it?"

B: "Yes it is. We were married on January 1, 1948."

No response.

B: "Do you remember how we always celebrate our anniversary on New Year's Eve? We eat dinner by candlelight with lobster tails and champagne. Ice cream bars for dessert. Just you and me."

R: "Oh."

B: "That will be tonight."

She was listening.

B: "So tonight will be our anniversary celebration, and we will feast on lobster tails."

R: "Did you buy them?"

B: "Sure did. I ordered them. And we'll have champagne, too."

R: "Did you buy that, too?"

B: "Yeah. Well, really, Dick got it for us. Do you remember how hard it was snowing yesterday? Dick did some shopping for us then. I asked him to pick up the lobster tails from Groben's [seafood store] and buy some Mumm's champagne. It's good stuff."

I continued. "Did you know we got married on January 1, 1948?"

R: "No."

B: "Well, we did. That's fifty-three years ago."

R: "No wonder we're so tired."

With that our conversation ended.

Roberta was extremely interested in the process of preparing the lobster tails. I had been thawing them for a couple of hours, so they were ready to cook at about five o'clock. She watched me as I dropped them into a large pot of water that I had brought to a rolling boil, letting them cook for five minutes.

Meanwhile, she helped me by correctly selecting and placing the flatware on the dining table, without my help. I was busy melting a half-pound of butter, heating the little dishes in which it would be placed, scooping some cocktail sauce into other dishes and opening a can of whole kernel corn.

Once the tails were partially cooked, I removed and cooled them, snipped off the bottom shells with a scissors, and detached the meat from the upper shell. Turning the upper shells over, I placed the meat on them, dabbed them with butter, and positioned them in the electric oven to melt the butter and broil them for a few minutes. Sprinkling a little paprika on them, I arranged them on our blue Japanese fish-shaped dishes, and filled the side dishes with corn. For the proper atmosphere, I lit the artificial log in the fireplace and the candles on the table, and put Mozart's *Eine Kleine Nachtmusik* on the CD player.

When the meal was spread on the table, we looked it over with great satisfaction.

"Doesn't this look great!" I said. She agreed. Folding Roberta's hands in mine and asking a blessing on our celebration, I then uncorked and poured the champagne. It looked particularly beautiful in the tall flutes that I had purchased years ago just for these celebrations. Rising from the bottom, the bubbles sparkled in the candlelight as they danced their way upward, skittering around on the surface, ready to tickle Roberta's nose as she drank. She rubbed her nose and giggled. Delighted, we toasted our marriage, the New Year, and then our marriage again.

From the way she assailed her lobster, it was clear that Roberta had not lost her enthusiasm for food that night. We both discovered how surprisingly well whole-kernel corn goes with lobster. One time she dipped her morsel of lobster into the dish of corn instead of the drawn butter, until, realizing that something was not quite right, she asked me what she should be doing. I suggested that she first dip the lobster into the butter and then into the dish of corn. She did so and was satisfied.

For dessert, Roberta served each of us one of the brownies that Christy had left after her post-Christmas meal with us; I added a dollop of ice cream as a crowning touch.

I cannot recall a more memorable wedding anniversary celebration than this one, all the more unforgettable because of Roberta's total engagement in it. Afterward, she remarked several times how much she enjoyed it. I, too, had delighted in each moment even as I resolutely tried to deny entry into the portals of my heart the awareness that this would probably be our last such festive anniversary celebration.

Later that night, Roberta touched me awake, after I had been asleep in my bed for a while, telling me that she couldn't sleep. This was an invitation to come to bed with her and comfort her until she dropped off. While we were dozing, she said drowsily, "I thought I should tell you again how much I liked that meal, instead of letting you lie there thinking that I grouse at you all the time."

"Thanks, Roberta," I muttered to myself. That's just what I needed in the middle of the night. And yet, why not? This, I knew, was the last meaningful wedding anniversary we would ever celebrate together, and spending a few more moments with her in its afterglow was not too much to ask.

Often, when Roberta could not fall asleep, it probably meant that she was about to be afflicted with restless legs. Sure, enough, after a while her legs began to twitch, at first a small jerk, followed in about ten seconds by another little twitch. And so on. If it was allowed to continue she would have to get out of bed and pace the floor for relief.

Remembering my prior experience with RLS and answered prayer, I reached over and placed my hand on her thighs and slowly massaged her legs, praying as I did so. Soon the twitching stopped. I let my hand rest on her leg. I could have achieved similar results of calming her restless legs by giving her a dose of Lorazepam, a sedative. But I preferred to relieve RLS without medication if I could, because it gave physical expression of my love for her. When a twitch occurred, I again slowly stroked her leg and before long she was asleep. After waiting long enough to be sure that she was soundly asleep, I returned to my bed for a wonderful night of rest. When I awoke very early and quite refreshed, she was still snoring peacefully.

IX

New Year's Day, 2001

Sue Rardin had called me on December 30 with a splendid proposal. She was hatching a plan, she said, to serenade Roberta and me in our apartment on New Year's Day morning. She would be joined, she continued, by three other serenaders—her husband Jerry, her sister and brother. They would take care of all the details. All we had to do was sit and enjoy. She needed my approval. What did I think of it? Would we like that?

I immediately fell in love with her plan but said I should talk it over with Roberta before giving a final answer. Knowing that she would initially reject the idea, fearing it would open up a whirl of confusion, I still needed to keep our partnership going and not make any more unilateral decisions than necessary. I did a "big time" persuasion job on Roberta, convincing her that when it was over she would have enjoyed the experience. She reluctantly agreed to Sue's proposal.

Soon after eleven o'clock on New Year's Day morning the four of them arrived. There was a shedding of jackets, a presenting of gilded cardboard "Happy New Year" derbies for Roberta and me to wear, some arranging of chairs so that we could sit next to each other as an audience of two, and a shuffling of music. At last all was in readiness.

99

To set the stage for the first song, Sue asked me to tell them how Roberta and I had met.

For some reason, feeling a little mischievous, I drawled, "Wa-yell, Ah always war a lag-man myself, and when Ah saw them thar paar of lags on the stairs ahead of me, Ah says to myself, 'Them's for me.' Wa-yell, they turned out to be Roberta's. So hyar we aire."

Although they laughed, my flippant response was not what Sue wanted and her eyes blazed for a split second. I was momentarily sorry I said what I did. Without missing a beat, however, she said directly to Roberta that she hoped we had met on a moonlit night on our college campus, perhaps on *some enchanted evening*, because that was what they were going to sing about. After a little fumbling around with the pitch pipe, Sue's brother got them started.

Sue kept singing directly to Roberta, which worried me a little because Roberta had occasionally mentioned that she does not like women with a large heads of hair (like Sue's). But with her good voice and acting ability, Sue soon swung Roberta into the spirit of the song. Before long, Roberta and I were singing quietly along with them. Jerry's solo parts pleased Roberta immensely, and we applauded them vigorously at the end.

The next song, "The Lord Bless You and Keep You," was an old standby in the repertoire of every high school and church choir in our school days. Since Roberta and I were well acquainted with it, we joined them, she alto and I bass. The song moved me deeply, especially as I realized that it was a farewell song to us, sung in the best Christian tradition.

The Lord bless you and keep you;
the Lord make his face to shine upon you,
and be gracious unto you;
Amen (sevenfold).

The third song was announced as one Roberta would surely recognize. I knew immediately that they were going to sing the one that she had written and composed for children of our church at Christmas time long before—"A Child's Carol." Jerry loved it and always included it in a worship service during Advent season. It just so happened that I had found a copy of her song in a folder that morning. So I went to the dining room table where it lay and got out the copy, only to turn around and find Jerry kneeling by Roberta's chair and showing her the words from his copy. I should have let him continue with her, but when he saw me returning he went back to the group, and Roberta and I sang along with them from the sheet I held.

I want to make a point for the record, on behalf of Roberta. Some of the printed copies of the song give credit for the words to Roberta, but credit for the music to Michael Korn, organist and choir director at our church at the time she composed the piece. That is not the way it happened. Roberta did both; she wrote the words and composed the music. However, she asked for and received help from Mike to resolve a difficulty with the ending of the score. But the music and the lyrics are hers with an assist from Mike. Here are the lyrics and the music with the score:

A Child's Carol

Roberta Timmer DeHaan

Roberta Timmer DeHaan
and Michael Korn

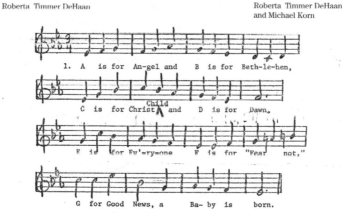

1. A is for An-gel and B is for Beth-le-hem,
C is for Christ Child and D is for Dawn,
E is for Ev'-ry-one F is for "Fear not,"
G for Good News, a Ba- by is born.

2. **H** is for holiday, **I** is for Icicle.
    J is for Jingle Bells, **K** is for Kiss,
    L is for Lovely Lights, **M** is for Magic,
    N is for Noise and Nonsense like this.

3. **O** is for Orange, spicy like Frankincense,
    P is for Pine Cones, astringent like Myrrh,
    Q is for quiet Night, quilted in candlelight,
    R for Reindeer with donkey-soft fur.

4. **S** is for Starbright and **T** is for Traveler,
    U "Unto Us," and "Venite" for **V**,
    "Double **U**," **W**ise Men and **X** marks the manger,
    Y is for "Yes" from A until **Z**.

The serenade was a huge success, altogether lovely, friendly, and heartwarming. The selection of songs was impeccable. I stand amazed at the creativity and generosity of people like Sue and the others who expended such effort to show their love and appreciation primarily on behalf of Roberta. A more delightful way to initiate the New Year was hard to imagine.

Before the serenade began, I knew that I could make this a still more memorable event for them as well as for us, with a little contribution of my own. Since Roberta and I had not finished the bottle of champagne at our celebration, I decided that we should use the remainder as an exclamation point to this wonderful occasion. Earlier that morning, I had gathered six champagne glasses and made them ready in the kitchen. After the conversation had settled down a bit, I told the group about our traditional wedding anniversary celebration and that I still had some champagne on hand from last night's party. I suggested to the group that we enjoy the wine together as a salute to this enjoyable event and a toast to the New Year.

To their applause, Sue and I retreated to the kitchen to bring in the glasses and champagne. Then it occurred to me that by adding orange juice to the champagne we could create a *mimosa*, the usual drink of Sunday brunches and just right for this occasion. (It would also stretch the champagne so each could have a generous glass full.) That idea scored big. After a great amount of pouring and mixing, we were ready. With glasses held high, and amidst much banter, we toasted our anniversary and drank to each other's health in the New Year that was upon us.

102

More wittiness and laughter followed when from the sidelines came the voice of Roberta, who was undoubtedly feeling left out of the merriment, "I'm getting tired of all this, folks." She was so innocent about it that no one took offense, and immediately our guests made moves to leave. More farewell embraces followed, and our serenaders were off.

While cleaning up in the kitchen after they left I was singing softly to myself, "Some enchanted evening."

Roberta chimed in, "But it's twelve o'clock."

I looked at her and then at the clock and sure enough, both hands were pointing straight up. "Not exactly an enchanted *evening* yet, is it?" I remarked, chuckling.

But she had already turned and was walking away like a champion boxer who has just floored his opponent, satisfied that she could deliver as clever a knockout remark as any of those people who had just departed.

Later that day, our longtime friends Szabi-Ishtai Zee and his wife, Rava, joined us for a final visit. This seemed to be the day for finishing remains of bottles of fine liquor, for they brought a partly filled bottle of Glenmorangie, single highland malt scotch whisky, which we had tasted earlier in the year at one of Zee's fabulous parties. It is a memorable potion, everything that the label on the back of the bottle claims for it. They also brought along a bucket of buffalo wings, since I had told them when they called earlier that we were out of goodies. Every visit we had enjoyed with these friends added another pearl on the string of memories that threads its way back several years through our lives. This was an especially poignant call, since we all realized that it was to be the last jewel on the string; they would never again see Roberta in any sense a whole person, if at all. It was particularly painful for Szabi and Rava to see Roberta's deterioration and to know that we would soon be departing from their lives.

Over the years Roberta had developed a warm friendship with Szabi. As an instructor in the GLCA Urban Semester, she had called on him regularly to discuss general systems theory, one of his many areas of expertise, with her student seminar. His lectures supplemented her presentations of *phenomenology*, a subject in which

103

she had become proficient while earning her Master's degree in Religion at Temple University. I have sat in on Szabi's lectures on occasion. Although legally blind, he has the uncanny ability to sense what is going on in a group better than most people with 20/20 vision.

Moreover, Szabi had been highly instrumental in my being offered the position of Director of the Master's Program in Human Services at Lincoln University in the early 1980s. We had maintained a personal and professional relationship ever since.

Still later our friends, Nancy Pigford and Alan Ankeny, fellow members at our church, stopped by to deliver a loaf of cranberry bread, Alan's annual post-Christmas gift to us, along with several substantial packing cartons and a wardrobe. Nancy added a batch of peanut butter cookies as her present. For the next several days we feasted on Al's bread topped with ice cream. Nancy's cookies lasted well into our trip to Michigan. A month later the cartons, filled with dishes, and the wardrobe, holding our jackets, arrived in Grand Rapids to remind me of the generosity of Al and Nancy.

The day after the big New Year's Day was extremely difficult for Roberta. She became rather bewildered and agitated and complained again and again of being confused. This was accompanied by what seemed like a stubborn resistance to look up and around at her world, as if raising her head and eyes was too much for her. She went through most of that day staring at the floor.

She did, however, watch me as I made dinner that evening, which involved preparing a frozen shepherd's pie, contributed by Ronnie Snowden. Sometimes Roberta was confused by a sequence of activities if she didn't get the big picture. So I explained to her that I was making dinner, that the frozen shepherd's pie—beef/tomato/mashed potato dish—was going to be the main part of the meal, and that I was going to heat it in our electric oven. This time, however, my explanation of the steps I was taking fell flat. She was suspicious of the whole proceeding; she kept asking what I was doing, and saying that it confused her and that it wouldn't work. She was right. Dinner was a disaster. Since the casserole was still cold in the center when I served it, this meal justified her suspicion.

Later that night, as I prepared Roberta for bed she got into her nightgown with little trouble, but she was still wearing her shoes. Sitting on the edge of her bed, she stared silently at another pair of shoes lying on the floor by her nightstand. "Take off your shoes now, Roberta." No response. Oblivious of me, she kept staring down. I urged her, instructed her, pleaded with her, all to no avail. I observed that characteristic Alzheimer's leonine cast to her face as she continued to be fixated on the pair of shoes by her nightstand. Finally, I reached down and unlaced her shoes, took them off, and placed slippers on her feet. Throughout this procedure, she was passive and pliable. I felt like I was molding a lump of clay.

The next step in our bedtime-preparation routine was for Roberta to go to the bathroom. This time she stood in front of the toilet simply staring at the bowl seemingly unable to figure out what to do next. Finally, I had to turn her around and actually sit her down on it before she could do her thing. Through this all, she kept saying in a resigned voice, "I'm mixed up," and, "I can't figure this out."

In bed, her confusion and agitation continued. Usually when she was ready to sleep, she would lie on her side and drift off peacefully. Tonight it was different. She lay rigidly on her back, staring at the ceiling. I tried to rock her body gently back and forth to relax her. When I finally convinced her to turn over on her side she did so, but still would not close her eyes. Instead of staring at the ceiling she was now staring at me lying next to her. Every so often, she reared up and looked intently down at her pillow. The pattern of leaves and flowers on the pillowcase seemed to bother her. She pointed at them, tracing them with her finger, making inarticulate sounds about them, communicating to me that they frightened her. I suggested she trade pillows with me since my pillowcase was unadorned. That satisfied her, and she put her head down peacefully.

Only a moment later she reared up with a terrified look on her face, staring at a pile of pillows and blankets on the bookcase near the bed, ready to be packed. I silently chastised myself for having placed them there without anticipating that the sight of them in the dark might agitate her. I climbed out of bed and moved them out of her range of vision.

Nothing I could do, however, brought her out of her agitated state. I sang "Rock-a-bye, my little owlet"[1] to no avail. Finally, I suggested that we go down to the kitchen for a mug of cambric tea (half milk, half boiling water, with several drops of vanilla extract). She readily agreed. When it was prepared, I gave her a Lorazepam pill, which she washed down without any question.

This medication works quickly, and soon after returning to bed, Roberta fell into a troubled sleep. Nights like this fueled my desire to be near an Alzheimer's treatment center as soon as possible.

The rest of the week following the glorious New Year's Day was one of unremittingly hard labor for Susan J. and me. We faced a hard-and-fast deadline—our departure date of January 9, the day Ray and Linda were to transport us to our destination, Grand Rapids. We wanted to complete as much of the larger packing job as possible, all the time recognizing, however, that we would leave with much of it still unfinished. During this time Roberta sat unobtrusively in her easy chair watching what was going on with no comment.

Fortunately, the first week of the new year ended on a positive note. Grace and Henry invited us, along with Ronnie, for our last "O be joyful" get together. We all knew it would be a time of good food and interesting conversation, of banter and tears, of joy and sorrow—and it was. As we left, Grace handed me a card with the following message, which I will treasure as long as I live:

Dear Bob and Roberta,

I've never been good at saying "good bye" to people. So I thought I would do it in writing.

First of all, you can not imagine how much Henry and I will miss you. In the more than 30!!! years we have lived here, you have been our very best neighbors, always thoughtful and kind, and ready to help in an emergency.

We'll miss Roberta's beautiful gardens and your outdoor

106

lights at Christmas.

We greatly appreciated Bob's saving the life of the oak tree and doing innumerable prunings and lopping of tree limbs.

As Ronnie once said, you have really been like extended family.

Bob, I am sure this is all very hard on you—leaving your church, your book club, and other activities. I'm sure your strong faith will carry you through.

Keep in touch by e-mail & we'll pass your messages on to Ronnie. Maybe I'll manage a farewell wave when you go.

Love,

Grace and Henry, too.

---

[1] Longfellow, H.W., *Indian Lullaby.*

107

X

Communion

The sacrament of Holy Communion turned out to be an unexpected source of spiritual strength as we journeyed into the shadows early in the winter of 2000. Roberta and I had grown up in our common faith community where the sacrament was taken for granted in worship, much as three meals were in our daily lives. It was not until we faced the crisis brought on by Roberta's disease that it became more than a regularly celebrated liturgical exercise. It grew into an essential conduit of grace for raising our flagging spirits and energizing us for the journey.

The Communion services that most steeled our spiritual determination had several things in common. They occurred at major transitions in our lives; that is, when we were about to set out on a journey. Each served as food for the journey, as well as concluding in a spiritual way our relationship with believers with whom we had lived and were about to leave. They occurred mostly outside the worship setting of the church, in our home or apartment.

These holy moments echoed another Communion feast brought to us years before by the Rev. Bill Hillegonds, Chaplain of Hope College in Holland, Michigan. I had been teaching there for twelve years, and in the spring of 1968 was about to move with my family to Philadelphia. The prospect of the move frightened my family more than I had realized. Bill must have sensed that, and several nights before we departed, he arrived at our home to administer the sacrament to our family. We sat around the kitchen table, our children with wide eyes and opened ears, while Bill, in his deliberate way, read the Biblical passage describing the Last Supper. He then passed the bread and grape juice to each of us, "proclaiming the Lord's death till He comes."

His presence was incredibly cheering, spreading confidence with every word of the sacrament. I'm not sure how much it stirred the children, but it made a deep impression on Roberta and me as we were about to make our exodus. The sacrament made the prospect of our journey less daunting by placing it in the perspective of Christ facing his greatest transition. It united us in grace and gratitude with Christ and with Christians of all time and by sealing our unity with Rev. Bill and, through him, with our friends and fellow believers at Hope College and in the city we were leaving behind.

Another memorable Communion service occurred on the afternoon of the church's annual Midnight Christmas Eve Service. Roberta and I had never failed to attend it in the past. The darkened chapel, "quilted in candlelight," as Roberta described it, the solemn gathering, gentle music, the pastor's grace-filled meditation, and the Communion service had always made this an especially solemn observance. However, since it started at 10:30 P.M., and almost always spilled over into early Christmas morning, we found it impossible to be present this one last time.

My disappointment at having to miss the Communion service that evening was assuaged by Rev. Jerry Rardin, joined to our church and long-time friend of ours, who came to our apartment that afternoon to administer the sacrament. Besides being a friend and pastor to us, he was a great admirer of Roberta. Earlier he had presented her with a book of Christmas alphabetical pop-ups, a companion piece to her song, "A Child's Carol." She treasured the book and enjoyed showing it to others.

Carrying the material for the service in a satchel, Jerry was well organized to make house calls of this kind to shut-in members of the church. While setting up the service, he showed us a special

110

bulletin cover produced by Bruce McNeel, one of the church's art-ists-in-residence. (It had been prepared for the special service held earlier in the week for people to whom Christmas was not a time of joy but rather one of depression and sadness. It was a service made to order for us, but I had known that we weren't going to be able to attend it. I had phoned Jerry, the clergyman in charge, and had excused ourselves from it.) Roberta was fascinated by the bulletin cover, looking intently at it as she held it in her hand.

Having arranged the Communion service on the coffee table, Jerry proceeded with the sacrament. No one could communicate better with Roberta than he. After the sacrament was completed, he knelt by her side and talked quietly to her for a long time. Only they and God know what he said, but Roberta listened with a fully engaged mind, as I could tell. This was the first of two Communion services that marked the impending transition in our lives and bound our hearts to Jerry.

I sent the following e-mail to Jerry a couple of days later.

Dear Jerry,

Thanks so much for that quiet, wonderful Communion service on Saturday. I was deeply moved. Did you notice how intently Roberta was paying attention after she stopped looking at the bulletin cover? She was really into it.

On Sunday morning, however, she woke up being quite irritable. She said so herself. "I feel grumpy this morning." She continued in this mode for some time.

Finally she remarked with great conviction, "Jerry was so nice to us yesterday that I don't feel free to be grumpy anymore." I smiled and gave her a high five. Then she shifted into the cheerful mode and stayed in it for a long spell.

I trust Christmas was rewarding for both you and Sue.

Fondly,
Bob (and for Roberta)

Soon after Roberta had been medically diagnosed with Alzheimer's disease, I began to feel a desire for a Communion service to consecrate our departure from Philadelphia and a new start in Grand Rapids. Remembering earlier transitions from Holland to this city, I wanted this major journey in our lives to be undertaken only after a final union with our pastor Ted and good friend Sam around the symbolic table of the Lord. Roberta agreed to the idea as I explained it to her, and I think she understood what I was proposing.

I wanted the service to be held on the last weekend of our life in Philadelphia so that it would be a fitting conclusion of gratitude for our time in this city and in our faith community. It would also be an appropriate beginning to our journey into the future. Thus as the segment of our life had ended in Holland thirty-three years earlier and a new journey begun with a communion service, in like manner would the Philadelphia era also be concluded, and our journey to Grand Rapids started.

Ted, being our close friend as well as our retired pastor, was the only person who could conduct this sacrament for Roberta and me. No minister in our lives has influenced us as deeply as has Ted; having him perform the sacrament would be a fitting way to be joined with him for the last time at the deepest spiritual level of our Christian faith. Although he was retired and no longer involved in church services or ministerial affairs, I was confident he would join us in this sacrament.

I intended to invite Sam to be present as well. He had become a brother to both of us over the years. Roberta, he, and I shared so many experiences and values that we could often tell without asking what the other was thinking regarding any issue, especially as it pertained to life at our church. I meant this to be a family affair for just the four of us and God.

Early in December I e-mailed the following note to Sam.

Sam,

Ted is coming over on Saturday afternoon, January 6, at 3 o'clock, to administer the sacrament of Communion

*to Roberta and me, and I hope to you. I told him you are
my unofficially adopted brother and that I had invited
you to join us on this occasion. Speaking of you, he said,
"You picked a good one."*

*I trust you will be able to make this date and time. I
gathered from your last e-mail that you would be in town.
This will be a significant event for Roberta and me in
our closing days at our church.*

Looking forward to the sixth of January.

Bob

I felt a little uneasy on Saturday morning, since the apartment, with the piles of packing boxes I had been stacking up, was beginning to look more like a warehouse than a residence, let alone a chapel. I covered the most conspicuous mound with a tablecloth handed down from Roberta's mother, which gave the unexpected appearance of an altar. I set two dining room chairs next to Roberta's easy chair for Sam and me, and a chair facing ours for Ted.

Ted arrived shortly after Sam, who had brought grape juice and a piece of pita bread. Ted held in his hands a beautiful ceramic chalice and platter, fashioned by Mark Smith, the unofficial resident potter of our church. Ted gave them to Roberta and me to memorialize this occasion and the sacrament we were about to observe. As I poured the grape juice into the chalice and placed the bread on the plate, I knew I would be forever grateful for this gift.

Gathered in the living room, we held the most relaxed and pleasant conversation old friends could ever have had. At Ted's suggestion we chatted about our experiences at church and the kinds of things Roberta and I had been involved in. We recalled Roberta's role in chairing the Music Committee in the hectic days of Miko Korn's tenure as organist and choir director, and of her unstinting efforts in helping him launch the Philadelphia Singers, one of the finest choral groups ever to sing in Philadelphia and the nation. We also relived the work that she and Sam had done as co-chairs of the Evangelism Committee, and remembered the wonderful meals we had at our home on Haines Street every New Member's Sunday, when new church members came together for feasting and fellowship.

We then conversed with pleasure about my work as chair of the Property Committee and how I had initiated the capital improvement program in the middle eighties. We reviewed the many improvements that the program had wrought in our physical plant. We also talked about how Bill Norton and I started the Religion and Race Task Force years before.

These were refreshing memories, and a delight to all of us. There was a sense of closure when our conversation came to this point. It was time to move on to the sacrament itself.

Although the afternoon was cold and damp outside, our apartment was warm with the glow of sacred expectation. As an introduction to the sacrament and to center our thoughts, Ted read the eleventh chapter of the Letter to the Hebrews, that outstanding treatise on the heroes of faith. As he read, his mind was so engaged, and his reading so expressive, that the Word acquired new depth of meaning in that room. There was no question that we all felt included among the heroes of faith memorialized in that chapter.

Ted then took the pita bread in his hands, broke off a piece, and pressed it into Roberta's hand, saying slowly and deliberately the familiar words, "The body of Christ, broken for you." He then turned to Sam, sitting next to her, and finally to me with the same act and words. While we were holding the morsel in our hands, Ted took the chalice and held it for Roberta, saying, "The blood of Christ, shed for you." She dipped her bread into the cup. And so with Sam and me.

Finally, Ted broke and immersed a fragment of bread for himself and, in silence, engrossed in our own thoughts, we ate with thankfulness the intinctured morsels, celebrating our Lord's death as Christians have done through the ages. It was a true Eucharist, a meal prepared in heaven by God, a time of giving thanks for our lives together in the church, the gifts we had shared, the grace that we had experienced. We thus sealed in this intimate way our oneness with two of our dearest friends and brothers in Christ, and committed our lives to the safekeeping of eternity. Thus comforted,

I felt that the final spiritual preparations had been made for the journey that Roberta and I were about to undertake.

After Ted offered a short prayer of thanksgiving and entrusted our departure to God, we sang all the verses of "O God Our Help In Ages Past." Ted embraced Roberta for a long time, then Sam and me, and gave us his blessing. I drew deeply from my well of tears as we held each other close for a few long moments. He murmured encouragement into my ear, but since it was the one that is stone deaf, I failed to hear what he said. I was, however, so deeply moved that I simply needed to let my emotions of thankfulness, sorrow, and apprehension flow. We both knew that this was the end of our physical walk together, but that nothing could break the bond of our shared spiritual unity.

Ted walked slowly out the door.

After his departure Sam and I were so overwhelmed by the experience of the Communion service that there was nothing we could say. Sam gave both Roberta and me a long farewell embrace. Though our hearts were being torn apart by our imminent departure, they were knit together inseparably by the experience we had just had.

The next day Sam wrote me in an e-mail entitled "O Love That Will Not Let Me Go":

> *Until all senses leave me, I'll never forget yesterday's moments with Roberta and you. For me, it was one of the most moving spiritual experiences I've ever had. Ted was at his joyous best, melding together—just for the DeHaans—all the sterling qualities he has: his compassion, his sensitivity, his insight, his tenderness, his Christianity—unblemished, cloaked as he was with the Scriptures, the mystery of the bread and wine, the spirit unshackled, embracing three dear friends. In a way, he illumined the room with all he has meant to us and what his gifts have been as candles and beacons on the jour ney of faith. How can I thank you for including me?*

Months later, Sam reminisced in an e-mail:

> *Often I think of her comment during the once-in-a-life-time communion service we had in your living room.*

115

> *Ted mentioned the Evangelism Committee, and I asked*
> *her if she remembered our working on it, and she re-*
> *plied, "Yes, that's when I first began to love you." Oh, my.*

As if that were not enough, the next day being the first Sunday
of the New Year and first one of the month (Worldwide Communion Sunday, which our church always observed), Roberta and I were
raised to still another spiritual peak. I awoke with shivers running
up and down my legs knowing this would be one of the most important Lord's Days in our life—the last that we would spend worship-
ping as a members of our church and our final Communion service
in this faith community. Moreover, the glow of the previous day's
Eucharist in our apartment still lingered in my soul, and I anticipated that this day would also be burned into my memory.

The day at church had begun inauspiciously in the Bible Discussion Group. Roberta had made a couple of unintelligible remarks
that everyone listened to out of love for her, after which she fell
asleep with her chin on her chest.

In the worship service, as a memorial to our departure, and in
honor of the Bible Discussion Group that Roberta and I had helped
start and which we both had attended regularly since its inception
several years before, some members of the group had been invited
to serve the Communion elements at the worship service. It happened by design that Tom Bartlow, whose friendship with us went
back to our early days at our church, and Sam, both also founding
members of the Bible discussion group, were assigned to serve at
the side of the altar rail where Roberta and I would be kneeling.
Noting this, I strongly suspected that Ann Marie Donohue, the staff
associate who was in charge of the service, had deliberately made
this arrangement so that Tom and Sam would be the ones serving
Roberta and me, bringing the four of us founders together for a
final brief, intense moment in the Eucharist.

My heart pounded as Roberta and I walked hand in hand down
the aisle to the altar rail. As we knelt, I closed my eyes in prayer,
and held out my cupped hands to receive the bread from Tom and
to hear his accompanying words. But I was waiting for the moment
when Sam would offer me the chalice. When he did so, I looked up

116

at him, and clung to his hand for a brief moment that seemed like an eternity, an experience that will follow me into eternity. Tears welled up in our eyes as he uttered the sacramental words, and I dipped my bread into the grape juice. Then he moved on to serve Roberta, and again heaven opened and their spiritual oneness engulfed them.

In the same e-mail that expressed his feelings about our Saturday Communion service, Sam wrote:

> *I can't tell you what it means to me to have been able to serve you the element of the wine of Communion. It was entirely different but equally as moving as yesterday with Ted. After serving Roberta, I couldn't see the next few people for the tears in my eyes. Later, Ann Marie came to me and said she was so happy that I had been able to give you Communion (she had been watching). I guess the most profound happiness is always tinged with bitterness and sadness. Oh, Stanley Kunitz is right, "How shall the heart be reconciled to its feast of losses?"*

> *Brother Sam.*

Through all these services Roberta was attentive and relaxed. Through faith I believe that God was murmuring to her in a still, small voice even as he was addressing Sam and me in ringing tones.

This Communion service was part of continuing drama that took place during that last Sunday of our life at our church. Other scenes from the day are replayed in the next chapter.

XI

Our Last Sunday at Our Church

With my antennae fully extended to catch every vibration of the Spirit, I approached the worship service and the Communion service that was described in the previous chapter. To my surprise, very early in the service Marion Taylor (co-lay leader of the congregation along with Sam) rose to the lectern to make an announcement. She proceeded to give the congregation a blow-by-blow, year-by-year account of how church member Bill and I had co-chaired a committee to develop a procedure for honoring persons in the congregation and community who had made outstanding contributions to social and racial justice through their lives and work. The idea of creating this award came from church member Sylvia Bolden, who also served on the committee. The award was presented each year at a ceremony on the Sunday before the national Martin Luther King Jr. holiday in January—one of the most important Sundays of the year for our church in Philadelphia. The award ceremony had become a tradition that added a new dimension to the multifaceted life of the congregation.

The committee, called the Awards Committee, had worked for several years, developing criteria for selecting recipients of the award from among those nominated by the congregation, producing an award lapel pin (designed by Bruce McNeel), ordering a permanent awards board on which the recipients' names would be recorded, and preparing procedures for making an annual public presentation of the award. Marion went on to recount how Bill and I had continued working with the committee on the process of selecting a recipient each year for three years beyond the planning stage.

As tangible recognition of our work, Marion announced that Bill, Bruce, and I were to be awarded the Social and Racial Justice lapel pin in recognition of our role in making the program happen. To the applause of the worshippers, Dick, a member of the Awards Committee, came to where we were seated and fastened the lapel pins on our jackets, first Bill and Bruce and then me. Tears welled up in our eyes as Dick and I embraced each other. I was completely overwhelmed by the honor of receiving this recognition and by being associated with Bill and Bruce in the work. I have suspected that this idea came from Dick, a man who has always looked for ways to make life more meaningful for people.

Roberta was also recognized and honored. The congregation stood and sang her song, "A Child's Carol." It has become better known as "Roberta's Song." Many people turned around and smiled at Roberta as they sang. I'm sure the hearts of the members went out to her as they saw her standing, small and bewildered, next to me. My only regret was that Roberta's immense contributions to the life of this congregation had not been presented as dramatically as my contribution to social and racial justice had just been.

Dick had informed me before the worship service started that, during the singing of the last hymn, he would escort Roberta and me out of the sanctuary and into Pilling Hall (the social hall) for a reception that was to follow the worship service. The reception had been planned by the clergy in recognition of our departure. While the congregation sang "O God Our Help in Ages Past," Roberta and I walked down the aisle, she on my arm, just as we had walked up the aisle more than fifty-three years before at our wedding. I was deeply moved.

A long line of people formed in the social room. They wanted to say goodbye and God be with us. Many of them wished to tell both of us that it was Roberta's or my friendship that convinced them to join the church and kept them coming. Many eyes were filled with tears, and the hugs were long and clinging.

Thinking that Roberta might not be able to endure the long stand at the reception, I had recruited Jonathan Hale Sills, a special friend of Roberta and me, to hover around the reception line. If she showed signs of panic or fatigue, he was to spirit her away to the lounge until the reception was over. Hover he did through the entire reception. Roberta, however, did not need his help. She carried on beautifully, being her best winsome self to each and everyone who wanted to hug her, tell her how much she meant to them and how much they would miss her, and finally to bid her farewell. Later Jonathan reported to me with a chuckle that at one point she had muttered to him, "All I wish is that we could get the hell out of here." Then with an impish smile she corrected herself, "I mean, get the heck out . . ."

Among many things that had endeared Roberta to the hearts of members of this congregation was her ability to distinguish between being *friendly* and being a *friend*. She was known for seeking out and greeting strangers at church. Often called on to sponsor new members, Roberta also followed them afterward, inviting them to our home for lunch or tea and keeping in touch with them for years. She especially enjoyed opening our house on Haines Street for the Sunday welcoming luncheon for members who had just joined the church. (Many such friends came to say "God be with you" to Roberta and me.)

The farewell that moved me the most was the last one, as I bid farewell to Dick, who was waiting at the side. With damp cheeks we approached each other for our final embrace. What a mainstay the man had been to both Roberta and me and to all his contacts within the church and the community. Hardly a program in racial or social justice can be found in which he is not a driving force, yet he also remains thoughtful of the merest details. The day before, with the help of Julie, his wife, he had hauled away our waste paper to the community collection center, knowing that I would be too busy to do it myself.

I was physically and emotionally depleted after the reception that lasted more than an hour, but not so much that I failed to thank

121

our friend Eleanor Lenz for the bouquet that she had prepared for the reception in honor of Roberta. It consisted of a bed of green foliage from which numerous flowers burst forth like fireworks. The soft green symbolized Roberta's healing powers and the burst of flowers represented her creativity, Eleanor told me as she handed me the bouquet.

That night I read with great interest the comments of our friends who had signed the guest book at the reception. Strangely, Roberta didn't want to hear any of them.

The following day, this e-mail from Sam was waiting for me on my computer. It had been written the day before.

O Love That Wilt Not Let Us Go

Dear Robert,

Your soul must be heaven-soaring, but your body must be completely drained of every emotion imaginable. An amazing flood of love engulfed you and Roberta today, a rare Sabbath-hours torrent of the deep affection and admiration in which the congregation holds you.

No one in this city will miss you more than I will. I can't even think about it without such a sense of loss. You and Roberta truly are brother and sister to me. How often have the fireside chats—with the round table behind us yielding oysters and Brie and champagne and fruit and love—been oases. Then there's our barely-off-the-ground tradition of lunch at Cuvee Notre Dame. And I know I'll not be able to sing unbroken notes again at the Gymanfa Ganu (the annual Welsh hymnsing), *especially "God Be With You 'Til We Meet Again" or "Lead, Kindly Light." Nor will it be easy to sing Roberta's favorite hymn, "There's A Wideness in God's Mercy." Thank God, though, that we can continue the e-mail.*

Surely there is a wideness in God's mercy, but it's somewhat blurred right now. I find myself getting angry about what has happened to Roberta. It's not anger against God because I know He doesn't cause these things to happen.

122

I know it's futile anger and will be displaced wherever I fling it. And I know that often the antistrophe to "WHY?" is often "WHY NOT?" Nor do I want to use the cliche "it's not fair" because I'm using only my perception of what's fair or unfair, extremely limited terrestrial parameters boxing in that perception. It's where faith is stretched, yet maybe that's the only way we grow. For a while, however, I think there's going to be some stunted growth.

Well, dear Bob and dear Roberta, too—there's no joy in Mudville tonight. There's dimmed joy, the dimming because you're moving away and because we're losing Roberta. The joy, though, is knowing you and loving you and remembering all that you have been to me and, of course, to the church. Words simply fail me now, so let me just say that you go to Grand Rapids on the wings of the prayers and love of all at our church, none more abundant or all-encompassing than my own for you. I won't even be derivative and quote one of the poets in my repertoire. You know how I feel. God speed, journeying mercies, and love, dear brother and sister.

Sam

I responded to Sam on Monday, January 8, 2001:

Sam,

You said it all in your note, Sam. It plucked at every fiber of my heart. As I read it the tears welled up from a reservoir that I thought had been drained completely dry by yesterday's events at church. It was a day that will stand out in my memory until all memories are gone, and your note etched it in all the more deeply.

Your serving the cup to Roberta and me was the union of our three souls for just a moment at the foot of the cross. The touch of your hand as you handed me the wine, and the same as you gave the chalice to Roberta, was a moment of grace that will bind us forever, and I am grateful.

123

As I said earlier, the people left behind do the deepest grieving. Know that I am praying for you as you are for us. May God bring peace through all the turmoil of emotions, both yours and ours.

Bob and Roberta

After departing Philadelphia, I wrote the following thank you note to our church family, which was printed later in *Tidings*, the church's fortnightly newsletter:

THANKS AND FAREWELL FROM THE DeHAANS

Dear Friends,

As most of you know, on January 9, 2001 Roberta and I departed for Grand Rapids, Michigan, birthplace for both of us and where many family members and friends still live.

I have often read notes in which people thanked others for their prayers during times of illness or stress. Now it is my turn. Only when I was in a position of needing such prayers did I come to realize how wonderful it is to have God's people praying for us and supporting us. Not only does it strengthen me psychologically that you were and still are all supporting me and Roberta in her illness and our move, but things happened that really can only be called answers to our prayers. I am deeply grateful, even awestruck, with the faithful prayers of you, our church family.

Specifically, I am enormously grateful to those who helped me organize and pack my household goods for our move to Grand Rapids, to those who made a project of sending out change-of-address cards for me; and to those who will monitor the loading of the moving van. I thank those who sat for Roberta when I was at my wit's end early on, and others who sat with her later. I am grateful to those who provided very welcomed soup dishes and other food, and to the Women's Group for the bounteous fruit basket.

I appreciate the advice from nurses on how to see Roberta through various medical procedures and how to care for her while traveling. To others who shopped for us, sent cards of encouragement, visited us, and did other helpful things in these past few weeks, I am grateful. Many thanks go to the pastoral staff for the consulting and consoling conversations and for the significant pastoral visits and the Communion services they provided us.

I speak for both Roberta and myself when I say thanks for the numerous warm hugs, the murmured words of encouragement, the squeeze of the hand, the pat on the back, the countless messages of good cheer on the Internet. I have received more offers for help than I could possibly use, and I thank all of you for them.

So now it's time to say good-bye again, or better yet, God be with you and us. You all will never know how much you have meant to us and how deeply you have supported and shaped our lives. Your legacy will live on with us as we take this important step in our lives.

On behalf of Roberta and myself,

Bob DeHaan

XII

The Transition

I remember the story of the building of the bridge over the River Kwai in Indochina during World War II. Hundreds of Allied prisoners-of-war were forced to construct the bridge under appalling conditions. Survivors of that prolonged atrocity reported that the only men who lived to tell about it were those who had paired up with a friend for mutual support. Having another faithful human being to stand by them was absolutely essential to their continued existence. Having a partner was necessary but, of course, not always sufficient. Many died notwithstanding the blessing of a supportive friend.

The truth that two persons standing together can endure immeasurably more adversity than one standing alone was constantly brought home to me in the fall of that final year in Philadelphia. How fortunate I was to have not just one ally, but many. There was no more direct and powerful manifestation of the grace of God in our lives than the encouragement and direct help given by members of our church family, our close neighbors, and our relatives.

Allies in the Battle

Two of the most dedicated were on hand on the last day of our life in Philadelphia. Sue Rardin came early to help with the final big packing push. She began by organizing boxes into three piles labeled "apartment," "storage," and "research."

Susan Jensen soon arrived on the scene and plunged with me into the effort, filling boxes with things that were still lying around. Later she joined Sue in packing pictures.

While all this hubbub was going on around her, Roberta was seated in her easy chair, silent and dozing part of the time. I sat down by her between chores and talked to her about what was going on. She nodded and quietly accepted what I had to say. Fortunately, she did not seem agitated by the activity swirling around her. Her medications were working well, and my attention to her also kept her in touch with our doings, although I am not sure how much she understood what was happening.

Early in the afternoon our nephew Ray and niece Linda arrived. The sight of them driving up to the house after their long trip from Michigan added another layer of reality to our move. It was now actually happening as we had planned. We were returning to Michigan! After embracing me and giving an especially warm hug to Roberta, they dove into the packing game. Their obvious goal was to get her and me organized for the trip, a goal which seemed to have escaped me. I had not been making sufficient progress toward leaving the next day, which probably hinted at my lingering ambivalence and anxiety about our departure. Taking one look at the cartons of odds and ends in my bedroom, Ray rearranged their contents and reduced three big boxes to two. He then proceeded to organize the clothes I would need. Linda and the two Sues took over the task of selecting, organizing, and packing Roberta's clothes, another necessary task that I had not accomplished.

By the end of the afternoon, Sue left, but not before giving both Roberta and me lingering farewell hugs. Her cheerful assistance during the entire fall, especially in sending out countless change-of-address cards, had lifted a heavy load off my back. Her New Year's Day serenade still brings smiles to my face.

128

After so many hours of stressful toil together, Susan and I later gave vent to our emotions in a long farewell embrace. We had filled a reservoir of emotions during our hours of hard work together, and when we came to the end of the day, the dam broke and the feelings poured out. How does the heart repay such devotion? Our embrace said without words:

"How can I thank you for helping me?"

"I knew you couldn't do it alone."

"You are a true friend."

"That's what friends are for."

"We're going to miss you and Carl."

"This place won't be the same without you two."

"God bless you."

"God be with you and Roberta."

After this last farewell ended, Ray and Linda left for their motel, leaving behind a stack of boxes and suitcases ready to be loaded into their SUV and my car when they returned in the morning.

These four people stood by us and provided the brains, muscle, and resources that made it possible for us to relocate. When I first thought seriously about moving back to Grand Rapids after Dark Thursday, I had no idea how to go about it and no notion there was anyone who would or could help us. These four came unbidden into our lives on wings of God's grace and ran what amounted to a rescue operation. Picking up two wayfarers, stranded where they could no longer continue to live, the rescue team provided the moving force for our transition to a new place, a new home.

Our return to our land of origin had become more of an Odyssey than an Exodus. We were not leaving the flesh-pots of Egypt and heading out to the promised land as Moses and the Israelites had done. More like Odysseus, we were returning to our close family, our lifelong friends, our religious heritage, and our cultural roots after a long adventure in a distant city.

A Last Supper

Starting shortly after Thanksgiving and through that Monday in January, we had packed up and disposed of a significant portion of our household goods. Much remained, however, for Susan to do before the movers would come to load the van later in January. She would continue to do most of the organizing, packing, and throwing out, helped by her husband Carl McHenry and a team of friends from church. This team had offered to pack all of our dishes, giving as their credentials that they had done this before for many other people on the move and had never broken a dish. I had accepted their offer with thanks and could report later that their record of unbroken dishes remained intact.

Left to ourselves late in the day before the move, I was already beginning to feel like a stranger in the stillness of our apartment. Piles of boxes cast unfamiliar shadows. In silence Roberta and I ate our final supper in the rooms that would no longer be ours.

This time, the shepherd's pie was baked to perfection. Often a good meal will perk up my spirits. The rapidly moving events of the day, however, left me in an emotional vacuum. I had no feelings left. I missed the consolation of being able to relive the day's activities with Roberta. How often in the past we had talked over events that had occurred, and in doing so enjoyed them anew and appreciated more fully God's presence in our lives. Roberta was undoubtedly bewildered by the events of the day, but she made no comment nor showed any signs of agitation. She was still a companion and a presence in my life, but a diminished one, leaving me rather lonely.

I pondered again, however, that only through the help of others had we come to this point in our journey. A line from "Amazing Grace" came to my mind, and I sang, "'Tis grace that brought us safe thus far, and grace will lead us home." Buoyed by my own singing, I tucked Roberta into bed and afterward dropped off to sleep.

On the Move

The big day arrived, Tuesday, January 9, the date that our life in the city and church that had been our home for more than thirty-two years would come to an end and a new one would begin. Rising early, I observed from the kitchen window that the roads were ice-covered, and I worried about Ray and Linda driving from their motel. Yet, I need not have been concerned. As veteran Michigan drivers, they knew how to handle icy roads.

As I mounted the stairs to waken Roberta for the trip I sang loudly, "There's a Long, Long Trail," to ward off the profound misgivings that swept over me just then. On the way I also had my last tussle with God. I actually shouted, "Why? Why do we have to do this?" I paused at the landing, white knuckles on the railing, angry and fearful. Then with the clarity of a hologram, the image of Dick standing in the pulpit rose before me, buoying me up: "Do not be afraid." Kicking myself into gear with his encouragement, I continued on my way to rouse Roberta and make ready for breakfast and the trip. She was docile and easy to dress and feed, as she often is after a good night of sleep.

Ray and Linda were twin dynamos as they loaded cartons and suitcases into their SUV and my Volvo, leaving me with little to do but put jackets and caps on Roberta and me. When we drove out of *La Grand Allée* for the last time, I was so busy settling Roberta that I forgot to check whether neighbors Grace and Ronnie were awake and waving goodbye.

The following is the "On the-Move" e-mail I sent early that morning to my network of friends and relatives:

Dear relatives and friends,

My nephew and niece, Ray and Linda Mulder, arrived yesterday in their SUV that will carry Roberta and me to their home in Grand Rapids, Michigan. Linda will drive the SUV, and I will take care of Roberta in the back seat, while Ray drives my car. We expect to make the trip in two days, and will stay at our nephew's apartment when we arrive.

We have said goodbye to our friends at church, and to our immediate neighbors, as well as various friends who dropped by to bid us adieu. These partings were painful for us and for them, but we were warmed and strengthened by the love and support they gave us in our new step forward.

I have been absorbed in the process of packing household goods over the past several weeks. I left much to friends who will come in to finish the job after we have left. They will also oversee the loading of the moving van toward the end of the month. Roberta and I owe a debt of gratitude to all of them.

Roberta has been very cooperative through all the hustle and bustle that has been going on around her. She seems to understand that we are going to move, and is willing to sit by and let the rest of us do our thing. She has had her good days and not-so-good ones. Her health is good. She is still losing weight, however, even though she has a pretty good appetite and eats almost as much as I do. Her medications are working very well.

I'll keep in touch with you either in transit, or soon after we arrive in Grand Rapids. We need your thoughts and prayers in the next couple of days.

Love to you all,

Bob (and for Roberta)

Although our trip as a whole was successful it was not an altogether easy one. The difficulties started with my seeing that the SUV did not have a bench seat in the back as I had expected, but rather had two captain's seats, separated by armrests and a space between. Thus my plan to hold Roberta close to me when she became agitated or needed comfort would not work.

Moreover, in the late afternoon on each day, the setting sun shone squarely into her eyes and into mine. Because of her seatbelt she could not get in position to escape it. I tried to shield her face with my hands and partly succeeded. But she was wholly miserable at that time.

Yet she bore up under the difficult circumstances with remarkable grace. I admired her, and gave her what comfort I could by word, occasional song, and long distance touching and caressing.

Carrying our suitcases into an Ohio motel on the evening of the first day, we felt colder wind than we had experienced since leaving Michigan thirty-three years earlier. It penetrated our jackets like ice picks. The howler reminded me that one reason Roberta had resisted moving back to our home state was her extreme dislike of the cold weather for which Michigan is notorious. The motel beds, however, were warm, and Roberta and I had a night of refreshing sleep.

After a second long day of travel, we arrived at the home of Ray and Linda. Unloading the cars went rapidly, thanks to Ray's can-do approach to things. With the large amount of closet and drawer space in our new bedroom in the lower level of his home, I had no problem finding places for our clothes. Roberta's precious medications went into our bathroom. There were plenty of phone jacks and electrical outlets throughout the lower level, so I knew I would have no trouble plugging in my laptop computer and accessing the Internet. The place looked fully as good as the description that Linda had sent me in November. I felt greatly relieved as I settled into this generous environment with so caring a nephew and niece.

Soon others in my family gathered. My sister Marguerite arrived, and the moment both of us had long been waiting for was on hand. We gave each other two big hugs and could not stop smiling at one another. How could I thank her for the support and encouragement she had given me in the past months? She then embraced Roberta, two wonderful women who have always loved each other. Roberta smiled at the meeting. Dinner was served from the pot of corn chowder that Marguerite had brought. Ann, daughter of Ray and Linda, joined us for the meal. Roberta ate heartily, the first of many wonderful meals she would devour at that kitchen table. With the comfort of being settled among such generous family members, Roberta and I later enjoyed a night of sound sleep.

Before going to bed, however, I sent off the following e-mail to my network.

Dear relatives and friends,

We arrived! We made it! We pulled into my nephew's driveway at about five o'clock this afternoon (Wednesday) after a hard but uneventful trip. Although Roberta

133

was uncomfortable most of the way, she did not complain. Once we arrived she settled in with no word about leaving or going "home." I am proud of the way she handled herself and how well she is taking to her new residence.

Ray and Linda were wonderful with Roberta on the trip. Their love for her showed in every action and word. I was impressed with their competence in managing this entire transition, and with their skill in driving.

Thank you all for your prayers and loving support. Your prayers and ours have been answered. Without them we would not have made it.

With love to you all, from Roberta and me.

Bob

XIII

The First Ten Days

On the day after we arrived, I was delighted with a visit from my sister Dorothy and her husband Nelson Vanderzee, who was also afflicted with Alzheimer's disease. The happiness of our greeting was tempered by sadness because our spouses were largely lost to this cheerful reunion. We four had often double-dated during our college days, and on many previous visits Roberta and I had stayed as guests in their home. Now Dorothy and I were looking at a dreary ending to what had started years ago so joyfully. It was four months since we had seen Nels, and he looked good compared to Roberta. It occurred to me that Roberta had already passed Nels in the descent into the valley of the shadows. He was still able to communicate reasonably well with us and seemed aware of what was going on. Roberta spent the visit in her withdrawn mode, which signaled to me that she was probably confused and upset by this encounter, and perhaps by seeing Nels, but she did not want to betray her condition by interacting with any of us.

It is sometimes said that Alzheimer's patients enjoy looking at old photos taken in their past. It presumably makes them feel good to be able to see pictures of things and people they had forgotten. I did not find that to be the case with Roberta. At one time early in the fall I had gone through a couple albums of photographs of her early family life and of her many aunts and uncles and of pictures taken even earlier. She would not pay attention to the photos and would only answer questions about them when I pressed her.

Her discomfort in the presence of old mementos was displayed once again when two friends from former days, Phil and Carolyn Lucasse, stopped by a few days later. Phil and I had been colleagues one summer long before in running a camp; Phil as waterfront director and I as program director. We had kept in touch with them since. They brought with them an album of photos from those days. The pictures fascinated me, especially the ones of our oldest daughter who was then about two-and-a-half years old. We all looked extremely young and innocent. I could not restrain my delight at seeing these pictures.

Roberta, however, was upset by the visit, probably because we three knew what was going on and what the pictures were all about. Roberta could not remember any of the pictures or follow our talk, nor was she aware who Phil and Carolyn were. It probably made her feel stupid and left out. While our two visitors were sensitive to Roberta's condition, it was hard, if not impossible, for us to include her in our reminiscing.

Afterward, Roberta mentioned to Ray and Linda, "They're nice, but they aren't my favorite people." There had been a time, however, when these two certainly were among her most favorite people.

A short time later Roberta's brother Jack Timmer and his wife Faye paid us a welcoming visit. Roberta recognized and conversed with them. My wife also recognized one of her dearest childhood friends, Jessie Gritter. Nevertheless, our conversations with our visitors invariably left Roberta in the dark; and after they left it took an hour or so to settle her down.

Sufficient sound sleep was an indispensable requirement for me. Since my top priority was avoiding an agitated, sleepless night, I looked for ways to have a quiet afternoon and evening. Because these visits left my wife agitated, I began to discourage people from dropping by late in the day even though I would have enjoyed visiting with them myself. On the other hand, it may not have been fair not to allow them to visit Roberta while she was still relatively intact. Still, I decided in favor of Roberta's peace of mind and the resulting restful night for both of us.

On January 20, I wrote an e-mail to my network about our first ten days in Michigan.

Our landing in Michigan has been a soft one, to borrow a current metaphor. Ray and Linda, my nephew and niece, have surrounded us with all the love and attention we needed to help us ease into our new surroundings.

The apartment in the lower level of their house is not a low-ceilinged basement room where you must duck your head to keep from bumping into hot-air ducts. It is rather an elegant living space, with eight-foot ceilings, crown moldings, recessed lights on a rheostat that allows for romantic dimming, thickly carpeted floors, a walkout door to a wooded area. The bedroom has a queen-size bed, ample closet and drawer space. Comfortable lounge chairs, a TV and a high-tech stereo are set up in the living area. The kitchenette, in which I brew my morning coffee, also includes a refrigerator, cupboards filled with kitchenware and food staples, and a telephone station, but no stove. Linda has offered to install a microwave oven, but I don't want to cook in the apartment. A bathroom with tub and shower round out the space. At the moment I am ensconced in a large leather wingback chair, my work station, as I peck out this e-mail to you.

We are welcome to enjoy the large upstairs kitchen and dining area, where we gather with the family for meals, and the family room with a huge sofa, gas-fired ceramic log in the fireplace, and a TV set.

This listing hardly conveys the extent of the resources at our disposal. More amenities than we can use are available to us, ranging from two warm futons, to a fax machine and copier, to a NordicTrack. I have not prepared a meal since we arrived, other than pouring out cereal for breakfast once or twice. Roberta has eaten more and better than she has in a long time, and is enjoying it.

137

Neither do these physical resources convey the affection that upholds and surrounds us here. Linda loves Roberta and attends to her every need when we are upstairs. Ray also takes wonderful care of her; just to hear him call her "Aunt Roberta" and talk to her like she was the only one that mattered puts a smile on my face. Both of them have hearts of gold.

We eat well in this place, and both Ray and Linda have made a project of bringing Roberta's weight back up to normal. They enjoy watching her stow away a big meal, and compliment her heartily as she does so. Ray is her one-man cheering section, saying to her with a smile, "Aunt Roberta, that was a great meal you just ate." She smiles back, pleased. They get so much pleasure from eating that Roberta is starting to do the same, and accepts bigger helpings on her plate from Ray than she would from me. Sitting at the head of the table, with her at his right hand, he holds up a serving spoon full of mashed potatoes, looks at her with a smile, and asks, "Do you want some more?" She can't resist. She responds by loving them in turn, and by consuming more food than I have seen her put away in a long time. Still, she continues to look small and frail.

I have learned from Ray and Linda that Roberta can do more than I gave her credit for. I have not been expecting enough from her, usually carrying out too many tasks for her. She has reciprocated by expecting too much from me. So I am beginning to give her more responsibility at all points, such as dressing and undressing, and eating. It is working better than I thought possible. She responds positively.

Bob

Roberta's bouts with restless leg syndrome continued to present a problem. I was in constant consultation with Ray and Linda regarding how to deal with RLS. It was controlled best when Roberta had an adequate walk. Our daily shopping trip in the giant all-purpose store and walks around the neighborhood provided the exercise we needed. These workouts, followed by a substantial evening meal, and still later by quiet togetherness in our apartment and a warm bath, were the essential steps to a good night of sleep.

Some old fashioned "necking" on the davenport in the family room when Ray and Linda were not home also relaxed Roberta. Such close physical warmth seemed to console her. It was also important for me to talk with her about anything on her mind that might be bothering her. Any perceived problem, if I failed to let her talk it out, might stay lodged in her mind all night and generate anxiety that would rob her of sleep. After concluding this routine with a bath, a sleeping pill, and other medications, we were off to bed.

Most of the time the above regimen worked. If any part of it was omitted however, especially the afternoon walk, we would pay for it with several hours of Roberta's tossing and twitching before sleep would finally take over.

During this transition I was getting on quite well. My appetite was good; I got sufficient sleep most nights; I was beginning to master the NordicTrack. My Internet correspondence kept me in touch with the outside world. We had not seen the sun since we arrived in Michigan, and it rained and snowed intermittently, so I needed the exercise machine. How I longed for the walking trails around the Wissahickon Valley.

Finding a Faith Community

Whenever we moved to a new city, it was as automatic for Roberta and me to seek out a faith community as it was to find the best supermarket. Our main criterion in selecting a church was whether we saw a working of the Spirit among the members of the congregation. Did they reach out to us? Were they active in matters of social and racial justice? Was the worship service spirited, the singing robust, the sermon spiritually and intellectually satisfying?

However, a new criterion now became paramount: whether Roberta would be able to relate to the worship service, to members of the congregation, and to the ambiance of the church.

On our first Sunday, we joined Ray, Linda, and Marguerite for worship in their church. Because it was a faith community that we might wish to join, I was eager to watch Roberta's reaction to it. When we arrived, worshippers were streaming into the large church, not by ones and twos, but by entire families. When the sanctuary was full, latecomers filled the choir loft. The crowd was impressive. Because a large physical renovation and expansion project was underway, the gathering of the congregation was probably less orderly than it normally would have been.

Organ, piano, and a quartet of trumpets provided the music. The congregational singing, as one can imagine, was magnificent. The Dutch are only half a step behind the Welsh in their hymn-singing prowess. The brass was somewhat overwhelming, but I was informed later that sometimes an entire brass ensemble was on hand, so I thought it best not to grumble.

Biblically oriented, spiritual and well crafted, the sermon was about our struggles with a host of forces in this world that seek to do us in but can be met with the force of God's faithfulness. I resonated to that.

Afterward I met a woman with whom I had taken a typing class in high school, a man who had my father as his high school math teacher, a retired faculty member of Calvin College with whom I had corresponded, and others. All were good people and friendly. Everything looked satisfactory from my standpoint.

Roberta's reaction, however, was predictable: "Don't take me there again." It was overwhelming for her. I could understand her bewilderment and could see she would not be able to handle this church. Since it would not meet her needs, it was not for me.

On the following Sunday, we attended the church a block away from where I had grown up, now an African-American neighborhood. In my youthful days the church had been the one of the spiritual hubs of the Dutch-American neighborhood. Quieter and more composed than the one we had first attended, the church looked like a better fit for us. Roberta was comfortable there. My sister, Dorothy and her husband were also members there, forming another tie.

140

Like our church in Philadelphia, many Christian Reformed churches in Grand Rapids have made a conscious commitment to remain in the city rather than to close their doors and move to the suburbs. I was pleased that many of them were concerned for social issues in the city and with environmental matters, as well as with their historic Christian faith and worship. People from these churches were thoughtful, concerned, committed Christians of the Reformed persuasion. I felt at one with them. They made me realize that I have two favorite institutions: the *church* and the *city*, and especially the *church in the city*. Finding so many faith communities with which I could affiliate added to my feeling of being in the right place.

Return of the Ring

Later my delight abounded when I received a call from Susan informing me that she had found Roberta's wedding ring while cleaning behind the toilet bowl in the powder room of our apartment in Philadelphia. Roberta had lost the ring the previous fall. When I asked her about it, she had looked at her left hand, seemingly noticing for the first time that it was gone. Showing no concern about it, she passed it off without comment, offering me no clue, of course, to where it might have fallen.

The ring was a beauty. In 1992, we had reset the diamond I had given her in her uncle's apple orchard a half-century before in a broad, plain gold band. It replaced her original wedding band that had worn so thin it had been about to break. Roberta had loved the new ring, and I had taken pleasure in seeing it on her hand.

Between Alzheimer's disease and arthritis, her fingers had become so emaciated and her knuckles so bent that the ring seemed to dangle from her finger. I berated myself for not having rescued it before it fell off. After conducting a cursory search in and around her bed and the drains of washbowls to no avail, I had decided that further search was hopeless.

I mourned its loss. Wasn't Roberta losing enough already? It was one more reminder of how rapidly she had been losing her personhood.

Before leaving Philadelphia I had alerted Susan to what had happened and asked her to be on the lookout for the ring as she was packing up our goods. My thanks to Susan could not be deep enough to express the joy I felt on receiving her good news. She returned the ring to me, heavily insured, by registered mail.

Deciding the ring was safer on my person, I slipped it on the little finger of my right hand where it was a companion to the silver moon-face ring I was already wearing. Even when I showed it to Roberta on my finger she evidenced no interest in it. Wearing it gave me the feeling that I had regained an ephemeral but vital connection with her.

Our situation changed radically ten days after we arrived. Ray and Linda left for a six-week vacation in Florida. Now we were on our own, beginning a new segment of our life together, in an unfamiliar environment, with an uncertain future, but supported by strong sisters and a host of relatives and friends available for help when needed. Over all was the umbrella of God's faithfulness working through all these people.

XIV

Settling In

Until we relocated I had never given much thought to how many services and amenities had been available to us in Philadelphia. By merely touching a few buttons on our phone, or by driving a short distance, we could reach an extensive network of personal and family services. As the people associated with them served our needs, we developed longstanding, warm relationships with many of them—store clerks, doctors, a dentist, insurance agents, church members, attorney, and with such institutions as the bank, favorite supermarket, dry cleaners, and library.

Having arrived in Grand Rapids and not having even one of these services located anywhere near us left me feeling out of touch and anxious. Roberta and I were living in an expanse of suburban houses, with commercial centers reachable only through a labyrinth of highways. What we had found and utilized during thirty-three years of living in Philadelphia I now had to reestablish, starting from scratch—and quickly.

Even before Ray and Linda left on their vacation, I plunged into the process of reestablishing the services I would need, including:

- Replacing our Philadelphia-based HMO with Medicare-plus insurance for both of us. This was a high-priority requirement, and I felt we were quite vulnerable without it.

- Replacing Roberta's Medicare card which I had lost in our move. I later discovered I had also lost her Social Security card.

- Finding a primary care physician for Roberta through the Holland Home system and setting up her first appointment.

- Locating a pharmacy and transferring Roberta's prescriptions from our Philadelphia pharmacy to a new local one.

- Making application and a down payment on a two-bedroom apartment in Breton Woods Terrace (a continuing care retirement community that is part of the Holland Home system), then under construction.

Even with Ray's help in finding what I needed, it took all of the organizational experience I could muster, and countless phone calls and automobile excursions around the city, to reestablish these services, while taking care of my wife and managing the household after my nephew and niece left. I brought Roberta along on all my excursions. Rebuilding our basic set of services took almost the entire time that Ray and Linda were gone. Finishing it went a long way toward settling us into our new environment.

Problems also arose in the immediate care of my wife. Before Ray and Linda went south, I e-mailed the following update to my network of friends and relatives:

Dear Ones,

A big problem, which we are now facing, is that Roberta simply cannot get warm in the lower level. I try to find the proper combination of layered clothes to keep her comfortable. I succeed to some extent. Part of the problem is that her circulation is not good, so that no matter what we do, she doesn't seem to feel warm. In addition, she does not have warm slippers. Cold floors were never a problem in our former residences because we did not spend much time in our basement. But the floor on the lower level here tends to be cool enough to chill Roberta's feet despite the thick carpet.

But aside from the problem of making Roberta physically comfortable we are doing very well. The best thing that has happened to us is my niece, Linda. She is a born comforter. She speaks kindly and respectfully to Roberta, and Roberta responds by wanting to be near her. I know no woman who has so opened her heart to Roberta as Linda has, and into whose heart Roberta has so willingly entered.

More than a nephew, Ray is a big Dutch uncle to her, the kind she loved as a child. At the dinner table he loads her plate with food and then applauds her for consuming all of it. He is a role model, enthusiastically finishing off his own generously ladened plate. Roberta has been eating as she did when she was well.

As you know, Sue Rardin had sent out change-of-address cards for me before we left. These are paying off with the many phone calls I am receiving from old-time friends in the West Michigan area. My sisters are rallying to our aid. Ray and Linda are magnificent. While the transition has only begun, the beginning has been propitious, but still far from easy for Roberta.

Love,

Bob

I was awakened from sleep one evening to find Roberta climbing into my side of the bed. Slipping over to make room for her, I felt her body trembling slightly. She didn't snuggle up to me as I expected her to do.

"I can't undo it," she said in her raspy, breathy voice, which I have learned to interpret as a sign of anxiety.

"Oh?" I said noncommittally.

A long pause followed with more fidgeting.

"I can't undo this whole mess."

Another long pause.

"I have tried sixty different ways and I can't undo it."

Knowing that she would not be able to answer it, I asked the question anyway, "What can't you undo?"

"All these little things," and she made some small looping movements with her hands.

She cuddled up close to me for a few moments and then drew back again. Her agitation and trembling continued.

I tried to reach her, by holding her close to me since words didn't seem to help. I reminded her that I loved her, that God loved her, and that He held both of us in His arms like I was holding her.

"If He loves me so much, why doesn't He help me undo this?" she sobbed.

I could not answer that, and nothing I said or did consoled her. "I'm so dumb today. So stupid. I can't undo it."

At last I began to get an inkling of what she was talking about— something in today's experience.

"Does it have to do with Marguerite?" I asked.

"Yes."

"And me?"

"Yes."

At last I divined what was nagging at her. My sister had come over late in the afternoon to help make dinner and to join us for the meal. She and I had spent an hour or so, peeling potatoes, snipping up broccoli, making gravy, dodging each other between refrigerator and stove as we made dinner. Roberta had stood by looking on, in turn disconsolate, bored, interested. We had given her little tasks to perform, such as putting the flatware on the table, throwing this or that into the garbage. Even these simple tasks required our cueing her, such as showing her where the garbage bag was. The conversation was mainly between Marguerite and me, with an occasional question or comment for Roberta.

Unable to keep up with us or break through the cloud of confusion that engulfed her had no doubt left Roberta feeling stupid. It was clear to her that she was not needed. Was it surprising that she felt dumb and left behind? While it was a great meal for my sister and me, my wife did not eat much. What happened before the meal probably reminded her of how inadequate she had become, particularly because we were doing things that she knew she had been able to do herself at one time. Because she was unable to participate in once familiar activities, she couldn't "undo" whatever it was that was engulfing her.

Sensing that she was telling me she felt left out and perhaps even unwanted, I changed my approach. Holding her close to me I said, "Do you know how much I love you and need you?" I continued, "I have loved you all my life. I need you to love me now. You may not think so, but I want you to stay by my side. Don't leave me. Just seeing you sitting in your chair makes me feel good. I really appreciate you." Surprised and even a little embarrassed at how dramatic I had become, I was driven by my need to assure Roberta as strongly as I could that I loved and needed her.

Gradually Roberta stopped trembling. I drew her relaxed body closer to me, and held her firmly. I knew that I had at last gotten through to her.

But the evening was not over. I felt that Roberta would need some medication to check her agitation and induce sleepiness. I went ahead of Roberta to the bathroom where we keep her medications. Benadryl and Diazepam were available. The first, an over-the counter antihistamine that also induces drowsiness, had been recommended to me by a pharmacist. The second medication was prescription Diazepam, a generic form of Valium. I had reservations about Benadryl because of the warning on the box against its use when psychiatric medications were being given. But I wondered whether Diazepam was potent enough. I requested a little guidance from above at this point.

A nudge in the right direction was provided in a remarkable way. When Roberta arrived moments behind me, she went straight to the counter where the plastic card of Benadryl pills was lying on top of its box. Without a moment's hesitation, she picked up the card and placed it inside its box, then laid the box back down on the counter. I had no doubt about what medication I should use.

I stared at her in wonder. What was going on here? Was she once again a conduit of the divine guidance I had requested even in this small decision? "Make of that what you will," as Leif Enger's character Reuben said after witnessing a miracle performed by his father.[1] I gave her a Diazepam pill.

Feeling like things were now on track, I suggested that we go upstairs and have a glass of warm milk and a snack. She loved the idea. After she put away a mug of milk, we returned to bed where she soon slipped into deep sleep.

As I lay next to her, listening to the burble of her snoring, I replayed the scene in the bathroom. Could it have been what I firmly believed it was—eternity dipping into time? I discerned in this evening's events an act of kindness of the Creator, who, billions of years after giving birth to this amazing universe, continued being concerned to make life a little easier for a couple of stressed-out but trusting ones. I accepted as a fact that God "spoke" with Roberta this evening in a scientifically inexplicable way and that she unknowingly responded to the still, small voice with her decisive action. I took this event to confirm the promise that, since not even a sparrow is forgotten by God, neither were Roberta and I in this small incident. The experience was faith strengthening.[2]

The verse of a hymn came to mind:

Lord of all gentleness, Lord of all calm,
Whose voice is contentment, whose presence is balm:
Be there at our sleeping and give us we pray,
Your peace in our hearts, Lord, at the end of the day.[3]

With that I, too, settled into a deep sleep.

I sent an e-mail to Marguerite the next morning, ending it as follows:

This morning Roberta told me, "I dreamed about Marguerite last night. Isn't she a beautiful woman. I don't know how she does everything she does."

I thought you might like to read that. Life with Roberta is always interesting.

It was wonderful having you around last night.

Love,

Bob

I began to see Alzheimer's disease not just as taking away memory, but as adding a very palpable mindlessness. The memory board was being wiped clean, but the board itself remained to remind Roberta that she was once full of interesting ideas, skills, and opinions. Like a feebly struggling moth caught in a spider's web, she was being imprisoned in filaments of futility. No matter how hard she tried, she couldn't undo this web that was enfolding her.

Roberta's behavior began to reveal to me another effect of Alzheimer's disease. It does not completely destroy all memories at first. Rather it seems to break them into fragments and scatter them through each other. I had imagined healthy, intact memories as consisting of numerous completed jigsaw puzzles in one's mind. Alzheimer's breaks up the memories, destroys some of the pieces, and intermingles them so that they no longer form coherent pictures. Confusion results.

The events of that evening later gave me occasion to reflect on what one of my doctors told me after I had informed him that Roberta had Alzheimer's disease. He said that at least one good thing about the disease was that the person was not aware of what was happening and felt no pain from it. That was not true of Roberta. She felt enormous pain and loss, judging from her frequent complaints about not being able to do things she formerly did, and her anxiety about being dumb. In the second stage of her disease, at least, her pain was palpable.

Finding a New Physician

Finding a primary care physician for Roberta was a critical challenge toward the end of January. However, this problem was trumped by a still more basic one—locating her Medicare card, which I had lost. Searching for it among the documents I had brought with us produced no results. Consternation hit me when I realized

149

that her Social Security card and driver's license had also disappeared. Before she had become ill, she had kept all of these in the little card-wallet tucked into her all-purpose purse. After her purse-emptying evening in our apartment the previous fall, I had lost track of the wallet. There was no use taking her to a doctor or getting medical help without her Medicare card since I was not in position to pay directly for such service.

Thinking that a trip to the local Social Security office would immediately produce a new card, I found myself sitting there with Roberta among forty or so other people, my "Take-a-number" slip in hand. I was soon brought up short by what I read in a brochure that I had picked out of a rack: I would need proof of Roberta's age in order to replace her Medicare card. Preferably a birth certificate, the brochure advised.

Muttering imprecations on all government bureaucracies I returned home with Roberta to search for her birth certificate. I had no more success in finding it, however, than I had in finding her Medicare and Social Security cards. Instead I made another discovery that delighted me: Mother Timmer's birth certificate. What a treasure!

I was delighted and called out, "Come see this, Roberta. I found your mother's birth certificate. Wow! Look at her name, *Egberdina*. Now that's a name for you!"

Underneath it, penned in blue ink was the name *Bertha*, which was the name she had gone by as long as I knew her. Who can blame her!

I read aloud further, with Roberta looking over my shoulder:

"Here it says your grandfather, *Father, Jerry Van Dellen.*

"Your grandmother's name was Egberdina, too. Look: *Mother, Egberdina Van Dellen.*

"And here's where they lived: *Residence: Plainfield Twp. Kent Co., Mich.*

"Your grandpa was born in Holland," I said, pointing to: *Birthplace of father, Holland.*

"And he was a farmer: *Occupation of father, Farmer."*

Roberta interrupted with a lightheartedness I had not heard since last summer: "*My* occupation is to eat whatever Bob DeHaan

150

cooks." Her smug smile told me she still had enough insight to know that she was buttering me up. Yet, what an accurate assessment of our current relationship—her growing dependence on me.

The next morning found us downtown in the office of the Kent County Register of Deeds requesting a copy of Roberta's birth certificate. The clerk returned from the files appearing concerned. "I don't have one for Roberta G. Timmer," she said. "This one is for *Alberta* G. Timmer." Finding everything else correct, however, I returned to the Social Security office, certificate in hand, hoping that a small mistake made by a clerk seventy-five years before would not jeopardize my mission. The young Social Security clerk behind the window smiled at my anxiety and assured me that all the information they needed to replace both Roberta's Medicare card and her Social Security card was stored on the computer.

Surprised, I asked, "You mean I don't have to show you her birth certificate?" She assured me that I didn't. "You will receive both cards in the mail in ten days," she said as she handed me letters certifying that I had made proper application for them. As a courtesy she even replaced my own frayed Social Security and Medicare cards with crisp new ones.

As I left, I made a 180-degree turn in my attitude toward Federal bureaucrats, simultaneously making an equal but opposite turn in my opinion of myself. Why had I failed to check on the supposed proof-of-age requirement before I had wheeled all the way downtown to obtain Roberta's birth certificate?

At any rate, we had now taken an important step forward in the "settling-in" process.

Toward the end of January, we solved one of Roberta's most persistent problems—keeping her feet warm. In our lower level quarters Roberta continually protested that her feet were cold. Her slippers that we had brought from Philadelphia were thin soled. Consequently, she had been obliged to wear her SAS shoes which, while being warm and good for outdoor walking, were rather clunky in the apartment, and could not be easily slipped on and off.

Fortunately, my sister, Dorothy, solved our problem by offering to loan Roberta a pair of oversized scuffs until we received new

151

slippers I had ordered from a catalogue. My wife tried them on and, despite initial skepticism, strolled around looking down with pleasure. "They feel fine," she commented, observing her feet as she scuffed along, and then added, "I hope nobody sees me in them."

These furry scuffs were the stuff of a clown's wardrobe. They looked much bigger than their designated size. Dark brown with black leopard spots, they made me think of the Abominable Snowman's feet. They appeared to be warm and comfortable, and evidently felt that way. For the first time Roberta did not complain of cold feet.

Early the next morning she stood in the bathroom in her nightgown and new slippers. I had offered her fresh underpants as her first step in dressing for the day. Leaning against the wall, she held the panties open by the waistband and tried pushing her right foot through, only to find that the oversized slippers would not easily slide through. After some stuffing, and restarting, she finally negotiated the opening and then encountered the more difficult challenge of getting her slipper through the smaller leg hole. After she almost fell over, I suggested that she sit on the edge of the bathtub. There she continued her efforts. Bending over to reach her foot required extra stretching and added to her difficulty. Then her nightgown slipped over her foot, making her task still more difficult. I never saw her labor at any task more diligently than she did at this one, and she had been a hard worker. Now this ordinary daily task was stretching her mental and physical abilities to the limit.

"Wouldn't it go better if you took off your slipper?" I asked. Either she did not hear me or did not understand; she continued trying to find the leg opening and cram her slipper through it. The panties seemed to conspire against her. Again I made my hint; again the same result. I should have known that the suggestion would not register with her, since Alzheimer's patients find it nearly impossible to follow even a simple two-step procedure.

The effort was comical (yet sad) because of her persistent effort, like a small child trying to pound a too-big peg into a small hole. Roberta did not appear to be frustrated or upset; she did not use bad language as I might have done. I could not help chuckling as she struggled, unwilling to give up the endeavor or ask for help, and yet unable to see a simpler way to do it. I had the feeling that she valued the slippers so highly that she wanted to show that she could handle them all by herself, lest they be taken away from her. "I can handle this job all by myself," was a line from a song she had occasionally sung at me in bygone years when I had mistakenly tried to show her how to do something that she felt capable of doing herself, if only I would get out of the way.

After much effort, she finally wiggled the slipper through the leg hole, and then went about just as intently pushing the other one through the waist opening and the second leg hole. Having finally succeeded in working the panties over the slippers, she stood up, hoisted them up to her waist, slipped her nightgown down over her legs, looked at her slippers and said in a firm voice, "There."

A little applause was in order, and I clapped my hands and gave her a high-five.

After this episode, I wondered whether Roberta was interesting and comical as a child. Doubtless she was. Her behavior now was so authentic that I am sure it arose out of some earlier established memory molecules and neuronal pathways that were still intact in her brain. What social and developmental forces caused her to abandon this naïve determination? Why was she not this innocently humorous as an adult? Perhaps she was, in the presence of others. Had I as her husband inhibited it in her? Did her earlier naïvete translate into her wonderful empathy for other people and their feelings? How little we understand about human development.

Glimpses of Humor

I wish I had had a tape recorder to catch the quality of Roberta's wry humor as it came out in ordinary situations. Early one morning I was, as usual, sitting in the corner of our living area, pecking away at my laptop. Looking forlorn and tiny, Roberta moseyed out of the bedroom holding her nightgown up around her thighs, in the manner of an eighteenth-century lady crossing a muddy street. Although I could not help smiling and wanting to hug her, I didn't dare because I knew the call of nature was urgent. Fearful of what she might do to the carpet, I hurried her as fast as I could toward the toilet, admonishing her along the way to hang on. Fortunately we made it. As she sat down, I skipped out to the kitchenette and picked up a Clementine orange, knowing she would enjoy eating a few sections of it. As I slipped one into her mouth, she didn't say "Thank you," or anything as conventional as that. Rather, she asked, "Do you carry those things around in your pocket all the time?"

At another time when Roberta was seated on the edge of bed, about to swing her feet under the covers she said: "Here goes me," with a smile in her voice, imitating the way our young children would say it when they were two or three years old.

Tucking her in and turning out the light on her bedside table, I asked her if she would like to have me keep the bedroom door opened a crack so that she could hear me working in the next room.

"Yes," she murmured sleepily. "So I can see where I'm sleeping." With that she yawned and settled down to her night's sleep.

As she dozed with the quilt tucked around her chin, she looked much like our youngsters had looked in their little beds. My heart went out to her as I kissed her cheek, whispering, "God be with you, Roberta." "And with you, Robert," she said softly.

Although Ray and Linda had stocked the pantry with large bags of broccoli and potatoes before they left, it was up to me to convert them into evening meals. I became the homemaker, a new and challenging role for me. Their son, Brian, was living at home, but we saw little of him. He was a vapor trail departing for work in the morning, and a congenial young boarder for dinner. His evenings were spent with friends. Although he was a good cook, I saw to most of that detail.

Partly because I was unfamiliar with and somewhat intimidated by Linda's large kitchen, with its microwave oven, beautiful push-button stove and high-tech dishwasher, I wasn't very good at the KP routine. Strange as it may seem, Roberta and I had never owned a microwave oven. She preferred our electric one. Now I was learning how to operate Linda's by a trial-and-error method, feeling well challenged.

I opened cans of soup, deciding not to make my favorite onion soup which requires scorching the onions while cooking them down.

Doing so in our ancient cast aluminum kettle was one thing; doing it in Linda's spotless teflon-coated cookware was quite another.

One of Brian's favorite dishes was steamed hot dogs with zucchini, which I prepared night after night. Both Brian and Roberta relished the mounds of boiled potatoes and brown gravy (from a package) that I set before them. Brian was always appreciative of my cooking.

Cooking took a lot of time and a great deal of planning. In my new homemaker role, I discovered how many management skills were involved in running a household. My admiration for my wife grew with each meal I prepared as I realized how many years she had spent cooking for our family. Roberta could give me little help. True to her acknowledged occupation, she ate, with fair appetite, whatever Bob cooked. Yet I could not generate the hearty appetite in her that Ray could.

Fortunately, a couple of cleaning ladies arrived every two weeks and gave the house the kind of cleaning that only Dutch women can give. Wasn't it Washington Irving who described how the Dutch housewives in old Knickerbocker New York rubbed the features completely off the brass door knockers with their furious polishing? The tradition is not dead.

Once when Roberta was getting ready for bed, I told her, "Brush your teeth now, okay?"

"Yes," she said, but did nothing.

"Brush your teeth now," I repeated.

"Now?" she asked.

"Yes. NOW," irritably.

"Yes," she said. Then after a moment's pause she asked, "What did I just say yes to?"

Shopping at a nearby supermarket was a form of recreation for me. I enjoyed this one-stop shopping in the store that advertised itself as "A million reasons, a single store." In addition to being a grocery "superstore," it also included a pharmacy, clothing store with women's, children's, and men's departments, an office supply, hardware, and sports section, a nursery, post office, several specialty shops, and other departments I had not yet discovered.

The store was so large that Roberta and I could get all of our daily walking exercise there while doing our shopping. She continued to sleep better at nap time and at night if she had a large daily dose of exercise. I overestimated, however, how much stimulation she could handle. Upset by the buzzing confusion of this thriving marketplace, she responded by complaining about her tired legs and constantly trying to find a place where she could sit down.

A new issue in my care of my wife was beginning to emerge—how to manage the amount of stimulation in her life. I was in a quandary. She needed exercise, I thought, in order to sleep well. Walking in this big store, however, seemed to agitate her because it took her out of the familiar surroundings of our apartment and the house. I now see that our shopping trips may have been counter-productive. Their value as exercise may have been negated by the agitation they engendered. Like doctors, tweaking her medications in order to find the right combination, I was experimenting with her daily exercise routines.

Slow Down, You Move Too Fast

It had been a long while since I had worked on my computer. Late one afternoon I was settled down in the wing-backed chair in the corner of our living area, computer on my lap, my feet on the hassock.

Opposite me, Roberta sat comfortably dozing in her lounge chair under several coverlets. At first she nodded off contentedly; later, she rose repeatedly to walk fitfully around the apartment. Thus, at times did the restless legs syndrome interfere with her relaxation, even during the day.

After one of her short walks, she stopped near me to complain of sore legs. I let this go without comment at first. After a couple more of the same woeful plaints, I suggested we take a short walk out of doors.

"Oh, no. Not that," she objected.

Overriding her objections, I said, "Let's go," and hustled her upstairs and into her jacket.

156

While doing so, I reminded her that as a massage therapist she had often advised her clients that they needed to exercise. Getting a massage for their aching backs, sore legs, and tennis elbows was not enough. By the scowl she gave me over her shoulder, I knew that she realized I had scored a point.

Later, while walking briskly down the Ashton Court roadway, she said pointedly, "You *said* it was going to be a short walk, didn't you?" The effect of this declaration was to forestall any tactic I might have contemplated to extend our walk beyond the next junction. She knew that I would sometimes coax her to take a short walk and then tack on additional segments as we went along. I dislike having people manipulate me that way, and I did not blame her for feeling the same way when I did it to her.

Yet I had to smile. I was delighted that her personhood still shone through. I gave her a poke on the arm, "O-*kaaay*! Just *to* Cascade Drive," I said trying to match her intonation.

When we arrived at the intersection, it became clear that we could not have crossed the drive even if I had contemplated doing so. As in Ben Hur's chariot race, a phalanx of cars was roaring by, whipped along by frustrated charioteers headed home after a hard day's work. In no place where I have traveled, with the possible exception of traffic circles in Rome, have I found drivers who streak down the highway at a more manic pace as they depart their workplaces than those in Michigan.

Roberta commented cheerily as we turned and retraced our steps up Ashton Court, "It feels good on the legs, if the legs can stand it." Later, however, as she watched me preparing the evening meal of "garden hot dogs" (a specialty of Brian's that consists of a bun with a wiener placed on a bed of lettuce, tomatoes, onions, with relish, catsup and mustard), she angrily accused me of tricking her into taking a walk. Although Roberta wolfed down two of these sandwiches she said she never wanted to eat another one. Never! A moment later, however, she added that she was sorry she had not said so while I was putting the ingredients together for supper. Still later in bed she surprised me by remarking how delicious the hot dogs had tasted.

The first lesson I drew from all this is that Roberta did not like to be manipulated. None of us does. Moreover, she still had plenty of selfhood left, at least at times. She was protective of her personal boundaries, and when they were transgressed, she became angry. Throughout her life she had been characteristically quick to respond whenever she felt stepped on. Some of that response still remained in her.

Having been manipulated, her anger carried over into our evening meal. Although her actions and her later admission showed that she enjoyed the hot dog, she was still angry about the walk and took it out on me by declaring war on my (and Brian's) special culinary creation. But what was equally remarkable was the self insight she showed when admitting that she should have spoken up when I was making the hot dogs rather than waiting until she had eaten them.

All of this posed a dilemma. If I were to go by her usual immediate objections to my suggestions to take a walk, go shopping, or whatever, we would do little more than sit around most of the day while she dozed. What to do? It seemed that the answer was that she still needed to be dealt with as any rational person wants to be treated—to be persuaded with reasoned words and at least have her objections heard. Using a tactic that hinted of manipulation or getting the better of her was wrong. I might rather have said, "I need to take a walk or I won't sleep well tonight," which was true. Or, "I'd like to have you join me so that you will sleep well, too." I think that would have worked better than throwing her own advice to her clients up at her.

Body language needed to be in line with the words. I would have done better speaking face to face, not over my shoulder while donning my jacket. In short, her personhood needed to be respected and enhanced as long as possible before the terrible disease wiped it out completely. Speaking slowly, facing her, giving sufficient time for a response would take time, but slowing down is essential in caring for any Alzheimer's patient.

I wrote occasionally to Roberta's friend and counselor in Philadelphia from whom she had sought advice on various personal problems. She knew about Roberta's RLS. The e-mail I sent her contained a summary of our life during our first month in Grand Rapids.

Lately Roberta rarely has RLS except in bed. But I might try the leg presses you suggested when night comes. It seems to me that RLS also occurs more often when her legs or whole body are cold. Do you have any thoughts about that?

I find that I need to be very careful about our regimen in the late afternoon, and at the close of the day. It is imperative that we take a vigorous walk before dinner. I do this by going shopping with Roberta in a monster store around four o'clock. While I walk around the shelves with her, looking for this item and that, she tags along with me, objecting mildly. Sometimes she looks around for a place to sit, and will even lower herself to an empty shelf if one is available. Getting her tired, however, induces sleep later.

Then I try to prepare as large a dinner as I can get her to eat. In doing so I am also trying to stop her from losing weight.

She is often cold, and I hold her hands and try to warm her up. As we engage in old fashioned necking on the davenport, cuddled under a warm coverlet of some kind, I sometimes sing the lullabies to her that we used to sing to our kids. Watching TV is a no-no. Talking heads and flashing ads agitate her. I have heard, however, that some Alzheimer's patients enjoy watching the tube.

I also need to find out what she is mulling over. I find that she just does not become sleepy if she goes to bed with unanswered questions, such as, "Where are my SAS shoes?" So I walk her over to where her shoes are, point them out to her, and explain why they are there. Seeing them and hearing about them usually resolves the problem, and she relaxes.

It is also necessary to find out if her whole body is uncomfortable. Roberta frequently complains about feeling "just awful." I do believe that her entire body is afflicted by restlessness, not just the legs although I have read no research to confirm this. In fact, I can tell at night that just before her legs get restless her body is also trembling ever so slightly. It seems that total bodily discomfort is a precursor to a night of RLS. When I have asked her about where she felt bad, she was unable to be specific. It seemed to be an overall, intense, hopeless discomfort. While these may be the psychological origins of her distress, I do not doubt that the disease itself is a major source.

Often, just my close bodily contact eases her discomfort and warms her.

I have found a warm bath before going to bed to be essential for keeping her RLS at bay. It does more than anything else to calm her legs. Stirring the water around her legs as I sit by the tub gives me something to do, and if I do it rhythmically I fancy that it has some soporific effect. About this time she often dozes off.

Prior to her bath I would have given Roberta the evening dose of medication recommended by the neurologist in Philadelphia. Adding a sleeping pill and a sedative for restless legs prescribed by her primary physician rounds out the medication menu. I have mixed feelings about this combination, but it works best so far.

Before she nods too long I help her out of the tub, sometimes having to step into it to lift her to her feet. Then I assist her into her nightclothes, and tuck her into bed. I have a concern that, as the disease advances, I will not be able to use the tub to relax her because I may not be able to get her out of it.

This regimen worked to perfection last night. She slept through the whole night with no restlessness and is still asleep this morning. I find that if I miss any part of the routine, the effect is diminished, if not lost altogether. I'm very pragmatic about this approach. If it works I use it.

160

She is sleeping more all the time. If I rouse her before 10:00 A.M., she will fall asleep in a chair after breakfast. My brother-in-law also has AD, and my sister says that he often goes back to bed after breakfast.

Thanks for your interest in Roberta. I know you care a great deal for her. Any help you can continue to give me I will appreciate.

With love,

Bob

Roberta continued her rapid decline. Most stressful were the nights when her sleep was disrupted by her RLS or the agitation of Alzheimer's disease. While she could sleep off a troubled night the next day, I could not. I was constantly dealing with the numerous details of settling in and taking care of her. At times my much desired after-lunch nap was sacrificed so that I could tend to her needs. Little did I know how much worse our nights would become.

Yet while caring for Roberta was stressful, I found it both challenging and satisfying. The disease is so awful, and she was so helpless, that nothing I could do seemed too much. Yes, I became very weary and frustrated at times. Yet I had never experienced as profound a love for my wife as I did at this time. Later, I was to learn that Alzheimer's patients induce the same deep feelings of affection, if not love, in professional caregivers, such as nurses' aides. Love of this kind undergirds the entire nursing profession, I'm sure, but I have found it especially evident in Alzheimer's care units. Perhaps it is akin to what most adults feel for small children. Caring adequately for Alzheimer's patients would be impossible without this emotional response to their needs.

I was pleased and thankful for Roberta's fine adjustment to this major change in our environment and social surroundings. Gone from our daily life were our neighbors, acquaintances, and church family in Philadelphia, all of whom had wrapped her warmly in their love. Yet, since Roberta had been gradually losing the ability to communicate with them, leaving them may not have been as traumatic for her as I had expected it to be.

A small but faithful band of family members in Grand Rapids filled the places that the Philadelphians had occupied. They were close to us and looked after us diligently. Friends dropped by and offered help. And as I was closer to my wife than I had ever been, my constant presence must have been one of the stabilizing effects in her life. Still, it had been an enormous adjustment for her to have made, and she carried it off beautifully. I was proud of her.

I felt a deep contentment at having settled in with my extended family and friends. Their promises that they would take care of us were being fulfilled every day. While I was often severely stressed by my occupation, there was never a doubt in my mind that we were in the right place for this time in our lives. Buoyed by the prayers and support of many spiritual as well as physical family members, by my faith, growing in response to God's faithfulness, by Roberta's reacting to the sound of the still, small voice, I realized that those everlasting arms were setting us gently down in our new land and were nudging me to proceed with assurance that all was well and would be well in the future.

The stirring words of the magnificent African-American national anthem, "Lift Every Voice and Sing," kept ringing through my head on those days. While neither I, nor any other European American, can match the depth of emotion that African Americans bring to it, singing with "the faith that the dark past has taught us," the words of the third verse gave voice to my experience of the past few years and for the future as nothing else did. James Weldon Johnson, lyricist, and J. Rosamond Johnson, composer, have given to their fellow African Americans, to the world, and to me the gift of stirring words and music. Here is the first half of the third verse that spoke so powerfully of my experience:

God of our weary years, God of our silent tears
thou who hast brought us thus far on our way;
thou who has by thy might led us into the light,
keep us forever in the path we pray.[4]

That became my prayer as I settled in and faced the future.

---

[1] Leif Enger, *Peace Like a River*, (New York: Atlantic Monthly Press, 2001), p. 48.

[2] John Baillie has words fitting this occasion, "O God of mercy, who so carest for me as if Thou hadst none else to care for, yet carest for all even as Thou carest for me . . ." *A Diary of Private Prayer* (New York: Charles Scribner's Sons, 1955). p. 67.

[3] "Lord of All Hopefulness," *Psalter Hymnal* (Grand Rapids, MI: CRC Publications, 1987) p. 558.

[4] "Lift Every Voice and Sing," (written by J. Rosamond Johnson and James Weldon Johnson), verse 3. Used by permission of Edward B. Marks Music Co.

XV

Putting Down Roots

Among the many beautiful Japanese art objects that Ray and Linda had acquired during their five years in that country were two very practical items—futons. When folded on top of each other they made a puffy pile on a chair in the bedroom that looked like a cumulus cloud to me.

At first I paid little attention to them. However, they provided a partial solution to my problem of getting sufficient sleep. After several consecutive nights during which Roberta was in and out of bed countless times until two o'clock in the morning, making it impossible for me to sleep, a novel solution to my problem burst upon me. Why not spread one futon on the floor away from the bed, lie down, cover myself with the second one, and turn over the bed to Roberta?

The next time Roberta went on an RLS jag, I spent a restful night sleeping on the floor. Surprisingly, she did not object to my absence or stumble over me on her nocturnal meanderings. Once, as she walked past me, I heard her mutter, "Be careful. Don't step on the man." At times I watched her out of half-closed eyes as she wrestled both in and out of bed with her sleep demons, realizing that there was nothing I could do to help her.

165

One night, after hearing several entreaties to help her lie down in bed, I rose from my cozy nest to find her sitting on the floor with her back to the foot of the bed, unable to lie down. Apparently, thinking she was in bed, she could not figure out why she was unable to recline. After I helped her climb between the sheets, she soon fell asleep. Sometimes I discovered her in the morning lying cross-wise on bed, occasionally under the covers, at other times on top of them.

In the fall before we moved from Philadelphia, Roberta had prepared an after-midnight snack for me on the coffee table in our apartment. It was one of those rare moments when she deliberately set out to show me in a romantic way that she loved me and wanted to take care of me.

Perhaps her romantic impulse was still alive. Or maybe it was just restlessness or hunger. After eleven o'clock one night, just as I was entering the wonderful dream-stage of sleep, she nudged me and said loudly, "I'm hungry. Let's make some of those eggs." I sometimes prepared scrambled eggs for brunch after she had slept most of the morning.

"Roberta, you've got to be kidding," I grumbled sleepily.

"I'm starved," she repeated, and would not be put off.

"Oh, all right. Let's go." I said, ungraciously. "I told you that you'd be hungry when you wouldn't finish your potatoes."

I stepped out of the warm bed into my cold slippers, and together we mounted the stairs into the cool kitchen.

She watched with interest as I whipped the eggs, poured them into the frying pan and scrambled them, loaded bread into the toaster, buttered and spread jam on the toast, warmed the milk in the microwave, and dished up the eggs.

It was a delicious snack, I must say, and we both ate voraciously. I had to admit that hers was a first-rate idea. I felt pleasantly warm and said, "Great idea, Roberta."

"Let's have some more," she responded, dabbing at her mouth with a napkin.

"What?"

"Let's have another helping of that."

Part of me protested this added chore. I was ready to return to bed. Another part liked the idea. So I prepared a second round of scrambled eggs, toast, and warm milk, which we consumed with as much relish as the first.

"How about some ice cream?" she suggested.

Strangely enough, I had been thinking the same, but had not expressed the idea, wondering if it might be too cold for her. Not so. Since by now I was completely converted to this midnight snack, I dished up ice cream for each of us, which we downed with a sense of satisfaction and closure.

As we cleaned up the dishes, the clock on the mantel struck twelve; we trundled back downstairs and went to bed. My wife was asleep in minutes. I replayed the occasion thinking how much like her former venturesome self she had been.

What began as a loving midnight snack in Philadelphia now developed into a frequent foray to the kitchen for food, companionship, and, in due course, a night of sound sleep. Recurrently, through February, either Roberta or I would suggest in the middle of the night that we go for a snack. Turning on as few lights as possible so as not to break the romantic mood, we would talk amiably about what a good idea this was and about how much we liked food that brought us close together. We snacked sumptuously—twice on pie *a la mode*, several times on hot milk and toast loaded with jam. Slathered with butter and heated fifteen seconds in the microwave, a plate of blueberry muffins that my sister-in-law brought us became one of the best snacks ever. Roberta usually started our evening venture with restless legs, or overall bodily discomfort if not agitation, and finished it able to drift off to sleep once more, relieved by our repast and companionship.

We were becoming a four-meal-a-day family: For breakfast, a huge dish of oatmeal, or fried potatoes, toast and jelly, for lunch, almost always soup and sandwiches; for dinner, boiled potatoes, gravy, some kind of meat, and a vegetable. Our fourth meal, the nocturnal sortie into the kitchen for a snack, was like one big dessert.

These snacks served an extremely useful function. My wife's getting a good night of sleep was a prime requisite for my continuing to give her adequate care. Without these snacks she would have been agitated most of the night, and I would have been sleep-deprived and bad-tempered or worse the next day. I accepted them as a gracious gift that sustained my caregiving.

One day, after I had cut slices from a banana onto our breakfast cereal, Roberta handed me the remaining tip end that was lying on the counter.

Somewhat annoyed, I asked, "Why do you give me your garbage?"

She smiled, "Because you're a garbage maker."

I peered over the top of my glasses at her like a schoolmaster eyeing a rambunctious pupil, and then returned her smile, pleased at her ability to joke at my expense.

Late one Saturday afternoon when the noise in the house had been deafening, with Brian enjoying at top decibels the hoopla on the TV that preceded the NBA all-star game, I decided that it was a perfect night to eat out. I was tired of cooking; Roberta showed enthusiasm for the venture. Waving a cheery goodbye to Brian, we headed out.

This eating-out experience, however, showed me how simple and not-so-simple mistakes had large consequences in my care for Roberta that evening.

Russ', a popular restaurant in the Dutch community, was the place for us. The food is always excellent and the meat loaf meal appealed to me. Knowing that Roberta could not eat a whole meal, I ordered one serving with two plates. All went well. She ate as she had done in bygone days, finishing her dinner, even while protesting all along that she had had enough. The cherry tart I ordered for dessert tasted as good this time as it had years before when Roberta and I would take my elderly mother to Russ' for an afternoon outing.

Then it happened. Who should walk past our booth but Steve Van Der Weele, one of our favorite people. A progressive, well read Christian with a delightful sense of humor, he had taught for many years at Calvin College. I flagged him down, and we greeted each other warmly. I told him that we had relocated in Grand Rapids, were staying temporarily at Ray's, and what Roberta's condition was. Pleasure registered on his expressive face at the first two pieces of news; shock and dismay at the last.

I asked him how things were going. His enthusiasm was boundless as he told me at length of his literary and journalistic activities in the Christian education movement.While this was going on, Roberta was nibbling away at the tart; she had consumed nearly all of it by the time Steve left to complete his interrupted mission of fetching a spoon for his wife.

Our meal eaten, Roberta and I were donning our jackets and preparing to leave. Steve rushed up and told us that friends from college days would like to see us. We were greeted warmly by Boyd Hoffman and his wife, Claudia. I gave her a big hug. She then turned and talked to Roberta, and I filled in Boyd about our situation. Following a short three-way conversation, Roberta and I departed. "Goodbye, see you later," I called over my shoulder.

Arriving home, we found the house empty of noise and Brian. I proposed that we spend some quiet time together on the big sofa, and Roberta liked the idea. I asked her if she would like to take in the "Lawrence Welk" show which, in Philadelphia, we had often watched with pleasure—she, however, more than I. She did not respond, which I took for assent. That was a mistake. Roberta required a good deal of time to make such a decision, a characteristic of Alzheimer's patients. Rather than waiting her out, as I should have, I plowed ahead, surfing the channels trying to locate "Lawrence Welk" on PBS. When I finally found the program, Roberta took one look at the quartet, singing in its typically sweet manner, and shouted, "That makes me mad." Taken aback, I quickly switched channels, realizing too late that Roberta had been seething for some time.

"Shut the TV off," she snapped. "I thought we were going to have a quiet time together." Her anger, I then realized, was caused not by the singers, but by my turning on the TV in the first place, and then fiddling around with it so long. What could I say? She was right. I had ruined the evening by turning on the tube. Switching it off, I started to make amends.

"Shut it off!" she repeated after a bit.

"It is off. See?" I clicked it on for a moment and then turned it off again. Satisfied only momentarily, she once again ordered me to turn it off. It then dawned on me that the light behind us on Linda's desk in the kitchen was reflected on the surface of the screen, and Roberta perceived that as a TV image. By switching off the desk lamp I resolved that little problem.

At last we were settled for some conversation. The first thing I did was to apologize for turning on the TV instead of just plain talking with her. That removed one item from the table. But her rigid body told me that all was not well.

"Are you still mad at me?"

"Yes."

"Why?" I then guessed, "Because of the people at Russ'?"

"Yes."

"The man at our table?"

"A little."

"The other two?"

"Yes. That woman."

"Claudia?"

"Yes."

After more questions it became clear that Roberta objected to my having hugged Claudia. I explained that my friendship with her went back to grade school days, but that I had nothing going with her, nor ever had. Yet my wife came back to this objection again and again, asking me, in addition, what I was planning to do next week. When I told her my schedule for the week, she asked again when I was going to meet with "those people."

Finally, I realized that since I had said "Goodbye, see you later," Roberta thought I was going to meet Boyd and Claudia next week. By vigorously denying that I was planning to see them and by affirming my love for her, I at last calmed her down.

Roberta's aversion to Claudia had deeper roots than the evening's encounter. Although we had never talked about it, I believe she was by then aware that her own face was less lively and her hair less attractive than formerly. Once while we were living in

Philadelphia, a woman friend with a beautiful hairdo, the picture of vitality, came bounding up the steps into our apartment for a visit. Later Roberta referred to her distastefully as "the woman with all the hair." Claudia's hair framed her face. Perhaps that bothered Roberta. Additionally, she may have felt abandoned by having to talk with Claudia, whom she no longer recognized, while I talked with Boyd. Moreover, we three had chattered like chipmunks for the few moments before Roberta and I departed, which left her feeling excluded and suspecting that I was planning to meet them again. No wonder this supposed getting together again enraged her!

Following further desultory conversation, Roberta took her medications and we went to bed where we continued our exchange in a quiet manner. Although somewhat relaxed, she was still periodically agitated and roused herself on her elbow to repeat previous objections.

We had returned home from Russ' at 7:30 that evening. It was 10:15 by the time we were finished dealing with my lack of consideration and Roberta's anger—almost three hours. What might have been a delightful evening turned into a night of wrangling, thanks to my insensitivity.

Marguerite and I had agreed that we needed to make a deliberate effort hereafter to include Roberta in our conversations and meal-preparing activities. We soon had an opportunity to put this decision into effect when she invited us to her home for Sunday dinner. In our conversations we talked *to* Roberta, not *about* her, or without her. Instead of my saying to Marguerite, "Roberta had a good day yesterday," I said to Roberta, "You had a good day yesterday, didn't you?"

She was able to respond appropriately most of the time; she followed what we were discussing and smiled readily. That was unusual for her, since she rarely smiled anymore and never laughed out loud. As a result of our including her in our talk, my wife was relaxed and ate the entire meal without help. Although my sister and I could involve her in our conversation, we would have had a more difficult time if other persons had been present.

After we returned home, Roberta and I hugged each other for a while on the sofa in the dimly lit family room. Completely relaxed,

171

well fed, and properly medicated, she went to bed with me. Yet, not until I gave her a warm bath an hour later was she able to drop off. I had no idea why she couldn't find sleep without the help of the bath. It might have had more to do with what was happening to her brain at that time than what we did together. So even when I did everything completely right, there were times when the internal state of her brain sometimes trumped our warm relationship and the conducive external environment.

During our first month in our new home, the project of moving our household goods to Grand Rapids was always on my mind. Our belongings, having been loaded in Philadelphia late in January, were stuck for more than a week inside a moving van somewhere in transit. I had selected, with Ray's help, an easily accessible, reasonably priced storage company, and had rented four adjacent 10' x 10' compartments for our goods. I engaged another nephew, Jim Mulder (Marguerite's oldest son), who generously agreed to help me with the unloading. Marguerite said she would sit with Roberta while this moving operation was going on. At last a delivery date was confirmed, and the movers arrived.

While Jim checked off the items, I directed the movers to the proper storage compartments in which they stacked our belongings. When we were finished and Jim and I were warming ourselves with a cup of coffee in his car, I felt that our move to Grand Rapids was at last complete.

A remarkable thing had happened, however, in the "restless legs department" of Roberta's life. During the two nights before the movers came to deliver our goods, she had experienced no problem whatever with restless legs. She slept soundly and continuously through both nights. I was blessed with two nights of solid rest in preparation for the stressful moving day and gave thanks for this miracle occurring just when I needed it. Talk about answered prayers not even prayed!

The night after our goods were delivered, however, Roberta's leg problem reemerged. She and I were awake several hours after midnight addressing it with a warm bath, a mug of warm milk, and a sedative. None of these worked very well until about four o'clock in the morning when she finally relaxed and went soundly to sleep.

I e-mailed my support network:

Dear Family and Friends,

Roberta has been holding her own in general, but just barely. She seems to be getting weaker lately, and has been experiencing more and more trouble getting up from chairs and from the toilet. She still manages to don her clothes, but I need to select them, and cue her on buttoning and zipping up. She eats fairly well, especially when I load her plate with potatoes and gravy. Ice cream is a favorite. She sits around most of the day with periodic walks around the house to stretch her legs. I rouse her to help me cook, or to go shopping. We still converse in a way, but there are longer periods of silence between us.

Let me say again that I would not have been able to make this move without the help of all you friends from church who organized it on the Philadelphia end, from the prayers and well-wishes of those of you both in Grand Rapids and in Philadelphia, from our nephew, Jim, Marguerite and Dorothy, as well as friends on the Internet. What a bunch of wonderful people! Thank you one and all.

From Roberta and me with love,

Bob

Daylight was still more than three hours away. Seated with my computer on my lap, I was reading and replying to messages on the Internet when a quavering voice sounded from the bedroom, at first faintly, then more insistently.

"Oh Bob, come and help me. Bob, help me. Puleeeease."

I hurried to the bedroom, replying as I went, "I'm coming Roberta. Hang on. Here I come." There I found her standing by the bed, looking forlorn, so pitifully beautiful. I held her close and pressed her head against my shoulder. Tremors ran up and down her frail body.

173

Snuggled deep in my arms, she sobbed, "I try to get it, but I can't make it out. I can't make it out." She repeated these words again and again.

"I'm so sorry, so sorry," was all I could say. For several moments we stood there, she holding on to me in dazed desperation.

"I think I have it and then I don't."

I could only hold her closer to me, distressed and furious at the demonic disease that was creating such havoc in her brain.

"Something has happened to me and I don't know what it is."

Feeling that some activity was needed to relieve the pain she was experiencing, I suggested, "Let's get some warm milk and cookies in the kitchen. How would you like that?"

"I would like that," she parroted.

Although it was closer to sunrise than midnight, we went through our now-traditional midnight snack routine of heating two mugs of milk in the microwave oven and opening a package of oatmeal cookies. Roberta downed half of one before the milk was warm. Munching what was left of the cookie, she mused in quiet desperation, "I can't believe that that's the way it is."

Even after the welcomed distraction of comfort food, Roberta kept pacing the floor muttering more to herself than to me, "I don't know how to make everything come out right."

Alzheimer's disease inflicted unimaginable pain on Roberta. Again and again in the course of a day she remarked, "I don't know what is happening to me," as she wrestled with her lostness. One can empathize with the pain embodied in that statement by imagining what it would be like to have all one's memories, plans, hopes, relationships, meanings wiped out of consciousness and replaced by inescapable blankness, fear, and foreboding of the moment.

Roberta would fall asleep, only to awaken and face once more the desperation of her pain.

One Sunday after church, Brian offered to make hamburgers for me, Roberta, and Marguerite, who was paying us an after-church visit. My wife was preoccupied with walking around the house in a driven fashion, and sensing that she was in no mood to eat at this time, I dissuaded him from making one for her. He then fried one for my sister and one for me; hamburgers are his specialty.

174

Roberta was absent from the table when he served them. When she approached, I asked her out of courtesy, if she would like part of my hamburger, cutting it in half, and offering it to her. She pondered for a long moment, as if contemplating a most disgusting object, then said, "*Eat that thing?*" Dripping with disdain and incredulity that I would even suggest that she eat it, she turned her back on "that thing." Her response was so surprising and fitting that my sister and I burst out laughing, and simply could not stop. Every time we tried to bring our mirth under control, a different nuance of her statement struck us—first the disgust, then disdain, and finally, incredulity—each shade sent us off again in fits of mirth.

It was easy to find humor in some of Roberta's comments, which, however, she might not always have meant to be funny, and which perhaps rose out of her inability to say what she really wanted to say. That was not the case in this instance. Yet, our laughter at her inadvertent, spontaneous wit might occasionally have added to her confusion. A child may find delight in having made adults laugh, but that was not necessarily the case with Roberta or other Alzheimer's patients. Still, it was a testimony to her inborn sense of humor that what she said was sometimes hilarious.

Early in the year Roberta still struggled to find a bridge over the chasm of forgetting, or a way around it, so that she might complete a sentence and convey her thoughts. It was most painful to have her start to tell me something, speaking forcefully at first, hoping, I think, to gain enough momentum to plow through to the end of the sentence, only to come up short. She might say, "Bob, please bring me the . . . " Or, "I was thinking about the ..." and be blocked in mid-thought, unable to name what she wanted me to bring or what she was thinking about. She could point to it, if it were within her vision, but she found naming it verbally almost impossible. Being unable to find the word she needed to finish what she had started to say, she would come to an agonizing halt.

With deep breathing, intense staring, and guttural sounds in her throat, she endeavored with all her might to articulate her thoughts. Her struggle would be intense, her voice forced, almost croaking. I grieved to see this woman, who had never been at a loss for words, striving so mightily to complete a simple sentence. During the pauses, I would try to suggest the word she was struggling to find. Sometimes I succeeded, but at other times I didn't; then she would stop me, probably because I was only confusing her and disturbing her efforts to remember what she wanted to say. The look she would give me at these times was one of desperation, not only because she was not able to come up with the word she wanted, but also because she understood, I think, the grave significance of her inability to do so.

Many other caregivers have commented on this phenomenon of missing nouns. It seems to be so universal that it is considered a fairly reliable everyday sign of Alzheimer's disease.[1] Since talking is such a common behavior it is not surprising that this symptom is so readily observed.

Roberta's inability to complete a sentence in the external world most likely reflected her inability to complete a thought in her internal world. Many thoughts, I believe, come as mentally formed sentences. She could not escape the frustrations of her conversations by retreating into her internal thought world. There she met the same problem, I am sure. She said she was confused. Why? Wasn't it because she struggled just as intensely to complete her internal thoughts as she did her sentences with me and others? No thought could ever be completed. Failing to remember a needed word, she would turn to another thought, hoping for better success, only to be blocked once more. Everywhere she searched, she encountered only the shadows of words that no longer had form, like ghosts seen out of the corner of the eye. When she turned to look directly at them, they disappeared. I pictured Roberta trapped in a dungeon with each possible escape route blocked by a guard armed with a pillow with which he smothered her every attempt to escape. Alzheimer's disease is a passive restraint, an amorphous loss. It is the ultimate jailer; no one to date has escaped.

Most of us, however, can deal with what Roberta experienced by finding a related word or starting a new sentence and talking about something else. But suppose with the next sentence we tried to formulate we would encounter this same impasse, and likewise with every subsequent effort. That was Roberta's experience. While we may fret, we know that the lost item of memory will return in

176

time, probably when least expected. Something will cue us in to it. Moreover, these memory glitches occur only occasionally, not continuously, as they do with the Alzheimer's patient. Perhaps the closest a normal person comes to the Alzheimer experience is trying to remember an elusive dream that dances out of sight as soon as one tries to bring it into focus.

Imagine what it must be like to have *every* thought, *everything* one wants to say blocked. Alzheimer's disease is like that—it never lets up; it never relents. She can never say, "I'll think of that in a minute." Or, "Tomorrow, I'll be OK." She awakens in the morning and goes to sleep at night with this horror. What an indescribably frightening world that must be. A friend said it best, "Alzheimer's disease is one's worst nightmare."

It is not surprising that the dreadful frustration arising from this situation would result in towering rage in some Alzheimer's patients, especially if they might be prone to anger in the first place. Moreover, since we do not know how the disease attacks the brain, with some patients, fury may be a direct result of the disease. Fortunately, Roberta had not been short tempered in her earlier life, and never flew into rage while I was caring for her. Later, however, when she became a resident in an Alzheimer's care unit she occasionally became angry enough to scream when forced to submit to something, such as having her diaper changed.

No wonder that Roberta felt ill, out of sorts, frustrated, and irritable at times. The hopelessness and inevitability of her illness was agonizing to me. I could only hold her close and tell her again and again that I loved her. The physical contact as much as the words seemed to lift her out of her dungeon of despair. Or we could take a walk or start some physical activity, such as cooking, that did not require verbalization. These were temporary measures, but they brought some relief to both of us.

Roberta was not, however, continuously afflicted with the unbearable frustration of not being able to form sentences with which to communicate or think. Medications worked wonders in calming her, although sometimes they left her staring blankly into space. On such occasions she might not have been struggling and may have even been at peace. Calmness may have come upon her because she was medicated or exhausted and unable to continue the struggle. Or the disease, encroaching ever more on her cerebral neurons, left fewer areas of the brain with which to think. Occasionally I even needed to shout to bring her out of her reverie.

It became clear to me in this period of pain that I needed the full embrace of the everlasting arms as much as Roberta needed my arms around her. I wrapped myself in the promise that nothing can separate us from the love of God in Christ Jesus. That helped. In the morning I read in Psalm 42, "By day the Lord commands his steadfast love," and when I retired with Roberta I recited, "and at night his song is with me, a prayer to the God of my life." In my simple way I believed that, even as Roberta sank ever deeper into the shadows, neither she nor I could be separated from that love.

---

[1] There is a short series of standard questions used as a rough screen for Alzheimer's disease, called a Folstein Mini Mental State Examination, that was described in an end note in Chapter 5.

XVI

Another Transition

A simple theory about the course of Alzheimer's disease has been proposed by social scientists who have been trying to improve methods of caring for Alzheimer's patients. This theory holds that the most recent memories and cognitive skills are the first to go; earlier memories are retained longer. In a catchy phrase, the theory says, "Last in, first out"—a sort of reverse development.[1] Roberta seemed to be following that course.

By the middle of the summer of 2000, my wife had clearly come to the end of the first stage of Alzheimer's disease, the stage she had already entered before Dark Thursday in 1999. About this time it seemed to me that she was well into the second stage of the disease.[2] Even before we had left Philadelphia, she had already forgotten many of the daily details and routines of our life—our walks in the Wissahickon Valley, the plans for the day, the way to church.

By early 2001 she had lost most of her cognitive skills as well as her memory. Her verbal skills were deteriorating; the range of her speech content was diminishing rapidly. Her social skills had markedly declined. The only psychotic symptom she showed, however, were occasional delusions and hallucinations. Now, also, her speech was becoming less coherent, she was becoming more confused and

179

agitated, and she was increasingly incontinent. While her restlessness was increasing, she was not verbally or physically aggressive. In sum, she seemed to be functioning at about the level of a preschool child.

Ray and Linda, who had returned from Florida, observed that she had lost considerable ground while they were gone. Her restless legs seemed to be untreatable. We had an occasional string of exhausting nights, and dog-tired, unpredictable days.

Early in February, with the help of the administrator of the Holland Home dementia centers, I located a geriatrist who also dealt with problems of dementia—a perfect fit for my wife. She was wonderful with Roberta, even being able to elicit a faint smile on our first visit, a tribute to the warmth and love that she imparted. (Roberta did not smile easily those days. Yet she tugged at the heart of everyone who saw her.) I observed the love welling up in the doctor's eyes as she dealt with her and me. After reviewing Roberta's medications and my report of what I was giving her, she concluded that my wife was being overmedicated. She dropped one or two drugs and made a substitution. Thus began a long process of sporadic medication adjustment, dictated by Roberta's current behavioral problems, a process with which all caregivers deal.

Finding a sleep disturbance specialist was also high on my to-do list. The doctor I found reviewed Roberta's list of prescriptions, subtracting one and adding one of his own. The two doctors seemed willing to coordinate Roberta's medications. But they still were not able to prescribe the right combination of medication to treat both her RLS and her Alzheimer's disease.

Roberta continued having good and bad days, restful and restless nights, periods of calm and times of agitation. I could discern no pattern in her behavior or cognitive abilities other than an uneven downward trend. It was not possible to predict what her conduct would be from one day to the next. Other caretakers have said the same about their stricken loved ones.

During our first two months in Grand Rapids I was getting along well physically, mentally, and spiritually. My mental health and spirits were continually pumped up by the responses of my extended network of family and friends to the periodic updates I sent over the Internet on Roberta's condition. They were my virtual support group. To those who had taken care of a stricken loved one or friend, I was especially grateful. Their firsthand experience corroborated mine and was encouraging. How a caregiver can make it without the sustaining love from family and friends is difficult to see. I concluded an e-mail to my network of relatives and friends with the following thanks:

> *I am deeply grateful to know that you are all out there thinking of us and praying for us. I feel as though we have a large cheering section urging us on in this challenging game. Please continue your cheering.*
>
> *With love, on behalf of Roberta and myself,*
>
> *Bob*

Toward the end of February, Roberta was still struggling to find a bridge over the chasm of forgetfulness, or a way around it. I tried to help her but seldom succeeded, as the following incident illustrates.

It was four o'clock in the morning late in February. Since I had always been a very early riser, I considered that I had had a good night of sleep. Unaccountably, Roberta had not been afflicted with RLS. She awoke at the same time I did, and together we climbed the stairs to the kitchen for one of our after-midnight snacks. Returning to our bedroom, I tucked her back in bed, telling her I would be in the next room, working on my computer, and she could come out if she wanted to talk with me. A few minutes later she was standing in front of me. She took the hand that I held out to her over the top of the computer screen, raised her gaze off the floor and smiled, a rare event.

"What's on your mind?" I asked her quietly. This question had often elicited meaningful responses in the past.

"I don't know," she replied, and turned away ever so slowly, back to the bedroom. In a moment she revisited me.

"Tell me, what are you thinking about now?" I asked, realizing that something must be bothering her.

Picking up my words, she said, "I'm thinking that I can't find any . . . " A long pause followed as she searched for the word she wanted, looking this way and that, eyes always on the ground. Finally she murmured,

" . . . any . . . anything." Again, turning slowly away, she returned to the bedroom.

Still later, she shuffled out to me again.

"What's on your mind now?" I asked.

"Shall we try for a . . . " Long pause.

I tried to fill in the gap. "Food?" Brow furrowed. "Bed?"

Looking around as if searching, lower lip trembling, she was the picture of sorrow. She shook her head, and turned slowly away.

Through all this, she was not agitated, just lost.

When she came out once more, I suggested, "Shall I walk you back to bed?"

"I would like that." I stepped to her side, offering her my arm as I had done when we walked up the aisle on our wedding day. She held it tightly. Smiling down on her as she looked solemnly at the floor, I escorted her slowly the long way around the living area, past the kitchenette and the bathroom, through the hallway to our bedroom. I tucked her in with, "God be with you, Roberta," and kissed her on the cheek.

When words fail, love fills in the gap.

I was awakened by a blaze of light that lit up the darkness of the early hours of a morning in March. No, it was not an on-the-road-to-Damascus encounter, such as that of the apostle Paul. The radiance emanated from the dome light in the hallway at the foot of the stairs, just outside our bedroom door. Shocked out of sound sleep, I leaped from my futon, knowing instantly that the brightness had to do with Roberta, and dashed to the stairs to see what was going on. Looking like a lost lambkin, Roberta came down the steps, followed by the large figure of Ray in his pajamas, smiling broadly. He might easily have carried her over his shoulder, like the Good Shepherd, bringing the wandering sheep back to the fold. Chuckling, he said, "She made it all the way to our bedroom."

"Oh, no!" I said as the situation became clear to me. "I'm sorry, Ray."

I was mortified that Roberta had escaped due to my lack of watchfulness and had extended her wandering all the way to Ray and Linda's suite on the second floor. At that moment Ray's good-natured love of Roberta struck me as being truly wonderful. (Roberta had recently taken to night wandering, always seeming to be looking for something, opening doors, poking around here and there. One day I found a half-finished can of ginger ale in our refrigerator that she must have nipped at during the night. Unfortunately, she had laid the unfinished can on its side, leaving me with the clean-up job.)

Comforted by Ray's calmly guiding her return, Roberta went meekly to bed and slept through the rest of the night.

Later in the morning, Linda told me that Roberta had opened the door of their bedroom, and asked in a quavering voice, "Robert, where are you?" This nocturnal intrusion probably scared Ray and Linda nearly out of their pajamas. Linda, wonderful person that she is, comforted Roberta and told her that Ray would take her down to Robert.

While this incident reveals the love of Ray and Linda for Roberta, the lostness and fear behind her trembling question, "Robert, where are you?" were telling signs of her interior torment.

The tale did not end there. Early on the following day, I was working at my laptop in the sitting area. Roberta made numerous appearances, looking forlorn and asking to be taken to the bathroom, or just wanting to be embraced and escorted around our apartment area before being brought back to bed. After she showed up the fifth or sixth time, I tucked her in with strong words about staying there. She responded that she would do so. Thinking that I had bedded her down for an extended slumber, I went back to work.

A half-hour of quiet aroused my suspicion. I looked into our bedroom hoping to find Roberta there, yet I was not completely surprised to see that the bed was empty. A quick inspection of our living area revealed no sign of her. Reprimanding myself, I hustled upstairs to find Linda clipping coupons from the paper, telling me, with a smile, that Roberta had returned to their bedroom and was snoozing sweetly on their bed. "Come and see," she said. Sure enough, there she was in peaceful repose.

In a half-hour or so Roberta appeared in the kitchen where I was preparing breakfast, seemingly unaware that she had been sleeping in the wrong bed; it may have seemed "right" to her! Clearly, I needed to block the stairway even while I worked early in the morning, or she would continue to use it as a getaway route to another land.

Later, I wondered: Is the wandering that is so characteristic of Alzheimer's patients a search for something with which to orient themselves in their sea of confusion, an attempt to locate an anchor to hold them against the riptide of forgetfulness? Or is the wandering driven by their agitation, a general urgent restlessness, with no specific goal? So often when Roberta had been agitated and restive in Philadelphia she had wanted to be taken from wherever we were at the moment, to another place, any other place. Perhaps her wandering into Ray and Linda's bedroom had been an attempt to find her way to the security of my presence, where she would not be lost.

Heavenly Guidance, Heavenly Rest

A night early in March started out in the worst possible way. Roberta could not slow down or go quietly to sleep. She was agitated, querulous, refused to lie down, and asked again and again, "What are we going to do now?" "What do you want me to do?" "What are we doing here?" She went on for a long time raising these impossible-to-answer questions. I said in as many different ways as I could, "We're living with Ray and Linda until we find another apartment for us alone." After a while I found myself raising my voice in frustration. (When I asked Linda the next morning if she had heard our loud conversation the night before, I was not surprised that she politely admitted that she had.)

I had given Roberta a warm bath, which was intended to relax her but which failed to achieve that effect. Having tried every persuasive device I could conjure up to settle her, I told her I was going to leave her in bed and go to sleep on the futons. At that point, all I could do was to pray, "O God, please slow her down."

Yet I was mindful that the last time I had slept on the floor in our bedroom, my wife had slipped away and had found her way into Ray and Linda's bedroom. How to prevent that from happening again posed a problem that was solved, I am convinced, by an answer to a prayer never even prayed. "Lay your futon at the foot of the stairs, and you will block her way," I instructed myself. (If I had been an Old Testament prophet, I might have claimed that the Lord spoke to me.)

This solution had its source, I believe, in my early and later religious education and practice. One of the best-known Bible stories that I have read countless times, is that of Jesus meeting his disciples at the Sea of Tiberias, one morning several days after his resurrection. The disciples had been fishing all night. When Jesus heard that they had caught nothing, he instructed them, "Cast the net to the right side of the boat, and you will find some" John 21:6 (NRSV). The cadence of my instructions to myself matched the cadence of Jesus' instructions to his disciples. That *cadence* was as deeply embedded in my nervous system as the words were, I believe. Internal cues as ephemeral as this can serve as answers to prayers, even unspoken ones, and may act as one source of creative problem solving.

The idea was a winner. I slept soundly on the floor of the hallway with my back against the closed stairway door. There was no way Roberta could get to the stairs without climbing over me. While I was sleeping there she continued her wandering, apparently unaware of me. With half-closed eyes, I occasionally saw her scuffs as she padded past me. In the morning I woke, having had the most restful night in a long time.

I had now devised an escape-proof lower level apartment. If sleeping with Roberta became impossible, I would leave our bed and take up quarters on the futon at the foot of the stairway. Before settling down I would wedge the backs of chairs under the doorknobs of all the closet doors, to discourage her from poking around in them. If my wife padded by me very often, I would get up and take her to the toilet. If she was still restless, I would roll back the futon and we would go upstairs to the kitchen for an after-midnight snack. My strategy worked superbly many nights, and we both obtained some quality rest.

While I was congratulating myself on having contained Roberta's night wandering, my sister Marguerite saw the situation quite differently. She later told me that she thought I should have been seeking ways to commit Roberta to an Alzheimer's care center rather than continuing to care for her under these conditions.

Alzheimer's disease is a fickle jailer. Occasionally it allows its prisoner a short leave of absence from the dungeon of dreary, befuddled agitation.

Such a leave was granted Roberta on an evening early in March. It started with a wonderful meal prepared by Linda—baked fillets of ocean fish caught by Ray on their Florida vacation. Roberta could not get enough of them. Steamed zucchini with sautéed onions complemented the fish, along with boiled potatoes topped with butter. For dessert, Linda scooped a large dish of butter-pecan ice cream. Roberta ate the whole meal with obvious relish, applauded by cheerleader Ray.

After we finished, Roberta offered to help Linda clear the table and wash the dishes, while Ray retired to the family room to watch his evening TV financial report. I descended to the lower level to watch "The News Hour with Jim Lehrer." Thus we reenacted with modifications the Victorian custom of men withdrawing to the parlor for cigars and brandy after the evening meal, leaving the women to clean up the mess.

Having finished the domestic chores with Linda, Roberta came downstairs, excited and full of words. "I helped Linda with the dishes. We washed the pots and pans. And it was fun." Three complete sentences, no hesitation, no forgotten words, spoken with a resonant voice! She was her old companionable self once more.

So relaxed was she that she was able to unzip her warm sweater and unbutton her flannel shirt without my help as she prepared herself for bed. Usually, she had such tremors in her arthritic fingers, exacerbated by agitation, that she could not manage these undressing chores on her own. She soon fell into a sound sleep without medication or a warm bath and slumbered beautifully all night.

The next morning, Ray, Linda and I reviewed the remarkable events of the previous night. Linda and I toyed momentarily with the hopeful idea that this might be the beginning of a trend toward healing, knowing full well, however, that it could not be. Ray confirmed our latter, more sane judgment, saying, "Consider it a gift for the day." That was good advice. I was learning to accept any good day with thanks and not to expect it to carry over to the morrow.

After another great dinner the next night, Linda invited Roberta to help clear the table and wash the dishes. But none of the beneficial effects of the previous night followed. She remained agitated most of the evening, and had a very difficult time getting to sleep. Once again the jailer had slammed shut the door of the dungeon; her leave was over.

Conditions of the two nights, however, were not comparable. The most obvious difference was that on the previous evening, Roberta had volunteered to help Linda, whereas on this night, Linda had invited my wife to help her. Volunteering itself was an indication of a positive mood. But perhaps this difference was not significant. The most generally valid thing that could be said was that Alzheimer's disease makes the person erratic. It is next to impossible to predict tomorrow's responses on the basis of today's behavior.

Alzheimer's disease can gradually interfere with such a simple act as getting into bed. I'm not referring to the rather complex sequence of getting undressed and ready for bed, a feat that usually took Roberta at least a half-hour to accomplish with my help. Rather, I'm referring to the seemingly uncomplicated series of steps one takes in order to put oneself down in bed and under the covers for a night of sleep.

Roberta was occasionally unable to do that, and I would have to help her with this task. As she sat rigidly on the edge of the bed, I would slowly tip her over like a wooden doll until her head was on the pillow with her feet still outside the bed. Then I would lift her bent, stiffened legs on to the bed, straighten them out, slide them between the sheets, and pull the blankets over her shoulders. After this maneuver she would be lying awkwardly on her back, with her head raised, slightly above her pillow. Slowly, while I gently massaged her legs, she would relax her neck, drop her head, and unwind her whole body. Bending over her I would kiss her, saying, "God be with you, Roberta." "Thank you," was her unvarying reply.

As I retreated out of the door after one of these sessions, she complained bitterly, "Going to bed isn't easy." It became even more difficult for her as the weeks rolled along.

Communication with Roberta was often a matter of giving directions, cueing her on her more complicated tasks, and asking how she was doing. This functional language became rather boring at times, and I found myself falling into tedious patterns, the way mothers probably feel as they communicate with their very young children. For a while I was using the word "okay" so often that I became tired of hearing myself say it. I began employing it because one day Roberta told me to stop asking her if she understood what I was saying every time I explained something to her. I had been saying, "Da . . . da . . . da . . . *Do you understand?*" She said, "Yes, of course I do. Stop asking me that."

I then started to substitute the word, "Okay?" for the question, "*Do you understand?*" I would say, "It's time to get ready for bed now. Okay?" But I was also implicitly asking, "Do you agree? or "Will you do it?"

Soon I found another use for the word—to catch her attention. I'd say, "*OKAY*, now Roberta, it's time to get up." And, "*OKAY*, Roberta, let's go for a walk." That greatly expanded my use of the word, since I spent considerable time trying to get her attention.

The word also evolved into a reward and a sign of approval, as when she pulled on her jacket by herself. "You did that *okay*, dear." With emphasis on the last syllable, it was meant to convey strong appreciation as, "You really did *okaaay!*"

Much of my dealing with Roberta was devoted to cueing her while she was in the process of doing a sequential activity, such as getting dressed. "Okay" became a useful cueing word. When she was buttoning her blouse, I would say, "Okay, now do the next button. As she fastened each one I rewarded her with "Okay."

Even as I dealt with my own actions I began to use the word involuntarily. I would say, "Okay, now I need to get the dishes washed." Or "Okay, now I'm done with that." In this way I would cue myself on each step when I had a number of items on my agenda.

Okay became a tonal word. Its meaning depended on the inflection of my voice, and the context in which it was uttered.

With a rising intonation it asked for *assent*—do you agree, or will you do it?

When said loudly at the start, it meant, *pay attention.*

With stress was laid on the "kaaay" it meant *approval.*

When said in a purring voice it meant, *that's fine, keep on doing it the way you are doing*, especially when it followed each successful step in an action sequence.

In speaking to Roberta, my tone of voice was all-important. I tried to keep it flat. Matter-of-factness went a long way to keeping her calm. "Oh, you wet your underpants a little bit. That's no problem. I'll get you another pair," as if this was an ordinary occurrence and nothing to raise my voice about.

If at times I needed to raise my voice to get her attention, I tried to follow up immediately with an approval. "*OKAY, ROBERTA!* BUTTON YOUR BLOUSE!" followed by an approving, "Okaaay! You finished it. Nice going!"

I e-mailed this discussion of the word, okay, to our daughter, Joanne, a linguist, and asked for her comment. She responded:

Hi Dad,

Interesting. The word seems to be functioning like a miniature sentence. An interesting thing about inflection is that it is the first thing children learn. Long before they learn words, they learn the inflections of their native language. It sounds from your account as if maybe word sound is also retained longer than word meaning.

Love, Jody

189

I e-mailed the following response to her:

Jody,

That's a helpful insight. I hadn't thought of it. Thanks. I think that during this time I have been actually treating Mom as a child, perhaps because she was retrodeveloping to her childhood level.

How dreadfully sad.

Dad

I could not help adding the last sentence even though I had reminded myself all along not to look back at how Roberta used to be, but to accept her as she was, day by day.

Joanne responded:

Hi Dad,

I don't think it had anything to do with how you were treating her. It's just that inflection is very deeply embedded in the mind. It is retained when other language learning is lost, and it is something we all respond to at a very elemental level.

A single repeated word with very clear intonational cues is probably an effective means of communication. When you talk with her now, she probably hears the tone patterns of your conversation, knows they are familiar and loving, and responds to that, whether or not she picks up on any of the words.

And yes, it is very sad.

Jody

I wrote in response:

Good morning, Jody,

I agree that inflection is probably very deeply embedded in the mind, and it is to that very primitive stage of language development that Mom has regressed, due to the disease. I began to rely on inflection because that is what she seemed to respond to.

Many words remain as a faint shadow in Mom's mind, I believe. When she initiates a sentence that she can't finish, which is almost always the case, and I try to finish her thought with a word I think she may be searching for, she will pause for a moment, and then give her assent. I can tell that the shadow has become a real word to her (1) if the pause is short and she agrees. I believe then that I have hit on what she was trying to say. (2) If there is a long pause followed by her assent, I don't think that I have succeeded, but that she is agreeing because she doesn't know how to disagree. (3) If the pause is long with no assent, I know I have missed completely what she wanted to say. We either stop the exchange, or I try again. But often it is too late if I fail on the first attempt, because she has already forgotten what she wanted to say.

Thanks for your suggestions,

Love,

Dad

Spring was in the air, and we were on the move again. After Ray and Linda returned from Florida late in February, I began putting my mind to the problem of locating "interim" lodging where Roberta and I could reside for a year until the now independent living apartment I had selected for us in Breton Terrace (of the Holland Home system) was ready for occupancy. Linda and my sisters stood ready to help with all that goes into making a successful move.

But first, I needed to obtain an overview of the apartment scene in Grand Rapids. I had no idea what was available. So on an afternoon early in March at Ray's suggestion, the four of us—Ray, Linda,

Roberta and I—piled into Ray's SUV and looked over six apartment complexes in the southeast part of the city.

After that survey, events moved rapidly. By Friday of that week, I had completed a preliminary application and plunked down a security deposit on an apartment in a lovely complex. A ground-floor, apartment was available, with an up-to-the-minute kitchen, a pantry (!), washer and dryer, two bedrooms and two baths, adequate closet space, a small office, a dining-living room area with windows on two sides, air conditioning, and a doorway to an old-fashioned front porch. From the porch, the apartment overlooked a beautiful little pond with a fountain in the middle and a fringe of woodland on the other side. The view would make an attractive water color painting.

Now to begin the big move into these new quarters. A major challenge I faced was to extricate the basic household goods I would need from the jumble of possessions that the movers had jammed into my four storage units. Ray and I checked out the storage compartments to get a handle on how to do this. An outfit I hired would do the heavy lifting, pulling out a table here, a chair there, a box underneath, and all the rest, which they would then load on their truck and deliver to our new apartment. Before the weekend was over, the Lord willing, Roberta and I would be settled snugly in our new abode.

We did not have the trouble I had anticipated locating the articles I wanted from my storage compartments. With advice from Ray, I selected what I thought we would need and the movers extracted them without great difficulty. It was like being reunited with old friends after a long absence. We emptied two of the compartments completely, and I hoped in the near future to distribute or discard enough of my goods so that I could get by with only one storage unit.

What amazed me was that Linda had taken it on herself to work for two days in our apartment, covering every shelf in every cupboard in the kitchen and two bathrooms, with shelf paper. When she was finished, the cupboards looked like new. She told me later that she did not feel good about my having to use those cupboards that had been used before without covering the shelves.

192

I hung our clothes in the closets and puttered around, while Ray supervised the placement of all the furniture that the movers were unloading. Ray and Linda organized my kitchen down to the last piece of flatware. The energy and organizing skill of my nephew and niece recalled to my mind the way they had taken charge of the last stage of our preparations for leaving our Philadelphia apartment.

Below is a snippet from an e-mail I sent to family and friends:

How is Roberta taking all this? While she expressed initial objections to the move, she readily accepts my explanation of why we need to make it, and what the new place will offer us. I suspect she does not understand all this, but accepts my word that we need to do it and that the move will turn out all right. Her problems are generally not with the external environment, but with her internal confusion. She is almost always confused, even worse, lost. Only when she is involved in some kind of action, like taking a walk, is she not troubled.

Two major problems have recently emerged in her illness. One is her more frequent incontinence, and the second, her increase of night-time wandering.

Late in March a nurse is scheduled to make a medical/ psychological/social assessment of Roberta's status, and to give me recommendations on what steps I need to take in the light of her evaluation. I face this session with the same trepidation that accompanied her MRI in November—hoping for the best but fearing the worst. It has been my fervent hope and prayer that Roberta will be able to remain with me in our new apartment at least through the summer and perhaps into the fall.

Your continued cheers, thoughts, and prayers are most welcome as we enter this new phase of our life together. Thanks to all for your strong, palpable support. I'll keep you posted on how well the move goes.

With love, on behalf of Roberta and myself,

Bob

A few days later I received an e-mail from a concerned friend counseling me not to move again after such a short period, pointing out that it is really hard on Roberta. I responded:

Agreed. We're settling in this new apartment for 12, maybe 14 months. That was the plan all along. Roberta is taking it remarkably well. I saw very little discontinuity in her behavior as we moved from Cherokee, to Ray and Linda's home, to this new apartment. Hers is a slow, bumpy descent into the dark shadows.

I am fully convinced that my moves have succeeded as well as they have because of the faithful prayers of God's people, like you and scores of others. If God, by implication, promised to hear the prayers of the importunate widow because she kept banging away at him, how can God refuse to hear and act on prayers of dozens of people who are doing the same for me and especially for Roberta? I think God has a special warm place in his heart for her.

Love you,

Bob

I left our snug nest in Ray and Linda's home with mixed feelings. On the one hand, I would have liked to stay there until our apartment in Breton Terrace was ready for occupancy. Much about the living arrangement at their home had been attractive; I would miss their company. But staying on was wishful thinking since the completion date for the Terrace was more than a year off. And my original understanding with Ray had been that we would live in their place only until I could find another apartment.

On the other hand, having found our beautiful apartment, I was eager to move into it. I looked forward to being alone with Roberta, giving my full attention to her, being reunited with our own familiar household goods, and trying my hand at housekeeping. Even though I felt the tremor of anxiety that I always experienced when making a move to a new stage of life, I was ready to face the challenge.

Our stay at Ray and Linda's had been a shelter in a time of storm. Without their generosity, I could not have returned to Grand Rapids. There is no way that I can thank them adequately for being such a wonderful nephew and niece.

The new apartment became home to me with the arrival of the things that had previously helped to make our life enjoyable. With our furniture in place and the kitchen ready for use, having the TV and music center available (after Brian fine-tuned the tape deck) and my computer running, our move was complete. I was pleased with the entire setup, and felt thankful to Ray, Linda, and Brian for their indispensable assistance, and to Marguerite who took care of Roberta during the hectic day of the move.

After more than two months of living in Ray and Linda's home, we were in our own apartment. I wrote the following note to Sam.

Dear Sam,

Today we left our nest in Ray's home to make one of our own in our new apartment. Our last night at Ray and Linda's was uneventful. We didn't have a big farewell party. Mostly, I felt a sense of satisfaction that everything was going according to plan. Tonight will be our first full night on our own since we left Philly. I have some anxiety about it, as you can imagine. Wish me and Roberta sweet dreams tonight cradled in the everlasting arms.

Brother Bob

---

[1] David Vance, Cameron Camp, Martha Kabacoff and Linda Greenwalt, "Montessori Methods: Innovative Interventions for Adults with Alzheimer's Disease," *Montessori Life*, Winter, 1996, 10-13.

[2] James Dumerauf, "The Spirit in the Shadows: A Medical Perspective on Alzheimer's Disease," *Reformed Review*, 54:2, Winter, 2000-01, p.88.

XVII

On Our Own Again

Roberta had taken the move into our new apartment fairly well, even though we were still living with partly emptied boxes and suitcases for several days. She walked around the place without anxiety or stress. Yet unaccountably, one night, after a visit to the social worker in her geriatrist's office, she was completely disoriented about our new home. She claimed she could not remember ever having been in our living room where we were then sitting. She was not joking. It was as if she had never seen the place. She asked me to go over everything we did that day, and after I did, she began to remember her surroundings. Her amnesia may have been a residue of the stress of taking yet one more memory test, administered by the social worker, in which she failed to recall anything—the day, week, month, city or state in which we were—nothing. Our recent move to this apartment may also have contributed. When I later told her we had left Pennsylvania, she said, "Did we really?"

Dear relatives and friends,

April Fool's Day, and for the first time in what seems like a year, but is only four months (that's what fools

197

me), we are not facing a major move to some new digs, as the Brits call them. We have been living in our latest abode for two weeks, and already it feels like that many months. Roberta seems quite relaxed, although she sometimes gets lost and disoriented just trying to find our bedroom by herself, or any other room, for that matter.

The last time I wrote, I mentioned the trepidation with which I was facing the forthcoming visit by the nurse from the Holland Home on March 23. Actually the visit was extremely constructive. As a result of it, Roberta is now enrolled in the Home Care program of the Holland Home, a multi-service system that provides care for the varied needs of elderly people.

I had two appointments with a doctor at the Sleep Disorder Clinic, who prescribed a medication that has done wonders in calming down Roberta's RLS. He is coordinating his prescription with the geriatrist with the specialty in dementia, who is Roberta's primary care physician at this time. We have had several sessions with her and the social worker in her office. She asked me to write a detailed log of Roberta's activities for several days so that she and the social worker can study it in order to get a handle on Roberta's occasional extreme nocturnal agitation, which continues to be a serious problem. In short, I am connected with a network of medical people who are helping me with my main occupation at this time—taking care of Roberta. These arrangements are lifting a burden of anxiety from my mind and are giving me a new sense of security.

Roberta continues her slow decline, with more days of agitation and confusion than of calm and clarity. The questions that seem ever to be on her mind are, "Why am I this way?" and "Why am I so mixed up?" Some days she repeats them over and over as she paces the floor. Sunday, however, was one of those days when she was calm and companionable; we attended church, ate, walked, and talked almost like old days. Such days are a gift from God.

*As with all occupations, I sometimes tire of this one. But
I am holding up well, sustained by many contacts with
my family, visits from friends, even from one as far away
as Philadelphia. The prayers of all of you, your positive
thoughts, encouraging e-mails, and snail mails keep me
going. Please continue them.*

On behalf of Roberta and myself,

Bob

Rage Against the Night

During her bad nights Roberta was in and out of bed numerous
times. On each occasion, I would help her get back in and then she
would immediately slip out again. I put her to bed several times,
following the procedure I had used occasionally in Ray and Linda's
home, only to have her get up and scuff around again. Sometimes
after lying down, covering herself, and resting her head on her pillow, she would ask, "What do I do now?" She did not seem to understand me when I told her, "Just relax now. You're in bed." She seemed
to have no concept that going to sleep was a process of letting go,
that nothing more was necessary.

One time as Roberta was shuffling past my bed, I asked her
where she was going. She answered quickly, "I'm looking for a piece
of my lost cause." Lost cause? Where did that come from? Was it
merely an association of words that are coupled through common
usage? When one says "lost," some would answer "key" or "glasses."
Did Roberta, by chance say, "cause?" Perhaps. Be that as it may, her
snappy answer gave me the chuckle that I needed and thus softened my approach to her.

My soft approach, however, soon evaporated. After putting her
in bed as gently as I could several more times, I told her that this
was the last time I would do it for her. If she got out of bed once
more, she would need to tuck herself in all by herself. I was not
going to help again. I went on at some length about how ridiculous
it was for me to help her go to bed only to have her immediately
pop up to ask me to help her back again. I then flopped over in my
bed and turned my back on her.

199

True to form, she soon appeared bent down in front of my face, pleading with me to help her go to bed. "Tell me how to do it just one more time." I kept my eyes closed. (I recalled a technique used by our very young children when they wanted to ignore one of us. They would say defiantly, "I'm closing my eyes at you." That is what I was doing to her.)

After repeating her request many times to my closed-eyed silence, she sobbed in anguish, "Please, Bob. Help me." Not being able to resist that plea any longer, I heaved myself out of bed.

Clearly, however, a different approach was needed. So I told her I was going to *teach* her how to go to bed, noting in my mind that I would follow the procedure I had used years ago when writing programmed instructional material—breaking down the total skill to be learned into bite-sized pieces. Walking her back to her bed, I said, "Okay, I'm going to teach you how to go to bed. I'll show you how. We will take this one step at a time. Okay?"

"Now, step one is for you to sit down on the edge of your bed." This she did eagerly. "Step two. Kick off your slippers." (Stimulus.) After she did so I said warmly, "Okay. Good work." (Reinforcement.) "Now for step three. Lift your feet up on bed and slide them under the covers." She slowly followed my instructions. "Step four. Lay your head down on your pillow." Slowly she did it. "Okaaay. Good work. Now, step five. Pull the blankets up over your shoulders." Thus she completed the whole process of going to bed with no hands-on help from me, only cues and reinforcement, following a strictly Skinnerian stimulus-response approach to teaching.

"Now you need to stay in bed," I told her sternly. Soon, however, she propped herself up on her elbow and bent her knees, preparatory to getting out of bed.

"Lie down," I shouted, thoroughly upset with her. She promptly did so. "You're in bed now. I want you to stay there and go to sleep."

"I'm trying to." Her face was contorted with distress. Clearly going to bed and staying there posed extraordinary problems to her, difficulties beyond my comprehension.

Supporting herself on her elbow once more, she changed her approach and said brightly, "I have to practice going to bed, don't

I?" What could I say? A pupil who was so eager to practice what she has just been taught warmed the heart of the teacher in me.

So she got out of bed, with my silence communicating my acquiescence if not approval, walked to the end of the bedroom, turned around and shuffled back to her bed, growling to herself, "Time to go to bed." What an act! Her father, who often did things with a flair, would have loved it. She continued this routine a half-dozen times, performing it without a hitch.

Having successfully practiced the going to bed routine, Roberta suddenly dropped her head on her pillow and, with a relaxed body, drifted off to sleep.

The next morning when she arose she said that she needed to practice going to bed. She tried to do so and became confused in the process. Alas, she had lost the smooth sequence that she had practiced the night before.

It seemed to me then that what may have happened was that Roberta had a certain amount of energy to discharge when she went to bed or woke up in the middle of the night. She had to walk or talk it off until she became too tired to continue. Then she was ready to sleep. It could be that my "teaching" her to go to bed had come at the end of her energy cycle and that she had merely dropped into bed out of sheer exhaustion. On the other hand, not being able to learn and remember new experiences is characteristic of people with Alzheimer's disease.

Yet, taking a nap was sometimes quite easy for Roberta. Once, tired after wandering around for a while she said, "I'm going to take another go-to-sleep" and did just that with no difficulty.

Late one evening, as I leaned back in my easy chair, a yellow pad in my pocket, I decided to write my wife a little note. I found out that I should have tried this before—that she sometimes seemed able to understand written messages better than oral ones. Feeling whimsical I wrote, "*Roberta, I love you mucho. Do you love me too? Your own Bob,*" and handed it to her as she was walking by.

She came behind me and kissed me on my forehead and said, "I do."

Later I handed her another note. "*You are a wonderful, sexy woman. Love you. Bob.*" She read it, smiled, and scuffed on her way.

201

On another night, as I reclined in my easy chair, Roberta pestered me to help her back to the bedroom. Telling her that I could no longer help her, I would send her back on her own. After I had pointed out the direction and got her started, I would see her turn mistakenly to the left into the kitchen or to the right toward the outside door. If she would have taken only three more steps straight ahead, she would been at the turn in the hallway. From there she could have seen the glow from the night light and followed it back to her bed. But finding herself in the darkness, she would panic and make the wrong turn before reaching the final one. She would then return and plead with me to help her.

It occurred to me to write out directions for her to return to her bed.

"Go straight ahead."

"Turn the corner and go on again."

"Go through the door to the bedroom."

She held the note up to her eyes, and after I set her on her way, she followed it and returned to the bedroom, and presumably back to her bed. I fell asleep without hearing whether she got out again or not. I did not have the occasion to try out this note-directive idea again, so I am not sure it would have had any permanent effect.

The last Sunday night in March turned into the kind of night I had dreaded and had known would be in store for me since Dark Thursday. Roberta was out of control.

The day had been difficult but not so bad, I thought, that it accounted for her unmanageable agitation at bedtime. The weekend visit with our daughter Joanne, her husband Omer, and their sons Mike and Ken had been delightful. Roberta had recognized all of them, and, as we ate a Saturday breakfast in a restaurant with Ray and Linda on hand, she acted like her former warm motherly/grandmotherly self, making the rounds, putting her hand on a shoulder, smiling and saying a word or two to each person. On Sunday morning I had prepared a hearty breakfast for us all before we headed to church. Roberta's ability to stow it away kept pace with the best of them.

Her restless legs, however, had made her miserable in church that morning. Again and again she had whispered hoarsely enough for surrounding worshipers to hear, "Let's get out of here." And, "I can't stand this a minute longer." And, "This is crazy." (Since she had been afflicted with RLS all her life, it is a wonder that worship services, where the symptoms invariably struck, had meant anything but discomfort to her.)

After church Joanne's family bade us farewell, our daughter with tears in her eyes. Much relieved of the pressure that a visit even from our loved ones placed on us, we each took a long, restful nap, followed by a quick walk in the cold, blustery afternoon, some TV watching, and a light dinner. Then it was bedtime.

At that moment the day ended and the nightmare began. Although she had been relaxed all evening and became sleepy sitting on the couch, when Roberta faced the prospect of going to bed, everything changed. She froze at the sight of it. A horde of demons descended upon her.

"Help me get into bed," she pleaded repeatedly. So I went through the Skinnerian procedure once more. Her performance was not as crisp as it had been earlier, but she managed to make the transition into bed. As usual, however, she soon propped herself up on her elbow, which is invariably the first move toward swinging her legs around and leaving the bed. No sooner was she up than she again asked me to tell her how to go to bed, as if it was the first time. This went on and on.

At one point, after she was lying down, I seated myself on the floor by her bed with my face near hers. She said she loved to look at my face. I talked as gently as I could about how much I loved her and how she could relax now and go to sleep, only to find her suddenly, despite all of my sweet talk, propping herself up on her elbow, preparatory to standing up and asking me again to tell her how to go to bed.

I adamantly refused, leading her to plead with sobbing voice for me to help her, to show her how to do it *just one more time.* When I acquiesced, with the proviso that this would be the last time I would do so, she went through the procedure, only to pop out of bed and implore me once more to show her how.

Roberta provoked me so much that I told her, much as I loved her, I could not help her, and that I was going to sleep on the couch in the living room. At Ray and Linda's home I had found that it was sometimes I who was the source of stimulation that led to her agitation. My presence kept her chattering nonstop. If I removed myself from our bed by sleeping on the futon in the hallway, she would soon slow down and find her way back to bed and to sleep. I hoped it would work again this time as I lay down on the couch and drew our Philadelphia church's bicentennial coverlet over me.

But it was not to be. Soon I heard her pleading with me from the bedroom, repeating again and again, "Robert, come back. I need you." With an expletive on the tip of my tongue, I dragged myself back to the bedroom, only to elicit a screech of terror from her as my hand touched the door knob. Her startle reflex, so strong throughout her entire life, set her screaming at the sound of the door being pushed opened.

This scene of husband struggling with Alzheimer's wife dragged on for three hours, until almost two o'clock. The rage I felt was not unlike that which I had occasionally felt when dealing long into the night with a ceaselessly crying baby.

Finally I gave up. Lacking energy to know or care what she did the rest of the night, I fell on my bed and slept. When I woke at daybreak, I found her sprawled out on her bed, as if she had flopped there, completely exhausted. I knew that she had no remembrance of what I had "taught" her about going to bed.

Sometimes I had thought that she was putting me on, seeking my attention with her "show me how to go to bed" routine. For this reason I occasionally tried to send her to bed by telling her firmly, "You know how to do it, so just go ahead and do it."

I have since come to realize that her asking me to tell her how to go to bed was a bona fide plea from her. She had actually forgotten how to do it from one transition into bed to the next. Going through our five-step routine lasted only for that specific time. I should have known that, since she had failed the simple two-step test in the doctor's office of folding a sheet of paper and placing it on the desk next to her, she actually could not have learned the five-step procedure of going to bed.

For the first time I began having doubts about how much longer I could care for Roberta by myself.

204

On the next night, I asked Roberta why she always propped herself up on her elbow, after she has been lying with her head on her pillow for a moment. She said with great sincerity, "It's because I am afraid."

"Afraid?" I asked. "Of what?"

She paused, deep in thought. She cried at last, in tears, "I don't know. I'm afraid all the time." The nameless fear that seemed to be haunting her, day and night, was held at bay during the daylight hours with various kinds of activities, but it relentlessly filled her total being at bedtime. I wondered if by propping herself up she might have been trying to see something that would not be frightening to her.

"Are you afraid of your pillow, too?" I asked, on a hunch.

"Yes. I am."

Terrified by an indescribable fear lurking just out of sight, exhausted yet unable to rest, it is little wonder that going to bed turned into a frightening ordeal for Roberta. Terror, bafflement, and sorrow coursed through the shadows of her mind where the healthy memories that had made life enjoyable for her once resided.

Many times when Roberta started to become restless I had suggested that we try singing, and I would start right in with "Shall We Gather at the River." Soon she would join in, and I would follow immediately with "God Will Take Care of You," and then "There's a Long, Long Trail." By the end of this song she usually had had enough and would call it quits. Gradually, however, singing, like warm baths, hot milk, and the cookies with which I used to ply her, had ceased to calm her spirit. Then she would begin a long session of restless wandering and getting in and out of bed, with the now familiar sound track of disjointed questions and comments.

One evening Roberta started to say to me, as she had done so many times:

"Bob, when you brought the . . ." (Pause)

"I can't think of the word." (Pause)

Roberta's face contorted and she broke out in tears. Soon they were streaming down her flushed face.

"I can't think of it. Oh, what's the matter with me?"

205

More sobbing.

"I'm so stupid." (Pause) "I can't talk to people," she said, doubt-less referring to the fact that she could not remember the words she needed.

"What's the matter with me? Can't you help me, Bob? Can't you help me find the word?"

More tears and clinging to me.

This scenario went on and off during the entire evening. Some of it may have been an obsessional repetition of words that had lost their meaning in the repeating. But the pattern must surely have originated in the pain of knowing that she could not communicate what she wanted to say because she could not remember the words that would complete her thought, and then there was the additional ache of having lost the thought altogether.

Roberta's pain did not leave even at night in her sleep. One night as I lay in my bed next to hers, I heard her muttering in her raspy voice, "What's the matter with me?"

"I'm so mixed up."

"I can't think."

"There's a dumbness in my brain today."

"I can't figure out what my trouble is."

Here was my wife, still struggling with the relentless shadows that were slowly swallowing words that had once lit up her life. The darkness was overwhelming; confusion unremitting; lostness her constant companion. Unable to find words with which to con-verse with me, she could only call out for help. In times like these, Ted's words would come to my aid. "Fear not," I could hear him say. But that message was for me, not Roberta. She had every reason to be afraid. The night was engulfing her. Although I murmured, "Don't be afraid, Roberta," it was through my embracing arms that I tried to impart to her, as best I could, the heaven-sent fortitude that my human tongue could no longer adequately convey. "God, go with her," I entreated as she journeyed ever deeper into the night.

Giving In, Getting Help

Toward the end of March, it was becoming clear that I was not go-ing to be able to care for Roberta much longer. Her nocturnal wandering and agitation were beginning to take their toll. Although I thought that I was holding up fairly well, my relatives cast a worried eye at me.

I finally called the Holland Home and told the admissions counselor that I needed to place Roberta in one of their Alzheimer's Care Units in the near future. I was informed that there were nine applicants ahead of her in the unit that was the closest to where we lived.

But the counselor said the Home would send out a nurse to evaluate Roberta's condition and determine if she was eligible for placement and/or for home care service. I thought another evaluation was ridiculous because I already had a diagnosis from a medical doctor. Evidently, their own evaluation was a necessary part of the admission process.

In a few days the nurse came to the apartment, interviewed me about my experience with Roberta, and made an assessment of her. She was apparently satisfied that Roberta was a candidate for placement and the home care service, so she said that she would send out a person who would make arrangements for us. This offered respite for me through the help of an aide who would sit for Roberta while I did whatever I needed to do for my own well-being—shop, read, nap, take a walk—a bargain at twenty dollars an hour.

The first aide was sensational, a bundle of energy and good will. Having shampooed Roberta's hair, a personal service that Roberta needed badly, but which she refused to let me do, the aide mopped the kitchen and bathroom floors and vacuumed the carpet throughout the apartment, all beyond the stipulations of her contract. Despite all these activities she still won Roberta's affection and received a hug from her when she left. The next two aides that were sent to me, however, were so unsatisfactory that I discontinued the service.

A mental health nurse from the Holland Home service gave me the most help. She made her first visit early in April. I cannot speak highly enough of her. She was wonderful with Roberta, and Roberta took to her immediately. Twice a week she visited us to check on Roberta and to talk over my caregiving problems. After discussing

Roberta's medications, she would phone Roberta's geriatrist on the spot if changes needed to be made. As a nurse she could obtain modifications more readily than I could.

Roberta's night wandering was of special concern to the mental health nurse. She pointed out how vulnerable my wife would be if she managed to slip out of the apartment. I had a gut feeling for this danger, having once lost track of her among the tall shelves of the Home Depot where we were shopping. I spent several anxious moments before a kind young man brought her back to the service desk from where I had sent out a call.

She was such an experienced nurse that for every problem I presented she had a bag full of practical answers. From her I learned much about myself. I wasn't the iron man I thought I was. Although I had managed to care for Roberta without seeming to compromise my own health, I soon encountered health issues that proved our nurse right.

She gave me useful information regarding Roberta—she was further advanced in Alzheimer's disease than I had reckoned—and offered me invaluable tips on Roberta's medications, and how to treat her with "tough love." I also looked forward to her visits because our conversations would range far beyond Roberta's disease—from Methodism, to the Dutch community, to comparing notes on our experiences raising our families.

The nursing service also provided a hot line on which I could call her or some other psychiatric nurse on duty for advice at any time, even in the dead of the night when I needed it most desperately. I availed myself of this service several times.

XVIII

Journaling for Insight

In March 2001, shortly after we moved into our new apartment, I met for the second time with the social worker associated with Roberta's geriatrist, to discuss some of the problems I was having as Roberta's caregiver. On a prescription sheet she summarized the actions that I could take to enhance that role.

- Let her sleep on the couch if she wants to.

- Take all the knobs off the stove.

- Check on getting a smoke alarm. (I found that I have one.)

- Secure both outside doors at night.

- Keep a log of Roberta: Record antecedents of the behavior, the behavior itself, and the consequences. (The social worker wanted to know, in detail, what happened before agitation started, when medications were given, how often, what time was dinner, etc. The assumption seemed to be that Roberta's agitation was the result of external stimulation.)

With the log of Roberta's behavior to study, the doctor and so-cial worker expected to be able to make a more informed assess-ment of our situation and more exact recommendations for Roberta's care. They hoped to be able to find connections between her agitated behavior, her medications, and my treatment of her.

This chapter is based on that log and gives a day-by-day ac-count of Roberta's behavior for several days and of the actions I took as her caregiver. Those who are interested can find complete information on her medications in a table in the chapter end notes, including dosage, time of administration, and for what symptom each one was prescribed.

Wednesday, March 28

I started the log immediately after picking up Roberta from Marguerite's home, where she had been during my session with the social worker. I noted that Roberta was relaxed. She said that she had had a good time at Marguerite's and expressed appreciation for the care she had been given. My sister mentioned that Roberta had napped part of the time. They had a cup of tea together, which Roberta drank one spoonful at a time. I later learned that Marguer-ite had served regular black tea. She expressed regret when I told her that caffeine, found in black tea, aggravates Roberta's restless legs syndrome.

On the drive back to our apartment I reminded Roberta that Susan Ellis from Philadelphia was coming for dinner that night. I asked her if she remembered Susan, and she said that she did.

Roberta was at loose ends while I whipped through dinner preparation, making stuffed mushrooms and other goodies for the visit. Although she did not seem to be agitated, nor did she com-plain about being confused, she needed to walk. She alternately stretched out on the couch and on my bed, but dozed off only once. She no sooner picked up the *USA Today* and made as if to read it than she laid it down, no longer capable of reading a newspaper.

I expressed surprise that she wanted to go outdoors when later she suggested that we should take a walk. "Oh, no," she said. "I mean walking around in here." So we took several turns around the apartment, arm in arm.

One of my most important responsibilities as Roberta's caregiver was to administer her medications on schedule. They were to be given according to the times specified by the doctor and the mental health nurse. Shortly after 5:30 P.M. I gave her her "sundown" medication for mood disorders. Late afternoon is often a restless time for people with Alzheimer's and this "sundown" medication was given to counteract agitation at this time.

Susan arrived early in the evening carrying a large pot of beautiful daisies. Roberta smiled at her, and they gave each other a big hug. Susan offered Roberta a cheerful, "How are you?" She responded with a smile and a wispy, "Just fine."

The three of us sat around the table for the light meal I served. Although Roberta was not seriously restless or driven, she left the table and wandered around the room. She joined us for a toast to the apartment and our future—Susan and me with wine, Roberta with apple juice. We continued our conversation, trying to include Roberta wherever we could. She responded briefly each time and then again drifted away from the table, at one time even lying on the floor.

Susan told me later that, while I was preparing the meal, Roberta had said to her, "I don't understand everything that's going on, but I trust Bob and will do whatever he says. I know he will do the right thing." I was deeply moved upon hearing this. Roberta was aware of her incapacity, yet felt secure in the care I was giving her.

Susan left after a couple of hours and I loaded the dishwasher, with Roberta bringing things from the table at my request. She did not need to be cued into the task and soon had the table completely cleared. We chatted about what a good time we had had, and what a great person Susan is.

Having finished the dishwashing, I gave Roberta her medications for the night: a pill to relieve anxiety and cause drowsiness, one to retard memory loss and thinking ability (which I call her "Alzheimer's pill"), and two to relieve her RLS. Returning to the living room, Roberta dropped into her reclining chair and I into mine. She was relaxed and sat without comment while I made a call on my cordless speaker phone (my new toy) to a friend in Philadelphia. After a half-hour Roberta began to nod her head, so I suggested that we retire for the night. She agreed readily, and we walked arm-in-arm to our bedroom. She showed no signs of agitation at this time.

She unbuttoned her shirt on her own and got out of her bra with my help. After donning her new nightgown with buttons running down from the neck line, she pointed to them and said something inarticulate. I could see she was dissatisfied with the gown and asked her if she would rather wear her older one with the plain front. She said yes, and I helped her into it. In a half-hour we had completed our undressing process without further incident and were ready for bed, both commenting on how tired we were.

Roberta got under the covers without my help and put her head down on her pillow. Only once did she rear up as if to get out of bed. I told her to stay where she was. Relaxing once more, she was asleep in ten minutes. I drifted off soon afterward.

About an hour after midnight I awoke to find the light on my bedstand lit, the door open and light streaming in from the hallway. I hurried out to find Roberta standing in the hallway wearing my green zipper-front sweatshirt over her nightgown, which told me that she had raided my clothes closet.

"What are you doing out here?" I asked. She gave no answer, and when I walked her back to her bed she readily climbed back in. I pulled the covers over her shoulders and went out to assess the damage. I found the light on in the second bedroom, which I was using as a study, and in the bathroom across the hall from it. She had removed the folding chair that I had jammed under the door handle of the outside door, which now stood unlocked and slightly open. The kitchen light was on; there on the counter was an orange and a dish of left-over gravy. A light in the living room was also lit.

Back in the bedroom, I found Roberta standing by my bed. I suggested we get something to eat and, on the way to the kitchen, I gave her the prescribed sleeping pill. While I was microwaving two mugs of milk, she told me what she had been eating. She showed me the meringue partly eaten off the lemon pie in the refrigerator. A piece of cheddar cheese, scraped away at an angle, lay on the counter. On another counter I found the cheese shredder with cheese and a bit of meringue stuck on it. She said that she had also eaten a slice of bread and some applesauce. In spite of her heavy raid on the refrigerator, she repeatedly said how hungry she was.

After we had downed our mugs of warm milk along with some cookies, I said we should go back to bed. She got into bed without assistance. As the sleeping pill began to take hold she yawned and drifted off to sleep. So did I. By then it was 2:00 A.M.

Thursday, March 29

Roberta woke up about 8:15 A.M. and shuffled into the study where I was entering the log on my computer. Her brow was knit in a questioning way. We hugged for a moment, and then she beckoned me to come into our bedroom. She had already made my bed; hers was still rumpled. Pointing to her bed as if it were a problem, she tried without success to articulate what bothered her. "Let's make it," I said. She assented and we soon had it done. Then she lay down on my bed and prepared to sleep. No sooner had I placed a coverlet over her, however, than she roused up again. Shortly thereafter, I gave her the prescribed morning medications.

Not wanting to get dressed yet, she allowed me to slip a robe on her. While I prepared breakfast, Roberta walked around the apartment and lay down on the couch a couple of times. She ate without help the large bowl of oatmeal I served her. At the close of the meal she said to me, "Something is wrong with me, isn't there."

"Yes." I replied, "There is."

"What is it?" she asked.

"Something is wrong with your head."

She rose from her chair and looked at me with what for the first time looked like fear in her eyes. "That's scary!"

"Yes it is," I agreed.

After a long pause she said quietly, "Well, I guess we will just have to go on."

What a soldier she is!

Like so many things in the recent past, however, that short conversation may soon have been forgotten. I believe, however, that the fear remained.

Roberta watched me as I washed the dishes, and, after I helped her dress, she walked around the apartment for a while. Before shaving I had found an unflushed bowel movement in the toilet, and her dry diaper on the floor by the side of it. Knowing that she disliked wearing the diaper I was not surprised that she had stepped out of it. Indeed, having to go to the toilet may have been what started the nocturnal wandering episode. I was thankful that she had still been continent at that moment. While I was shaving she returned to my bed, where she slept for an hour.

After that, while I was phoning my sister, Roberta alternately walked around, sat down, and sometimes lay down, until just before noon, at which time she took another nap on the couch. During her wandering she had come to me several times with something to say, which, however, she couldn't complete, such as, "We have to get those . . ." She paused, tried to remember what it was, and then made motions with her hands, but she could not verbalize what she wanted to say. "Yes, I guess we should," I replied, not knowing what she was talking about. That affirmation satisfied her, and she went on with her walking.

At lunch she showed her usual resistance to, or perhaps fear of, food, asking me again and again if it was all right for her to eat the minestrone soup and toasted cheese sandwiches. And as often happened, she walked around in the living-dining area between each bite of food.

I napped for an hour and she for three with a half-hour break midway through. Late in the afternoon we left to shop for household things, and to get some exercise by walking in a large superstore. Unfortunately, the old-fashioned doorstop with which to secure our bedroom door against her nighttime wandering was not to be found there.

We returned in time for me to give Roberta her sundown medication for emotional and mood management, followed by a glass of ginger ale and a few cashew nuts.

Determined that Roberta would not go to bed hungry as she had apparently done the night before, I prepared an evening meal of pork chops cooked in stewed tomato sauce and peas, my mother's recipe. I also prepared a side dish of boiled potatoes and gravy. For dessert I served slices of the lemon meringue pie, which bore traces of her nocturnal snacking. She cleared the table while I loaded the dishes into the dishwasher; it was reminiscent of the style of working together that we used to enjoy.

While I watched the "News Hour," Roberta was agitated and surely not ready for bed. Halfway through the program I gave her the evening medications. She took off her sweatshirt, saying she was hot. A little later she took off her shoes. She alternated between walking around and snuggling up to me on the couch while I continued watching TV, which Roberta said she found "scary." During the commercials we strolled through the apartment with my arm around her. She responded positively to these physical contacts. Several times she declared that she was confused and didn't know who she was. I responded that all I could do was to hold her tight. She relaxed when I did so.

At 9:30 P.M. we got ready for bed, and by 10:00 P.M. we were in bed. She lay down quietly, without any fussing about my helping her, and within fifteen minutes she was asleep. I jammed the bedroom door with a spatula from the kitchen serving as a makeshift doorstop (easily removed if we needed to exit the room in an emergency).

Well after midnight Roberta woke me up, asking to get in bed with me. I consented, but within a minute she was up and out again. This went on a couple more times. At last I suggested that we go to the kitchen for a mug of warm milk. She was delighted with the suggestion. On the way there I took her into the bathroom and gave her an over-the-counter sleeping tablet, which I myself occasionally use. We chatted amiably as we finished the lemon meringue pie and warm milk.

Once again she bedded herself down without my help. I heard her tossing and turning, however, and she was soon by my bedside asking to come in to bed with me, addressing me as, "My lord."

"May I come into bed with you, my lord?"

"Is it all right if I walk around, my lord?" I must say, being addressed this way tickled me. She repeatedly got in and out of bed to shuffle around the bedroom. She seemed not to be agitated, and did not ask for help in getting into her bed. I inquired if her legs

215

were restless, and she said that they were. She asked me several times if she could get in bed with me (my lord), and when I declined because, I said, she would just get out again in a minute, she was not upset. She merely said, "All right," and went on her way. Perhaps she thought it best not to upset his lordship. Because her legs were restless, I debated whether to give her another tablet to ease her restless legs syndrome, but decided against it. Moreover, she did not approach the bedroom door at any time. Apparently my prior strong words about not leaving the bedroom at night had registered and were retained. I fell asleep while she was still up and around.

At about 4:00 A.M. I woke up and saw, as I got out of bed, that she was soundly asleep. I went about my devotions and customary early morning activities of reading and responding to my Internet correspondence and, now, writing this log.

Friday, March 30

At 9:00 A.M. Roberta woke up looking very sleepy, having nothing to say. She did say, "Yes," when I asked, "Would you like a glass of OJ?" After drinking the juice, she went back to bed while I showered and shaved. When I returned to the bedroom she said, "I don't know what is the matter with me. Can you help me? Do you know what it is?"

"Well, I know the name for it," I said. "It's Alzheimer's disease. But I don't know what it is."

Later she said, "I'm not doing well. Help me!"

I hugged her. "I'd like to. Just let me hold you."

After a moment or two she said quietly, "I'm okay." Again, her strength, in the face of the awful future, which I felt sure she knew awaited her, brought tears to my eyes. I was frustrated at my inability to carry this discussion to a more fruitful end.

About 9:30 A.M. we had breakfast of scrambled eggs, sausages, and toast and jelly. She wolfed it down, including spearing a sausage off my plate and transferring to her own. I gave her the usual morning medications.

216

The mental health nurse from the home care program called at 10:00 A.M. saying that she would be visiting us in a half hour, so I got Roberta dressed. She was very agreeable about the clothes I suggested and, in general, was quite pleasant.

At 10:30 A.M. Roberta resumed her morning nap.

I consulted with the nurse from 10:30 till well past noon. Then Roberta walked into the room. The nurse asked her how she was, and she said, "I'm fine." She responded positively to the nurse's conversation, and to having her blood pressure and pulse taken. When asked what her name was, she replied "Roberta Geraldine DeHaan." She had not used her given middle name for years, giving instead her maiden name, Timmer. When asked, however, what day of the week it was, she did not know. She did not know what 100 minus 7 was. What a fall from our first math class in college, I thought. When the nurse told her "93," Roberta got out of her chair and walked away. For the rest of the visit she alternated between sitting and pacing around.

After the nurse left at about 12:30 P.M., we had lunch of my homemade onion soup and hot garlic bread, which Roberta ate without once getting up to walk around.

At around 1:30 P.M. I began my nap, as did Roberta. I woke up an hour later to find her still lying on the davenport. She told me she had looked at me as I napped but decided not to disturb me. I also noted that her chair had been moved, indicating that she might not have slept much.

We left to do some grocery shopping at 3:00 P.M. As we made our rounds of the aisles, she pushed the shopping cart, using it as a walker; I pulled and steered it from the front. Soon after we started, she complained of being tired and began looking around for a place to sit down, which she continued to do during the entire shopping trip.

Returning home at about 4:30 P.M. she sat down and/or wandered around while I put the groceries away. After I finished that chore, we had a glass of ginger ale and some cashews. She sipped and nibbled but didn't finish either.

I gave her a "sundown" medication at 5:00 P.M. While I puttered around the kitchen area making supper, she paced the floor and flopped down on the couch, seeming to be mildly agitated.

After our supper of boiled potatoes, gravy, boiled carrots, and sliced tomatoes, which she had to be encouraged to finish, we sat down on the davenport and watched the news. Roberta tried to make herself comfortable by having me hug her and hugging me in return, by lying with her head on my lap or with her head on a pillow, and by walking around. She said she was very uncomfortable. At 7:30 P.M. I gave her the scheduled evening medications. After we had a dish of ice cream at 9:00 P.M., we started to get ready for bed.

Going to bed did not go as smoothly as it had the night before. Roberta complained of being cold, so I allowed her to get in bed with me. I felt her body warm and begin to jerk a bit as it sometimes does while falling asleep. After about fifteen minutes I suggested that she go to her own bed so that I too could get some sleep. She complied, but as soon as she laid her head on her pillow, she roused up saying, "I'm afraid." Looking down at her pillow she said, "This makes me afraid." Feeling that this was more of a mantra than a genuine complaint, I told her that she had nothing to fear because I was taking care of her. This calmed her momentarily. She roused up again and again, wanting to know exactly how she had come to bed. I recounted how it had been. Pulling her blankets up to her chin, turning over on her right side, then her left side, then on her back, she told me again how uncomfortable she was. She wanted me to tell her how to go to sleep. I said, "You get in bed and go to sleep." She made a cadence out of it, saying it over and over to herself. At one point she exclaimed, "God, why is everything so complex?" Several times she got out of bed, asking me to hug her, which I did. She also asked to get in bed with me again, which I refused saying it wouldn't work. Finally, at about 10:00 P.M., I heard her snoring lightly and, looking over at her, I saw her lying on her back sound asleep.

Saturday, March 31

At about 7:30 A.M. I heard Roberta calling me quietly, and went to her bed to see what was up. She was full of questions, "What are we doing here?" and "What are we going to do next?" I asked her if she would like a glass of juice and, while she was relaxing and sipping the juice, I got dressed. Since she seemed wide awake I suggested that we have breakfast. She liked the idea. During breakfast I was momentarily away from the table getting her morning medications, which I thought she might take with her breakfast, when I heard her call, "Bob, come here quick. I need you." The tone in her voice told me this was an emergency. She was standing in the hallway, holding up her nightgown. "Do you need to go to the john?" I asked. "Yes," she moaned. I got her there just in time. Going back to where she had been standing, I saw a small mess on the carpet, and as she was finishing up in the bathroom, I swabbed the carpet clean.

After that mishap I finished breakfast with her, put the dishes in the dishwasher, and gave her the morning medications. Then, having shaved and dressed, at 8:45 A.M. I came out of the bathroom and saw her asleep on my bed.

She did not sleep long. She was soon up and around for the next couple of hours, while I did chores around the house. Then we took a walk down to the apartment office to pay our rent. Back at the apartment, she paced the floor, sometimes lying down on the couch or my bed, sometimes sitting in her chair, repeating her chant over and over again, "What is the matter with me?" and, "I'm so mixed up."

She had to be persuaded to eat her soup, sandwiches, and milk at lunch time, questioning again and again, "May I do this?" before taking a bite. Although I took a short nap after lunch, she did not sleep. During this entire Saturday, Roberta did not take a nap.

We drove to a hair salon at about 2:30 P.M. for Roberta to have her hair shampooed, colored, and cut. It was badly needed. I should, however, have given her a medication for emotional and mood disorders to calm her agitation. Mindful of restlessness, I circled the shopping mall with her, trying to walk off the problem before going into the salon.

The actual process was worse than I feared. Fortunately, I was allowed to stay with her as she sat in the chair, waiting for the hairdresser to begin. Once the service began Roberta was extremely uneasy. Getting her hair colored and sitting under the hair dryer, terrified her. Her mouth trembled, she clutched my hand, her legs were restless, she frequently started to get up and walk around. Finally, I could no longer talk her out of it, and occasionally allowed her to get up from under the dryer for a short break. About a half hour later (which seemed more like an hour), her hair was colored, shampooed, trimmed, and blown dry. Throughout the ordeal, the hairdresser had been very reassuring, but Roberta was as near to panic as I had ever seen her.

After this ordeal we stopped at Ray and Linda's home. We no sooner entered their house than she wanted to leave. She was still agitated, and even though Linda tried taking her for a walk outside twice, and inside around the rooms several times, she would not calm down. Three-quarters of an hour later we left.

Although the first thing I did back at the apartment was to give my wife her medication to calm her, it did not help much. While I sat on the davenport, she alternated between sitting next to me, putting her head on my lap, wanting to be hugged, and hopping up and pacing around. I decided I might just as well watch the Michigan State–Arizona basketball game.

Later, I prepared dinner, which she needed help to eat. She was agitated throughout and spent the time pacing around, stopping by the table to get a bite from me. Sometimes I loaded the fork and set it on her plate; when she came by she picked it up and ate the food. At other times I would actually feed her. She finished the entire meal in this manner and then helped me clear the table.

I gave her the evening medications at about 7:30 P.M. She was on a talking binge, asking questions I could not answer, such as, "What are we doing here?" No matter what I did she continued to be agitated. I asked her if she would like to watch the "Lawrence Welk" show. She said she would, but then paid no attention to it. She tried sitting next to me, having me hold her, putting her head on my lap. None of these activities lasted more than a few seconds, however, and she would be up and pacing again. So I chatted with her as best I could while keeping one eye on the TV.

After eating some ice cream for dessert at about 9:00 P.M., we both agreed it was time to go to bed, although I knew she was not really ready. We slipped again into the pattern of her wanting me to show her how to do it, telling me she was afraid, and my telling her I couldn't help her. To interrupt this sometimes heated conversation, I suggested we have a snack of hot milk and an oatmeal cookie. She downed these enthusiastically. I then told her she could sleep wherever she wanted to—on the couch, in my bed, or her own bed, (as per instructions from the social worker). She said she only wanted to be next to me. (So much for that instruction.) Not knowing what else to do, I again turned to the TV and watched a basketball game while she paced around, asking me to help her. I walked her to the bed a couple of times, and after that told her she would have to put herself to bed while I slept on the couch. That did not work, either. From the bedroom she begged me to help her, or she would come out to the living room to make her urgent request. Finally, I said that if she would get herself as far the bed she could call me and I would come and help her in. Remarkably, she went all the way to the bedroom, but then I heard nothing. Was she in bed, sleeping? After a bit I peeked into the bedroom, and there she lay, under the blankets, fast asleep. It was 11:00 P.M. when I tumbled into bed.

Three hours later, I heard Roberta shuffling around. With half an eye I watched her as she walked back to her bed and with ease got into it, lay down, and pulled the covers up to her chin. Although she tossed and turned awhile, she eventually went to sleep.

Sunday, April 1

I decided to waken Roberta at about 8:00 A.M., rather than letting her sleep, even though she had had a rather short night. I had decided that we should go to church that morning instead of sitting around the house, depressed, in the dreary early spring weather.

To my surprise, she woke in a wonderful mood, expressing appreciation for the glass of juice I brought her. As I prepared breakfast, she continued to doze in bed. Before escorting her to the table at 8:30 A.M., I gave her the morning allotment of medications. She ate the entire breakfast with little help from me.

Since I told her we would sit on an aisle seat in church so that we could leave easily if her legs became restless, she was very co-operative in getting dressed and did not object to the prospect of attending the worship service. Occasionally a complex explanation like that will click with her. In church she had no problem sitting still, and dozed repeatedly during the sermon.

Roberta continued in her pleasant mood after we returned home around 11:30 A.M. She did not pace the floor but did lie down occasionally on the couch while I prepared lunch. During the meal, she ate without pacing around the room, needing little help or cues to finish the meal.

I slept soundly during my nap until 2:30 P.M., but Roberta said she did not sleep much. At about 4:00 P.M. we took a walk around the apartment complex, she all the while complaining how tired her legs were. When we returned about a half-hour later, I gave her the sundown medication and her RLS pill. We drank some ginger ale and then had dinner shortly after 6:00 P.M. For the third time that day she ate her meal without leaving the table and also with little prompting or help from me.

That evening, I asked her if she would like to watch "60 Minutes," and she said yes. Midway through the show, I gave her the Alzheimer's medicine and vitamin E for her restless legs. We returned to the davenport and dozed off and on in each other's arms for the next hour or so, glancing occasionally to the TV. Later in the evening Roberta asked for another helping of potatoes left over from dinner. After I heated a serving in the microwave and generously buttered them, she downed them as if she had not eaten an evening meal.

Following the TV show I made the mistake of offering her ice cream for dessert. I suspected it may have loaded her system with too much sugar and kept her from falling asleep easily. Although she went to bed without difficulty at about 9:00 P.M., she did not drop off to sleep. She became more and more active until I suggested we have a mug of warm milk and a cookie. Upon downing the first cookie she asked for another. Not wanting her to ingest

222

any more sugar, I persuaded her to have some peanuts instead. That snack did the trick, and she fell asleep around 9:30 P.M.

Hearing her padding around at 1:30 P.M. I awoke and again suggested a round of hot milk and a cookie. On the way out of the bedroom, I noted that the door had been opened about an eighth of an inch, indicating that she had tried to exit the room while I was asleep, but had been prevented from doing so by my improvised doorstop. We stopped at the bathroom for an over-the-counter sleeping pill. The snack and pill did the trick, and she was soon back asleep.

With this, I ended the log.

Five days later, I spent what must have been my worst night ever with Roberta. The day had been a busy one, and by about 8:30 P.M. we were in bed. Roberta rested quietly on her back for a few moments, then roused up on her elbow, sat up, and finally swung her legs to the floor. Knowing what lay ahead, I felt my heart sink with apprehension. Roberta was soon pacing the floor in an agitated shuffle, muttering mostly unintelligible remarks to herself and me. Occasionally she asked if she could get in bed with me. After allowing it a couple of times only to have her pile out in about thirty seconds, I finally refused. This pattern repeated itself until 11:00 P.M.

At that time I gave her medication to relieve anxiety and cause drowsiness, hoping to slow her down. It made no difference. Finally, I told her that I had to get some sleep, and I was going to do so in the living room. She paid no attention. From my reclining chair I could hear her pacing back and forth until about 1:30 A.M., at which time I stole back for a look. Like a caged animal, she strode back and forth down the hallway between her bed and the little office beyond the master bathroom. She stared straight ahead and did not seem to notice my standing in the doorway. At one point she mumbled, "Well, I guess you know where I'm going. I'm going home. Good night, everybody." I wondered, sorrowfully, where she imagined she was. This driven, delusional pacing continued for about thirty minutes.

At one point she came toward me as I was standing just inside the doorway to our second bedroom. Coming within two feet of me, she looked into the room, unaware of my presence. The hair on my legs prickled as I could almost feel the heat of her body. "Okay, who's there?" she barked. I held my breath. Slowly she moved on. Still hoping to get some rest, I returned to my easy chair.

As I stretched out in my chair to sleep, with only the dim glow of the night light in the room, I could hear her calling to me from the bedroom, "Please, Bob. Come and help me." I did not respond, determined to ignore her and let her settle down on her own. Soon, however, through half-opened eyes I saw her wraithlike figure come around the corner of the hallway. I heard the soft shuffle of her slippers and watched her feel her way down the darkened corridor, searching for me, ghostly in her white nightgown. First, she looked toward the outside door; then she peered into the kitchen. My spine tingled as I watched her dim form slowly approach me as she called shakily, "Robert, are you there?" I held my breath, hoping she would give up and return to her room. When at last she reached me, however, I was ready to hold her hand and say, "Here I am." The eerie spell was broken. I knew that Roberta had just enacted her journey into the shadows, hoping to find someone or something to help her find her way out. I put my arm around her and led her to the bedroom.

After fussing around back in the bedroom, trying to get her to lie down, I hurried her, none too gently I admit, toward her bed. Then, for the first time ever, she lashed out at me, smacking me on my shoulder with her fist. "Don't you ever do that to me again!" she snapped. "I'm not going to bed." When I did finally convince her to lie down, I sat on the floor next to her bed as I had done before, with my face close to hers, talking quietly, making amends for having pushed her. She seemed to relax, and my hopes rose, thinking I might have calmed her at last. Seconds later, she popped up on her elbow, saying, "I've got to get up so I can go to bed," again failing to grasp that she was already there. Later while lying down she asked, "When should I go to bed?" Some part of her still tried to please me and to do what I wanted her to.

224

Still she could not get to sleep. It was 2:30 A.M. when, exhausted as I was, I decided to give her a prescribed sleeping pill as a last resort, along with some warm milk and peanuts. One of the side effects of over-medication, I had been told, is that the patient becomes unstable and loses balance. So it happened to Roberta. She went lurching back and forth between the little office and her bed, sometimes bouncing off one wall and then the other. I stood by ready to catch her; and after thirty minutes or so, as the side-effects of the pill began to wear off, she started to regain her balance and walk normally.

I could stay awake no longer, and at about 4:00 A.M. I drifted off into an uneasy sleep. Roberta fell asleep sometime during this period and slept until 7:00 A.M.

I was hardly ready to face the next day. Fortunately, the mental health nurse was scheduled to visit us at 10:00 A.M., and I looked forward to discussing the previous night's events with her.

Her comment on my tale was that Roberta's agitation and apparent hallucinations had probably been precipitated by the previ ous day's excitement. My take on the night, however, was that the medications didn't do anything to stop her agitation, which, once started, fed on itself and took on a life of its own. After consulting with Roberta's geriatrist on the phone, the nurse came back to me with a new schedule of medications and instructions to slow Roberta down during the day.

This I did. I had already given Roberta her morning medication for mood disorders. I was instructed to give her another one at 2:00 P.M., a tablet to relieve anxiety and cause drowsiness at 5:00 P.M., and a prescription sleeping pill at 10:00 P.M. The doctor ruled out the restless legs medication, saying that she feared it made my wife agitated. I disagreed, but was willing to give her new regimen a try. I did nothing all day but pay attention to Roberta. We took two short drives. One to a deli to pick up some milk and a half-gallon of vanilla ice cream (no chocolate, which is a stimulant). The second drive took us to our storage area, where we picked up a small table for the living room. We had a quiet lunch—with no TV, and none of my scurrying around the apartment doing chores.

The result was totally wonderful. That evening Roberta got ready for bed with no resistance whatever and lay down quietly on her bed. We sang, "Shall We Gather at the River," and she sweetly dropped off to sleep. She woke at 11:00 P.M., and when I gave her the prescribed sleeping pill, went back to sleep immediately. At 2:30 A.M. she awoke again, so I gave her an over-the-counter sleeping pill, plus warm milk and an oatmeal cookie, and once more she promptly slept. I enjoyed the blessing of almost a full night of sleep and wakened much refreshed, ready to face the day with enthusiasm.

The unhurried day and the new schedule of medications had worked wonders for Roberta during the previous night. Now I had to figure out how to finish the task of sorting the stack of mail that Ray and Linda had brought over, go shopping for necessary groceries, finish the half-read newspaper, and plan to have occasional visitors, all without upsetting Roberta. In short, I concluded that if I spent my entire day caring exclusively for her, we could probably continue to have peaceful nights. Feeling it was worth the effort, I determined to do what I could to meet the challenge so that we could continue living together as long as possible.

The mental health nurse had recommended that I find an adult day-care center to which I could take Roberta a couple of days a week. That would free time for me to do necessary household chores. I resolved to locate such a facility by Roberta's birthday on April 22.

One of the benefits of a slower pace of living was that Roberta not only calmed down, but also became more companionable. While she continued to hallucinate occasionally, she also had extended spells in which she seemed to be in touch with the real world. On Saturday evening, while I fried hamburgers for supper, we chatted amiably as I told her about each step of the meal preparation. Then, during the meal, we both commented on how good the hamburgers tasted.

If our medication schedule would hold up, and if I could keep our days simple, I hoped to be able to enjoy life with Roberta for whatever length of time God would give us together.

Fast forward: Months later, after I had committed Roberta to an Alzheimer's unit and was living alone in the apartment, I was occasionally flooded with a surge of panic as I turned out the lights in the living area before retiring for the night. The darkness still called forth the ghost that shuffled toward me in the dark shadows of the hallway on that night early in April. A residue of the dread still rose in my chest. I would gladly part with that apprehension when I moved from this apartment.

Roberta's medications

The medication regimen on the following page was in effect during the time that I kept the log. The list was modified as the doctor and nurses tried to find the right combinations to address her multiple problems—Alzheimer's disease, restless legs syndrome, and the other problems implied in the last column. This is provided to readers as an example of one patient's regimen and in no way represents a recommendation for pharmaceutical treatment. Caregivers should view this only as anecdotal material and consult their physicians for individual treatment.

Medication	When administered/ Dosage	Effects
Risperdal	At breakfast, 0.50 mg 5:30 P.M., 0.25 ("sundown pill")	Treats emotional and mood disorders
Aricept	8:30 P.M., 10 mg	Treats loss of memory and thinking ability associated with Alzheimer's disease
Lorazepam	8:30 P.M., 1 mg	Relieves anxiety and causes drowsiness
Atavan	Replaced Lorazepam	Relieves anxiety and causes drowsiness
Mirapex	8:30 P.M.	Eases restless legs syndrome
Vitamin E	8:30 P.M., 800 IUs	Eases restless legs syndrome
Iron Folic Plus	At breakfast	Eases restless legs syndrome
Evista	At breakfast, 0.5 mg	Retards bone density loss
Synthroid	At breakfast, 0.125 mg	Treats hypothyroidism
Ambien	8:30 P.M. and at my direction	Treats insomnia (short-term)
Unisom (Doxylamine Succinate)	At night at my discretion	Treats insomnia (over-the-counter)

XIX

The End of Companionship

Despite my hopes, as April wore on, it became increasingly obvious that I would soon need to place Roberta in the Alzheimer's care unit. Her agitation and wandering at night were taking their toll on both of us. Sleep deprivation and physical exhaustion were draining me. Moreover, having nine applicants ahead of Roberta on the waiting list made the situation increasingly desperate. My feelings of having come to the end of my ability to continue caring for her by myself crested on Wednesday, April 18. The next day, however, events happened that convinced me that the everlasting arms were not only around us, but were working for us. I sent the following e-mail on the Internet.

Dear family and friends,

It started with several bad nights in the past ten days in which I was up with Roberta until three or four o'clock in the morning, with her pacing around, talking incessantly, and repeatedly asking me questions I couldn't answer. These nights left me not only completely exhausted but also depressed. They told me that I had come to the end of what I can do for Roberta and that profes-

sionals who could carry on the next stage of her care needed to take charge. It was not an easy conclusion to reach, as you all can imagine.

On Thursday I received a call from the Director of Admissions informing me that there was an opening for Roberta in the Verblaauw[1] Alzheimer's Care Unit of the Fulton Manor, part of the Holland Home system. Did I want to act on it?

It was a call that I needed desperately. Yet it hit me like a physical blow to my chest. I crumpled on a chair for a moment, holding my head in my hands. Being suddenly confronted with the necessity of making this decision left me unable to function for awhile. Although I had known that there would be an opening someday, I did not expect it so soon. I felt a deep sense of guilt at having to make this decision while she was completely unaware of the outcome. All the while she was engrossed in her deadly struggle with the relentless foe within herself, and I was unable to help her in this fight. Anger and sorrow flowed through me as I realized that she could not and would not be able to win the war.

This is truly the beginning of the end.

I'll keep you posted on the events as they unfold.

Bob

I asked the mental health nurse who visited us later in the day whether it was time to place Roberta in the treatment center, based on her experience and what she knew of Roberta and me. Her answer was strongly affirmative, as if she had been waiting for me to ask the question for a long time. My relatives also agreed. They all confirmed the answer that my head had been trying to tell my heart the past few days.

One reason that the call from the admissions counselor had caught me by surprise was that, having been informed earlier that nine applicants preceded Roberta on the waiting list, I had settled down for a long haul of caring for Roberta. I later learned that there were only four ahead of her at the Verblaauw Unit, on the Fulton campus, another division of the Holland Home. I also found out from the nurse that admission is not based solely on first-come-first-served status. *Need* is also an admission criterion. I suspected that my imminent collapse, probably communicated by the mental health nurse to the admissions committee, tipped the scales in favor of Roberta.

On the next day, Sam sent me the following e-mail, with the subject line reading, *"Of the End, perhaps . . ."*

Dear Bob,

Oh, my, my, such a heart-tearing e-mail from you. All of the shadows have gathered too quickly about dear Roberta, though they have been lurking there all along. What I think is happening to you is that whatever you may have been holding out as inklings of hope have now been dashed upon the jagged rocks of reality, and the realization has come that we—you, especially—are losing this lovely soul. When Arthur John Gossip, noted Scots Presbyterian preacher, lost his wife, who died suddenly during surgery at age 36, he mounted the pulpit the following Sunday and preached a magnificent sermon: "But When Life Tumbles In, What Then?"

And dear Robert, you don't need me to remind you that life has tumbled in on you. I'm quoting from Gossip now:

"Some things have become very clear to me. This to begin, that faith works, fulfills itself, is real; and that its most audacious promises are true. Always we must try to remember that the glorious assertions of the Scriptures are not mere suppositions and guesses. There is no perhaps about them. These splendid truths are flowers that human hands like ours plucked in the gardens of their actual experience. Why is the prophet so sure that as one whom his mother comforts so will God comfort all hurt things? How did the Psalmist know that those who are broken in their hearts and grieved in their minds God heals? Because, of course, it had happened to them, because they had themselves in their dark days felt His

231

unfailing helpfulness and tenderness and the touch of
wonderfully gentle hands. And it is true. When we are
cast into some burning fiery furnace seven times heated,
we are not alone, never alone; but there is One beside
us, like unto the Son of God. When our feet slip upon
slimy stones in the swelling of Jordan, a hand leaps out
and catches us and steadies us. 'I will not leave you
comfortless,' said Christ. Nor does He. There is a Presence with us, a Comforter, a Fortifier who does
strengthen, does uphold, does bring us through somehow from hour to hour and day to day. Pusey once wrote
that when his wife died, he felt 'as if the rushing waters
were up to my chin; but underneath the chin there is a
hand, supporting it.' And that hand is there. And as the
days go by, what grows upon one more and more is the
amazing tenderness of God."

*God does comfort all hurt things, and he does not leave
us comfortless. Depend upon it. Nearly two years ago
now, when I first shared with Ted that I was very concerned about what was happening to Roberta, he, as I've
told you before, advised me to talk with you. For some
reason, I thought that would indeed be intruding, so, as
you know, I did not. But something else he said has stuck
with me; he ruminated that in your hands Roberta could
have no finer care. And that is what you have done—
cared for her lovingly, unselfishly, devotedly. And now
relinquishing her to the trained and professional care
in an Alzheimer's center is the finest care you could possibly provide for her.*

*I wish I could offer words that will help you. I don't know
such words. But do know that you are surrounded by the
prayers and love of a host of people who want to share
your burden. Your cross is too heavy to carry, Bob. Angels are being sent to strengthen you in your agony.*

Love,

Sam

In response to his e-mail I wrote:

Dear Sam,

How can I thank you enough for the comforting and strengthening words of your last post, and those of Arthur John Gossip. You are a tower of strength, and absolutely right. The time has come to give Roberta more than I can give her—tender, professional care. I have made my peace with this decision . . .

Having come to terms with my own emotions, I called the admissions counselor for the Verblaauw Unit and told her that I was prepared to have Roberta admitted. She said that the room would be ready for her on May 3.

The next day I sent an e-mail to my network of relatives and friends announcing my decision.

A flood of e-mail from family and friends filled my Internet mailbox. Those who had passed through deep waters with loved a one were particularly helpful to me. Here is a sample of what I received:

. . . My heart aches for you, and even though you made the correct choice, it is a lonely and frightening place to be. "Could we have done more?" "Should I have done more?" "There must be other and better choices!" You can not help but think this way . . . for this is your heart speaking. Then your head answers, and as harsh as the final answer is, you slowly begin to realize it is the right one. . . .

. . . My mother was in the Verblaauw unit—they were gentle, caring people. It was good for me, too. I could be caring and supporting when I visited. My knowledge of my mother and her background kept me still valuable to her care. Sometimes, because of our family history together, I would have special information to make me a unique advocate for her. . . .

That note hinted at a matter I didn't appreciate until later. The family must continue to keep in touch with their loved one, even in such a well run unit as the Verblaauw. There are times when the family members need to act as advocate for their loved one since

233

they alone know that person's history, and may need to make suggestions or ask questions about the treatment he/she is receiving.

> *. . . I grieve with you. It is so difficult to think of Roberta in her present situation. My mother went this way, so I can empathize. In fact, I relive that loss as you live this one. I suppose one thing that helped me was remembering that what her situation meant to my Mother was different from what it meant to me. That is, she experienced her life from inside while I experienced it from outside, and I tended to think she felt what I did about it. You were with Roberta during the most painful and frightening part of her decline and made that transition as loving and supportive as was possible for her. . . .*

> *. . . I'm so sorry I am not there to give you a hug, or hold your hand as you struggle and live these hard days and nights. Roberta seems to be moving on ahead of you, and many of us, to another place—literally and figuratively. But I do believe that we'll all be there together, again, someday.. . .*

> *. . . My heart goes out to you for having to make the decision to place Roberta in the facility. I think the emotional stress involved in trying to care for her at home alone supports the decision, but the fact that there is so much physical stress involved makes your surrender imperative. . . .*

When my sister and I toured the Alzheimer's Care Unit, my heart sank as we entered and saw a dozen of the residents in an exercise class in the lobby. Some of them were doing exercises to the direction of the leader, others were sitting with their chins on their chests. I had a terrible time picturing Roberta among them. It sank further as we looked into the room Roberta would occupy. It was carpeted and clean, sparsely furnished with a bed, a small chest of drawers bearing a table lamp, an easy chair, and a floor lamp. A toilet room with a washstand is shared with the resident in the twin room next door. The room seemed very constricting to me. The window looks out on a courtyard with a miniature Dutch windmill in honor of our Dutch heritage.

But my spirits rose as we talked to the nurse in charge of the unit. She is a warm hearted person, and I thought that Roberta would respond positively to her. I cheered myself knowing that Roberta would be in good hands among loving people. They will help her, and me, adjust to the new situation, I assured myself.

On the day before Roberta was scheduled to enter the Verblaauw Unit, Marguerite and I brought in the clothes that were required for her: ten pairs of slacks, ten blouses and shirts, six pairs of socks, bras and underpants, shoes and slippers, a few toilet articles. I brought in a bedside stand and small lamp. Later I placed some favorite pictures on her walls, and a large leafy artificial mock orange tree (on loan from Linda) on the floor.

The two events that marked the last ten days of Roberta's life with me were almost anticlimatic. The first was Roberta's seventy-sixth birthday on April 22. Our life was so steeped in sorrow that I completely forgot about it.

The second occurred on the last weekend in April, just before Roberta was to move into the Care Unit. I developed the worst migraine of my life. It started in the late afternoon on Friday when Ray, Linda, and Marguerite came over for an "O, be joyful" occasion. Roberta joined the group but drank nothing. I felt the migraine coming on, but stupidly drank a glass of sherry anyhow. By Saturday afternoon, I was in the medical center, unable to function. The doctor routinely took my blood pressure and became more concerned about it than about my migraine. His medication relieved my headache by Sunday evening, but the hypertension would take several months to bring under control.

I now had direct evidence of the heavy toll that caring for Roberta for the previous nine months had taken on my health.

On the morning that I was to move Roberta into the Care Unit I wrote the following e-mail to my two closest friends in Philadelphia:

235

Dear Sam and Ted,

Ted, the Communion Service you provided for Roberta, Sam, and me just before we left Philadelphia served its purpose well, that of giving us food for our journey, and reminding us of Christ's love. It didn't make leaving our church and the city any easier, but it did associate our move with a sacrament of eternal significance.

Now Roberta is leaving on a journey of her own, without me. Since she and I are opening a new phase of our life, without each other as constant companions, I once more experienced that gnawing hunger for a Communion service. Not knowing exactly how I would carry it out, I nevertheless went to the store yesterday and bought a can of frozen grape juice and a package of pita bread, intending to hold a Eucharist with her as our own Last Supper, as well as our last bedtime snack.

It was clear to me the customary Communion service format would not do. I feared it would only confuse Roberta and generate endless questioning about what we were doing.

So I decided that an enactment of the Last Supper would be more appropriate. As we approached the bedtime hour, I poured the grape juice into the ceramic chalice and placed a slice of pita bread on the platter—your gifts to us, Ted—and sat Roberta down at the table next to me. I began breaking off pieces of bread, handing some to her, and together dipping them in the grape juice and eating them.

"You know, Roberta," I said "This is what Jesus did with his disciples the last time He had supper with them before He was crucified."

She continued dipping and eating with relish.

"And He told them that the bread was His body and they should remember Him by it whenever they ate it this way."

She nodded.

"This is what we are doing now. We're remembering him."

The thing about this way of doing communion was that we went on eating the whole slice of pita bread, not just a bit of it as is done in the service at church. We broke off big chunks, holding them in the grape juice until they were thoroughly soaked and licking our finger tips afterward. Perhaps this was more like the way Jesus' disciples ate the last supper. It made a satisfying repast; Roberta enjoyed herself.

"Then Jesus said the same thing about the wine. We are to remember him when we dip our bread in the grape juice like this."

We continued our snack with long silences until the bread was consumed. Then we finished off the juice, she holding the chalice to her lips followed by me doing the same.

Roberta looked at me. "That was Communion," she commented in a calm voice.

"Yes, Roberta." I said. "That was Communion."

Today, May 3, I walked with my wife, Roberta, into the Verblaauw Alzheimer's Care Unit and commended her to the care of the professionals there. It is the last journey she will make in this life before the final one.

Bob

---

[1] The Verblaauw Alzheimer's Care Unit was named in honor of Cornelius Verblaauw. It was opened in 1992.

XX

Our Conspiracy of Silence

Five years before Roberta's medical diagnosis was made, we were still able to quip about the trouble we were both having with "senior moments." Or so I thought. As I look back on them now, however, I see that it had been I who was doing most of the joking, not Roberta. My own occasional memory blanks never bothered me. I was able to banter about my lapses; Roberta was not. She may have already sensed that this dreadful disease was lurking somewhere in her brain. Her memory lapses were no joking matter—they probably frightened her more than I knew.

Roberta had personal grounds for being alarmed by her mental failures, having lived with her father as he suffered through the trauma of electroshock psychotherapy for his chronic depression. These treatments, I was told, had erased most of his memories of youth and childhood. He never stopped struggling to recover them. Roberta was close to him at that time; she knew the pain that the loss had inflicted on him. The ghost of her father pacing the floor may have haunted her during the early stages of her disease.

She became increasingly silent about her memory difficulties and allowed no opening for us to discuss them in the way we had previously dealt with most of our concerns. But since at first her difficulties occurred so infrequently, I felt little need to deal explicitly with them.

The significance of Roberta's memory lapses was removed even further from discussion by an aspect of her individuality that now became more evident. She had a strong aversion to being wrong or admitting it, at least where our relationship was concerned. Being wrong, however, had not previously been her concern because she was usually right in what she did or said. Relying on her judgment, I had often been amazed at her ability to assess a given situation accurately.

Not wanting to be wrong, however, had not caused Roberta to tiptoe around her world, fearful of making a mistake. Needing to be right coexisted with the independent spirit that allowed her to flout conventions if she felt they were stuffy and unnecessary. One summer, on a family camping trip in the Rockies, we were hiking through the hills on a hot afternoon. To the astonishment of our young children, Roberta stripped down to her underwear, and sat under a small waterfall to cool off.

By the late 1990s Roberta's failure to recall a name or a past event carried the import of her being wrong, as well as being an ominous premonition of what these lapses foreshadowed. She now began to tread carefully, cautious not to make a mistake. As she was drawn deeper into the shadows, she did not act or speak out as spontaneously as she had done earlier. It was not because of her hearing problem, as our friend had thought after the meeting of ASA at Gordon College in the summer of 1999. Rather, Roberta gradually must have realized that at times she was not making sense when she spoke. As she observed pauses and quizzical looks, she became more reserved and less adventurous.

Resistance to discussing her increasing memory lapses was, in effect, our conspiracy of silence. We agreed, without ever saying so, that we were not going to talk with each other about her lapses and disorientations. Mention of Alzheimer's disease in personal terms was taboo. Although she willingly talked about the disease objectively, for example, whether we should make a contribution to the Alzheimer's Association, we did not make any explicit personal connections to the disease.

This conspiracy drove us into a state of denial about Roberta's illness. I added my own delusion to hers. Rather than acknowledge the fearful significance of her memory slips, I would focus on things that she was doing well, which, early on, far outnumbered her momentary failures. Thus I fooled myself into believing that she was aging like I was—albeit perhaps a little faster than expected. Meanwhile, the mental slippage was gradually gaining momentum.

I commented on Roberta's rapid mental deterioration to her primary care physician in the fall of 2000, while we were still in Philadelphia. The doctor claimed that there had undoubtedly been many indications of it during the past several years, but that I had failed either to notice them or to accept them for what they were. At first I was incensed by her suggestion, recounting to her how well Roberta had been conducting herself. But I have since come to see that the doctor was right. Roberta did a splendid job of masking the disease with her strong intellect and her will to be well. She was very quick with words; when she could not recall one, she usually extricated herself by finding a synonym. Dismayed at how fast Roberta had deteriorated in the fall, our friends, too, had been taken in earlier by her ability to dance around her lapses and disorientations and maintain the appearance of good health. Indeed, she was healthy in the main, except in what was happening to her brain.

It's not that we didn't talk about her other illnesses. In the autumn of 2000, early in what might be called the second stage of her illness, she knew that she was seriously, if not terminally, ill. However, she thought it was her feet, or alternately, her stomach that would bring about her demise. Fears aroused by her abdominal pain led her to believe she was going to die soon. At one time she said anxiously, in response to her pain, "I'm not going to get better, am I, Bob?" Later I was able to say, "You have a disease in your brain," and even, "It's because you have Alzheimer's disease, Roberta." But it did not register. I could find no way to say it helpfully. The conspiracy of silence had taken its toll.

Often I wish I could have talked openly with Roberta about her illness before it had advanced. I think it would have helped her if she could have attached a name to her fears. To be able to label the

241

vague thing that lurks in the shadows sometimes gives one control over it. Openness would also have also given the two of us the opportunity to plan together the good years that still remained.

The time just before Roberta's Dark Thursday was most difficult because the symptoms were not clearly defined. The disease still seemed far distant. Winslow Homer's painting, *The Fog Warning* captures the mood of that period better than words. I pictured Roberta looking fearfully over her shoulder at the encroaching fog, but rowing desperately to reach the safe haven of the mother ship before the fog bank closed in on her. Assuring her she was not going to get out of the fog was something I could not do.

Ted and Sam, as well as neighbors and friends at church and elsewhere, saw what was happening and were heartbroken, but they remained unable to crack our conspiracy. Ted made an overture one Sunday morning, and I put him off with a joke. These dear people all respected our privacy.

The conspiracy was a challenge for us, and perhaps for many others dealing with the very early stages of Alzheimer's disease. Families, churches, and the medical profession would do well to address it. When discussion of the uncertain symptoms is off-limits, how can a caregiver (and the person who is struggling in the early stages of the disease) be helped to face the reality of the disease and be supported and strengthened to face the awful future?

On the other hand, talking about Alzheimer's disease does not necessarily help the sufferer, since his or her rationality is severely impaired. A woman who had been the caregiver to her stricken husband told me that, even though they discussed his illness, it only added to their anguish. The knowledge didn't stay with him for long, and he would return to questions about his illness again and again in anger and frustration.

Another woman faced a similar situation with her Alzheimer's-stricken husband. He would not allow her to talk about his illness. Once when a public service advertisement appeared on TV briefly telling the story of the disease, she tried to take the opportunity to open a discussion of his illness with him. But he would hear nothing of it and ignored the subject. His denial was impossible to overcome.

Another difficulty arising out of denial is that it tends to interfere with constructive thinking. If one denies that a problem exists,
he or she is not likely to try to solve it. Because I was bent on ignoring my wife's Alzheimer's disease, I had little reason to reflect cre-
atively on how to talk with her about it. When I might have been
thinking about alternative ways of approaching our communication problem or finding out what other people might have suggested,
I was intent on covering up. Because Roberta had denied that there
was a problem and I collaborated on the denial, we missed an opportunity to find ways of dealing with the shadows.

Moreover, I feared that if I brought up her lapses and disorientations as reasons for believing she had the disease, she might have
contested my judgment and perhaps countered by reminding me of
my own failings, of which there were more than a few. We might
have gotten into an *I-forgot-this*, but *you-forgot-that* exchange, ending in a stalemate. I had no desire to pound her with evidence that
she had the disease. She would have resented me for having brought
up the subject in the first place. When she was still well enough that
we could have talked about them, her symptoms were not sufficiently severe to make a convincing case.

This raises another problem. I have read that it is desirable to
get an early medical diagnosis of the disease so that plans can be
made for the future. Yet the very problems I am discussing make it
difficult to obtain an early verdict. What if the person in the first
stage of Alzheimer's were to ask why he or she should go to the
doctor when the symptoms are not clear-cut? If that person is not
compliant and agreeable to obtaining a medical diagnosis, what can
the caregiver do? Moreover, doctors may not be willing to make a
diagnosis without obtaining an MRI, adding another layer of difficulty to an already complex situation. When I took Roberta to her
physician with her painful stomach problem in the fall of 2000, the
doctor might have suspected that Roberta was slipping. Yet she dealt
with the medical problem and paid no attention to the more threatening mental one.

Neither of us, however, was satisfied with our conspiracy of
silence. There were times when I wanted to discuss her illness with
her, but she did not allow an opening for me to do so. At other

243

times, she asked, "What's wrong with me?" Not having the presence of mind to seize the opportunity, I answered, "It's because your brain is sick. And it won't get better, Roberta." When I used the words, "Alzheimer's disease" they did not click with her. It was as if the words were not in her vocabulary.

Why was it such a problem to talk openly with Roberta about her Alzheimer's disease? Because facing Alzheimer's disease is the most shocking experience imaginable, short of being consigned to Hades. It is a sentence of death; indeed, it is the mother of all death sentences. First, there is the lingering death of one's self, and second, the subsequent demise of one's body. Even in dying by such a horrible disease as cancer, one's personhood does not depart before the body dies. Telling one's beloved that he or she has Alzheimer's disease is a death sentence that will be executed only at the end of a long agonizing march through the twisted undergrowth of mindlessness. It is that long passage that is so horrifying in prospect.

I regret that Roberta's doctors did not offer me help in facing my dilemma. David Shenk[1] indicates that, after the medical diagnosis is made, the physician in charge should send a letter to the patient, rather than informing him or her at the time the diagnosis was made. In the letter, the diagnosis is explained, and the patient is urged to come in later for a follow-up. Sensitively, the doctor explains the diagnosis further, tells what it means for the future, and answers questions.

I did not receive such help. The neurologist walked away from Roberta and me after our consultation, leaving it to a secretary to deliver the written medical diagnosis. I never saw him again. Neither did I receive a letter from Roberta's primary physician inviting us to confer about the diagnosis. Such a conference would have helped us break out of our conspiracy of silence.

It should not be left to the spouse or loved ones to convey the diagnosis. It is simply too shocking and painful. Being the bearer of the dreadful news may create a gulf between the stricken one and caregiver. It can be very difficult to offer the necessary comfort and assurance after telling one's loved one that he or she has Alzheimer's disease. I believe the diagnosis is best conveyed by a third party, a person who is vested with authority to do so. Nobody is in a better position to convey and explain this medical diagnosis than one's family or primary physician.

If my dilemma is similarly experienced by others, then it seems clear that at least some caregivers may need help from medical professionals in delivering this most difficult message to a stricken loved one. After that, it is the responsibility of the spouse and loved ones to help the Alzheimer's patient accept the diagnosis. That much I would have been able to do. Ministers, priests, and rabbis can help the suffering persons and their caregivers face the awful future constructively.

Where was God in all this? I have watched other Christians who were stricken with Alzheimer's disease and their caregivers, and have been amazed at the wide variation in the manner in which the latter have responded and exercised their choices. Some have cared for their stricken loved ones at home to the very end. More women than men provide for an ailing spouse in this way, I believe. Others have committed their spouses or parents to professional caretakers in Alzheimer's care centers. I have seen God honoring whatever style of care that is given by providing strength at the point where loving care addresses human need at its most basic level.

The role of the church, the family of God, in the early stages of Alzheimer's needs further consideration. I received incredibly strong support from my Philadelphia church family. They were sent by God to help me. The church, in my experience, and in that of others, is one of the main sources of strength and serves as the agent of God's grace to those hurting ones who are members of a faith community. But more needs to be done to make it possible for caregivers to receive assistance in the very early stages of the disease of their loved one, in order to change a conspiracy of silence into a flood of grace. Employing parish nurses, as some churches are doing, is a step in the right direction.

Since moving into the Breton Terrace independent living apartments, I received an open letter from one of the residents who has Alzheimer's. The letter that follows is a good example of what can be done in an open approach to the disease.[2]

245

Hi, my name is Jim Voss. I live in apartment #3000, with my wife, Judy, who is helping me write this letter. We just moved here in early September from our condo downtown. We are enjoying our new place and have felt very welcome here.

I am 63 years old and was diagnosed with Alzheimer's disease almost 3 years ago. I am in the mid-stages of the disease. We have worked with various doctors and had several tests done recently to help provide the best treatment plan. I am on several medications to help slow down the progress of Alzheimer's, but the disease continues to deteriorate me mentally. I can still walk, eat and do all of life's normal activities with supervision or instruction. Right now, I have a hard time focusing, conversing and finding my way around, but I love talking with people.

I appreciate any help you can provide me since I get bored staying at home (of course I can't drive). I sometimes display some unusual behaviors because of my disease. For example, when I am in an unfamiliar situation, I cannot always express myself the way I want to. I often have a hard time coming up with the right words and so I don't make sense. When you see me, please greet me by name and introduce yourself, as I might not remember you. If I am not making sense to you, you don't have to try to correct me. Just laugh, and smile and go along with what I am saying; perhaps try to change the subject.

Generally, I am a very happy person, despite my condition. In a large group, I might be a little quiet at first. It takes time to warm up. It might help for you to ask me a question or two, but don't expect the "right" answer!

Although it doesn't happen often, occasionally I might get frustrated and angry. At these times, try to change the subject and leave me to myself for a while (but make sure I don't wander off!).

I sometimes get lost, so I appreciate some help in find-
ing my way back to my apartment (#3000). I like to go
outside, but should not be outside alone.

Thank you in advance for your assistance. I hope to have
an opportunity to meet you soon.

Sincerely,

Jim Voss

I have come to several general conclusions about this conspiracy of silence. In most cases it is desirable that the diseased person be told that he or she has Alzheimer's disease. Bringing the disease out into the open may make it less dreadful, permitting loved ones to talk about it with less fear so that they can make constructive plans for the good years that remain.

Spouses and relatives may need help in informing the loved one that he or she has the disease. Doctors, having the authority of their profession, are the most suitable ones for this task. Ministers, priests, and rabbis may support the caregiver as he or she helps the stricken one accept the awful diagnosis.

Faith communities need to continue to offer support and love for Alzheimer's patients and their loved ones. Specific ways of doing so in the early stages of the disease need to be thought through and implemented.

In my situation, I did what I could best do. I held Roberta close to me and told her again and again that I loved her and that I would take care of her no matter what happened. I repeated that God loved both of us and would not let go of us; indeed, that God had big arms wrapped around us all the time. Her body relaxed and softened as I held her and talked to her in this way. I am convinced that the tactile sense, the strong encircling arms, the closeness and warmth of the protecting loved one speaks as profoundly, if not more so, than words. I felt God's grace most deeply in such quiet, intimate times. Thus, I made known my love to Roberta as never before.

My morning prayer was for strength for the day, and ease of mind and body for Roberta. Grace and strength poured forth as

247

water from an artesian well. If faith is the belief that God will honor his promises, then my faith was strengthened by the fulfillment of his promise that he would not forsake us.

---

[1] David Shenk, *The Forgetting Alzheimer's: Portrait of an Epidemic* (New York: Doubleday, 2001) p. 39.

[2] I am grateful to Judy Voss for her kind permission to reproduce the letter.

Epilogue

I began this book as a story about the love between Roberta and me and the love of God for both of us as she journeyed into the shadows of Alzheimer's. I was her constant caregiver and companion. Circumstances changed, however, after May 3, 2001, when I committed her to the Alzheimer's care unit. I now have my love for her but without her company. That is a great loss, and I miss her presence deeply. But through all this the love and grace of God have remained constant.

Roberta's early days in the assisted-living unit were difficult for her. She, too, missed our companionship. The nurses' aides told me that she often asked where I was. Yet my visits with her were usually satisfying to me, and I have many good stories to tell about them.

More than eighteen months have passed since I placed Roberta in the assisted-living unit. She remained there only slightly more than a year, after which she was transferred to the skilled nursing unit housed in the new Van Andel Pavilion on the same campus of the Holland Home.

This move was made after a great deal of back-and-forth between me and the head nurse of the assisted-living unit, during which

I voiced objections to the transfer. The report of the nurse who evaluated Roberta's behavior indicated that Roberta was ready for the move, largely because her irritable behavior made her difficult to manage. I did not think she needed to go to the skilled nursing unit, arguing that she was getting excellent care where she was and that the nurses' aides were successfully dealing with her problems. I also thought that Roberta's adjustment would take a nosedive when she entered the Pavilion because of the unfamiliar surroundings and all the new faces she would encounter. But none of my arguments prevailed.

So it was that on July 18, Roberta, the recreational therapist for the assisted-living unit, and I could be found trudging through the connecting hallways to the skilled nursing unit. I had hoped that we could enter the Pavilion with Roberta holding my arm, much as we had walked up the aisle on our wedding day; this, however, was no ceremonious entry. Rather, I clutched two of Roberta's favorite framed pictures with one arm while I cradled her close to me with the other. She quietly plodded along at my side. The therapist followed, pushing a shopping cart stacked high with cartons of Roberta's clothes and other belongings.

It turned out that I was wrong in my predictions about Roberta's decline. She made the transition in great style, adjusting well to the new surroundings, and to the loving care given by the nurses in the skilled nursing unit. She continued to be a nightwalker and at times did not sleep for a complete twenty-four hour cycle, after which she would spend a day catnapping. Roberta still recognized me, although on a couple of occasions she asked, "Who are you?" When I told her I was Bob, she picked up from there, and we carried on as usual. She chattered a great deal as we walked or sat on her bed, actually telling me about specific events or people, although she could not make it clear to me what or who she had in mind. I went along with what she was trying to say, responding now and again to an intelligible word. So the transition was made, and Roberta is now in the last stage of care, short of hospice.

I am taking notes and sending occasional updates to friends and family via e-mail on Roberta's life and mine, lived in the loving presence of God. It is my intention to gather these together into a second book that will chronicle our lives as we dwell in our different circumstances, Roberta in her world and I in mine. Our lives are connected by my frequent visits during which I enter her world of restless pacing, unresponsive lethargy, and often quiet chatting, occasionally interrupted by a blessed moment of lucidity in which she can hear me say, "I love you," and to which she may then respond, "I love you, too."

Appendix

Ten Warning Signs of Alzheimer's

The Alzheimer's Association has developed a list of warning signs that includes common symptoms of Alzheimer's disease (some also apply to other dementing illnesses). Individuals who exhibit several of these symptoms should see a physician for a complete examination.

1. Memory loss that affects job skills
It's normal to occasionally forget an assignment, deadline, or a colleague's name, but frequent forgetfulness or unexplainable confusion at home or in the workplace may signal that something's wrong.

2. Difficulty performing familiar tasks
Busy people get distracted from time to time. For example, you might leave something on the stove too long or not remember to serve part of a meal. People with Alzheimer's might prepare a meal and not only forget to serve it, but also forget they made it.

3. Problems with language
Everyone has trouble finding the right word sometimes, but a person with Alzheimer's disease may forget simple words or substitute inappropriate words, making his or her sentences difficult to understand.

4. Disorientation to time and place
It's normal to momentarily forget the day of the week or what you need from the store. But people with Alzheimer's disease can become lost on their own street, not knowing where they are, how they got there, or how to get back home.

5. Poor or decreased judgment

Choosing not to bring a sweater or coat along on a chilly night is a common mistake. A person with Alzheimer's, however, may dress inappropriately in more noticeable ways, wearing a bathrobe to the store or several blouses on a hot day.

6. Problems with abstract thinking

Balancing a checkbook can be challenging for many people, but for someone with Alzheimer's, recognizing numbers or performing basic calculation may be impossible.

7. Misplacing things

Everyone temporarily misplaces a wallet or keys from time to time. A person with Alzheimer's disease may put these and other items in inappropriate places—such as an iron in the freezer, or a wristwatch in the sugar bowl—then not recall how they got there.

8. Changes in mood or behavior

Everyone experiences a broad range of emotions—it's part of being human. People with Alzheimer's tend to exhibit more rapid mood swings for no apparent reason.

9. Changes in personality

People's personalities may change somewhat as they age. But a person with Alzheimer's can change dramatically, either suddenly or over a period of time. Someone who is generally easy going may become angry, suspicious, or fearful.

10. Loss of initiative

It's normal to tire of housework, business activities, or social obligations, but most people retain or eventually regain their interest. The person with Alzheimer's disease may remain disinterested and uninvolved in many or all of his usual pursuits.

Ten Warning Signs of Caregiver Stress

In addition to the "Ten Warning Signs of Alzheimer's," The Alzheimer's Association has also developed a list of symptoms common to Alzheimer's caregivers. Individuals who experience several of these symptoms should consider seeing a counselor, physician, or mental health professional, along with their pastor, for help.

1. Denial
About the disease and its effect on the person who's been diagnosed. *I know mom's going to get better.*

2. Anger
At the person with Alzheimer's or others: that no effective treatment or cure currently exists, and that people don't understand what's going on. *If he asks me that question one more time I'll scream!*

3. Social withdrawal
From friends and activities that once brought pleasure. *I don't care about getting together with the neighbors anymore.*

4. Anxiety
About facing another day and what the future holds. *What happens when he needs more care than I can provide?*

5. Depression
Begins to break your spirit and affects your ability to cope. *I don't care anymore.*

6. Exhaustion
Makes it nearly impossible to complete necessary daily tasks. *I'm too tired for this.*

7. Sleeplessness
Caused by a never-ending list of concerns. *What if she wanders out of the house or falls and hurts herself?*

8. Irritability

Leads to moodiness and triggers negative responses and reactions. *Leave me alone!*

9. Lack of Concentration

Makes it difficult to perform familiar tasks. *I was so busy, I forgot we had an appointment.*

10. Health problems

Begin to take their toll, both mentally and physically. *I can't remember the last time I felt good.*

Editors Note: The author and publisher recommend that those who suspect or believe that someone they know may be affected by Alzheimer's disease should contact the Alzheimer's Association at (800) 272-3900, on the web at www.alz.org, or your local chapter of the Alzheimer's Association for more information on the care of people suffering from Alzheimer's and to support the work of the organization.

Acknowledgments

Two people played major roles in this book writing drama. The first is Samuel Whyte, intimate friend of my wife, Roberta, and me throughout our years of residence in Philadelphia. His brotherly affection for both of us carried me though many trying days during Roberta's descent into the shadows of Alzheimer's. Moreover, he was the first to suggest that I gather into book form the e-mails that I had been sending to my network of family and friends about Roberta's disease. Having started me on this writing project he continued to support my efforts, most importantly by reading and making key suggestions regarding the form and contents during my writing of the manuscript. His comments, backed by years of experience teaching college students the skills of writing, have resulted in substantial improvements in the story.

The second person is Phyllis VanAndel, friend and classmate from junior high through college, who greeted me upon our return to Grand Rapids, with an offer to proofread the manuscript that I was writing about my wife's disease. Aware of her professional experience as a freelance writer and editor, as well as her artistic sense, I eagerly accepted her assistance. Her help soon turned into far more than proofreading. I light-heartedly dubbed her approach, "reconstructive surgery," as together we worked over an occasional sentence or passage that she had, with good reason, questioned or cut out.

Further downstream I was miraculously brought into contact with Dirk Wierenga, publisher and co-owner of FaithWalk Publishing. His enthusiastic acceptance of my unsolicited manuscript and his fast-tracking it into production are a continuous source of wonder to me. With sensitive editing, Louann Werksma, senior editor, has enhanced Roberta's story; it was Ginny McFadden who shaped the book into its final excellent form.

To this group of faithful friends and co-workers I owe far more than I can ever repay. They will, I trust, feel rewarded by the faith and love that this book may kindle in readers whose lives may in some manner be touched by the shadow of Alzheimer's.

Robert F. DeHaan
January, 2003

About the Author

Robert F. DeHaan, Ph.D., forged a distinguished academic and scientific career during which he launched and directed groundbreaking programs in education and psychology.

He graduated from Calvin College in Grand Rapids, Michigan, with a bachelor's degree in chemistry and education, and from the University of Chicago with a Ph.D. in human development, individual counseling, and group dynamics. He served for twelve years as professor and chair of the Psychology Department of Hope College in Holland, Michigan, before going on to establish and direct the Philadelphia Urban Semester of the Great Lakes College Association. He also directed the Master of Human Services Program of Lincoln University in Pennsylvania. He has authored five books and numerous articles.

Dr. DeHaan and his wife Roberta raised four children while managing productive academic careers and remaining active in many scientific, academic, and professional organizations. Underpinning and informing all their activities has been an abiding faith in Christ and an active church life.

Says Dr. DeHaan, "As a lifelong committed Christian and a churchman, I have learned to communicate well with people of faith and have been able to recognize and present the mysteries of divine grace that accompanied my wife and me on her journey into Alzheimer's disease."